CASE STUDIES IN BUSINESS, SOCIETY, AND ETHICS

Donation

CASE STUDIES IN BUSINESS, SOCIETY, AND ETHICS

Fifth Edition

Tom L. Beauchamp
Georgetown University

PEARSON
Prentice
Hall

Upper Saddle River, New Jersey 07458

Library of Congress Cataloging-in-Publication Data

Tom L. Beauchamp
  Case studies in business, society, and ethics / Tom L. Beauchamp—
5th ed.
    p. cm.
Includes bibliographical references.
  ISBN 0–13–099435–9
  1. Industries—Social aspects—United States—Case studies. 2.
Industrial policy—United States—Case studies. 3. Trade
regulation—United States—Case studies. I Title.
  HD60.5.U5B38 2003
  658.4'08'0973—dc21

                          2003012832

Senior Acquisitions Editor: Ross Miller
Assistant Editor: Wendy Yurash
Editorial Director: Charlyce Jones-Owen
Editorial Assistant: Carla Worner
Director of Marketing: Beth Mejia
Marketing Assistant: Kimberly Daum
Production Liaison: Marianne Peters-Riordan
Manufacturing Buyer: Christina Helder
Cover Design: Bruce Kenselaar
Composition/Full Service Project Manager: John Shannon, Pine Tree Composition, Inc.
Printer/Binder: Phoenix Book Tech

Credits and acknowledgments borrowed from other sources and reproduced, with permission, in this textbook appear on the appropriate pages.

Pearson Education LTD., London
Pearson Education Singapore, Pte. Ltd
Pearson Education Canada, Ltd
Pearson Education—Japan
Pearson Education Australia PTY, Limited

Pearson Education North Asia Ltd
Pearson Educación de Mexico, S.A. de C.V.
Pearson Education Malaysia, Pte. Ltd
Pearson Education, Upper Saddle River,
  New Jersey

10 9 8 7 6 5 4 3 2 1
ISBN 0-13-099435-9

For Zachary,

Young Entrepreneur

Contents

Preface

The thirty-six cases in this volume concern ethical and social issues surrounding business. Fourteen cases are new to this fifth edition. Of the twenty-two cases carried over from the fourth edition, fourteen have been extensively revised, five have been revised in minor respects (to clarify or update information), and three remain unaltered. The general Introduction to the volume has also undergone thorough rewriting, updating, and expansion. This Introduction treats the uses of cases and the case method, rather than the particular cases in this volume.

As in previous editions, the objective of this volume is to make students aware of situations that require moral reflection, judgment, and decision, while revealing the complexities that often surround moral choices and the formation of public policies. The book has not been produced to create a platform for moralistic criticism of the behavior of individual persons, corporations, or governmental agencies that play leading roles in the cases. Some cases contain dramatic instances of professional irresponsibility (the Andersen-Enron case being a well-known example), but it should not be inferred that the purpose of the cases is to teach what ought not to be done or that conduct in the profession under discussion generally follows this pattern. Irresponsible actions are occasionally featured because more is to be learned, in the circumstance, from wrongful than from rightful behavior.

However, learning through the study of wrongful or negligent behavior is not the primary orientation of this volume. The focus is generally on circumstances in which hard choices must be made under complex conditions of uncertainty or disagreement. More is to be learned from reasoning under circumstances of controversy, personal quandary, and incompleteness of information than from paradigmatic cases of irresponsibility.

The length and structure of the cases also deserve comment. Many cases that now circulate in the general literature of business, society, and ethics either are too short to contain enough detail for discussion or contain such a vast body of data that discussion is retarded by the particulars and their connections. Most of us encounter severe limitations on the amount of information we can study and remember about any sequence of events; and too much information often makes it difficult to find the essence of the problem. Accordingly, most cases in this book conform to the model of tidy cases that come to the essence of the matter without a massive body of descriptions and data.

Experienced executives and experienced teachers will rightly insist that the situations under which decisions are made in business are multifarious, perplexing, and short on relevant information. Executives see real-life cases as too intricate for short summary presentation. This point of view has its merits. Every student should appreciate that historical sequences of events are almost never fully captured by the facts mentioned in the write-up of the case. This is so even when cases are described at book length.

Many teachers of the subject matter found in this book prefer cases that take an *inside* view of a corporation or an institution under investigation in the case. They want to examine the decisions that managers must make and the strategies that they follow on the firing line. I endorse this form of pedagogy, and several cases in this book are so oriented. However, this approach incorporates only one profitable style of case study. An *outside* look at corporate activities is sometimes the only perspective obtainable. Moreover, it can be the best approach to cases that involve public policy. A variety of approaches to case writing is therefore used in this book, some taking the inside look, some employing the outside perspective, and some using a mixture of perspectives.

Some teachers and students like to see questions at the end of each case, in the belief that these questions focus reading and discussion on particular features of the cases. I believe that this practice is an editorial disservice rather than a service. A teacher may profitably circulate questions in a class for a targeted purpose, but the problem with this approach in the text itself is twofold: (1) Teachers teach the cases with very different approaches, purposes, and problems; and (2) students can easily be impeded in their own thinking by being channeled in a particular direction. For these reasons, no questions or aids accompany the cases in this volume.

Most of the cases in this book report actual rather than hypothetical events. That is, they are based on authentic incidents that occurred in a circumstance of business or during the development of public policy. Corporations involved are often identified by their true names, and historical dates and places are unmodified. However, in several actual cases, confidential material was used, or full documentation of some claims was impossible; in these cases, names, dates, and locations have been changed, and no identification of the corporations and persons originally involved occurs. In some of these cases, hypothetical elements have been added to highlight the problem and focus the reader's understanding of the situation. In two instances, a composite case was created from several actual cases by combining various features of the cases.

Acknowledgments

A talented research staff has assisted me for many years in the collecting and writing of these cases, and I have in turn been generously supported through previous editions of the book by several grants. Support came initially from the Exxon Educational Foundation and the Landegger Program in International Business Diplomacy at Georgetown University. The Kennedy Institute of Ethics has also supported this work. Through the Institute, work on new cases in the third edition was supported in part by BRSG SO7 RR 07136-18-20 grants awarded by the National Center for Research Resources, National Institutes of Health. I also acknowledge the support provided by the Kennedy Institute's library and information retrieval systems, which kept me in touch with the most important literature and repeatedly reduced the burdens of library research.

I am grateful for entirely new cases—or at least large blocks of cases—in this edition that were written by John Hasnas, John McVea, Roland B. Cousins, and Norman Bowie. Research on many other cases has been undertaken (in at least one of the five editions) by Michael Hammer, Sasha Lyutse, Dianna Spring, Joseph Folio, Ahmed Humayun, Megan Hughes, Jonathan Larkin, Jennifer Esposito, George Lucas, Jr., Stefanie Ann Lenway, Jeff Greene, Kier Olsen, John Cuddihy, Ari Paparo, Katie Marshall, Nicole Herb, David Parver, Katy Cancro, Jennifer Givens, Brian Tauscher, Jeffrey Kahn, Kelley MacDougall, Anna Pinedo, R. Jay Wallace, Martha Elliott, Nancy Blanpied, William Pitt, Barbara Humes, Louisa W. Peat O'Neil, Andrew Rowan, Linda Kern, Cathleen Kaveny, and Sara Finnerty Kelly.

Ted Moran and John Kline of the Landegger Program steered me in a number of important directions. Helpful criticisms and constructive suggestions in various editions have been made by Ed Epstein, Ruth Faden, Norman Bowie, Tom Donaldson, Theodore Purcell, Carl Kaufman, Lisa Newton, Robert Cooke, William H. Hay, Thomas L. Carson, Archie B. Carroll, George Lodge, Henry W. Tulloch, Vivian Weil, Michael Hooker, Deborah G. Johnson, David P. Boyd, Richard E. Wokutch, Burton Leiser, Homer B. Sewell, Stephen Klaidman, and John H. Bubar. Useful and substantive suggestions for improving the Introduction were made by Terry Pinkard, Ruth Faden, Judith Areen, and Alexander Capron. Michael Pritchard, Richard Wilson, Jonathan P. West, William Griffith, Artegal Camburn, and John Modschiedler have reviewed many of the cases and made suggestions for improvement.

Employees of a number of corporations discussed in the cases provided vital materials and criticisms. A couple of corporations threatened lawsuits, but most were extraordinarily kind and patient. They are acknowledged in the footnotes to the cases. I was also aided by several persons in organizations other than corporations, including a number of officials at federal agencies in Washington. They too are acknowledged in the notes. Several lawyers and media representatives enabled me to obtain (with permission) confidential papers from corporations. I regret that I am not at liberty to mention them by name.

REVIEWERS

Keith Robinson, Grand Valley State University; Norman Hawker, Western Michigan State University; Jonathan P. West, University of Miami; Otto Lerbinger, Boston University; Harvey James, University of Hartford; George P. Generas, Jr., University of Hartford; John S. Steiner, California State University, Los Angeles; and Keith W. Krasemann, College of DuPage.

T. L. B.
Washington, D.C.

Introduction:
The Uses of Cases

The cases collected in this volume emerge from the intersection of professional practice in business, economics, law, and government. These cases can be profitably explored from each of these disciplinary perspectives. The purpose of this Introduction is to investigate how perspectives in these disciplines affect our understanding of the problems embodied in a case, the nature and history of case methods, different types of case analysis, pitfalls in case analysis, and reservations about the nature of the "facts" that comprise the case.

DIFFERENT PERSPECTIVES
ON THE STUDY OF CASES

Many students and teachers who benefit from the study of cases agree that cases help to focus and to dramatize problems and, at the same time, to identify problems in real-life situations. Beyond this point of initial agreement, however, orientations and styles of case analysis are diverse and plentiful. Different disciplines direct a reader to identify different elements in the cases as problematic and deserving of analysis. This pluralism of approaches occurs in the broad territory of "business, society, and ethics" as a result of two distinct, though not incompatible, orientations: (1) the perspective of *ethics* and (2) the perspective of *business.*

   The ethics orientation ("business ethics") consists of the analysis of cases using categories such as justice, utility, rights, and personal virtues. Cases about discrimination in hiring, for example, are studied in light of theories of justice and social utility and principles such as equal opportunity. In this paradigm, a consideration of moral decisions, quandaries, and virtues is fundamental to a proper understanding of the case.

   The business orientation tends to categorize its endeavor as "business and society" and analyzes cases in terms of various relationships between business, on the one hand, and government and society, on the other. Cases about environmental pollution, for example, are studied by detailing empirical facts about pollution and disease and by examining social processes that have diminished the scope of decision making in business and have created new responsibilities through government requirements. The economic aspects of pollution control are central to this approach. (The cases in this volume of "How Reserve Mining Became Cleveland-Cliffs" and "Regulating Emissions: From Acid

Rain to Global Warming" can easily be studied in precisely this manner.) The responses of corporations to changing legal and regulatory situations are often heavily emphasized, as are the considerations of what has been and may become public policy. Tax policies and the economic consequences of proposed public policies may be studied in detail and are likely to be viewed as central to the analysis of cases. Ethical principles and moral philosophy may not be mentioned at all, just as those who examine cases with an ethical interest may ignore questions of good and bad management.

These different orientations are not mutually exclusive, nor is one orientation primary or preferable to another. The most constructive approach is to acknowledge that cases invite multiple forms of productive analysis.

THE CASE METHOD IN LAW

Just as different *perspectives* on cases prompt us to look for different ingredients, different *strategies* for analyzing cases yield different outcomes. The oldest and most extensive body of thought about strategies and methods for analyzing cases (apart from religious traditions) is found in law, where the case method has long been a staple of training and where case law establishes precedents of evidence and justification. (Two cases in this volume that offer transparent examples are "Violent Music: Sony, Slayer, and Self-Regulation" and "The Open Door at IBM: What Can Company Doctors Disclose?")

It is instructive to look to the history of legal case analysis, which has had a deep impact on the case method in business. The birth of the case method in legal training occurred shortly after 1870 when Christopher Columbus Langdell became dean of the law school at Harvard. He revolutionized previous academic standards and teaching techniques by introducing the case method. He intended this method to replace the prevailing textbooks and lecture methods, which he condemned as promoting rote learning and worthless acumen for passing examinations. Langdell's idea was to use casebooks rather than textbooks for the entire law school curriculum. The casebooks were composed of cases selected, edited, and arranged to impart to the student the pervasive meanings of legal terms, as well as the rules and principles of law.

This approach envisioned a Socratic style of teaching to reveal how concepts, rules, and principles are found in the legal reasoning of judges, as exhibited in the cases. The skillful teacher presumably could extract the embedded nuggets that are the fundamental principles of law, much as a skillful biographer extracts the principles of a person's thinking by studying his or her considered decisions over a lifetime.

Langdell was not a disenchanted teacher who disliked conventional lecturing. Rather, he had theoretical reasons for his reforms. In his view the law was no perfunctory profession that a clerk could learn by boning up on textbook wisdom. Langdell believed that the law is a science that rests on an inductive method modeled on the scientific method of the natural sciences. Teachers and students develop hypotheses in their dissection of cases and arrive at principles just as a scientist does. In law, he argued, one extracts from cases a select body of principles that frame the English common law.[1] Although the many particulars in cases vary and their judicial conclusions sometimes conflict, the principles of judicial reasoning remain constant. Also, one could utilize this method to study exactly how far a principle extends. In the process, the student acquires a facility and sophistication in moving from particular circumstances to generalizations and back.

Langdell's innovation horrified Harvard students, and they skipped classes in massive numbers. They disliked both criticism by dialectical questioning and the demanding preparation required for every class. There was also a faculty revolt, and the school's enrollment slipped. But, in the end, Langdell was victorious. The method was adopted and spread to other echelons of American legal education. Eventually every American law school of renown succumbed in some measure to the case method. This rapid reform was unfortunate because there were many unexamined problems and pretentious claims in the Langdell vision, especially the odd notion of making the law a science and reducing its essence to a few abstract principles. This vision tended to suppress such integral aspects of law as legislation, the politics of legislation, particular historical circumstances, and jurisdictional variations.

There were, however, good reasons why this method, with appropriate modifications, ultimately prevailed in American law schools. By making analysis of case law a basic component of legal education, teachers have a powerful tool for generalizing from the opinions of judges. Spanning the tangled web of details in particular cases are principles and fundamental doctrines. Moreover, training in the case method sharpens skills of legal reasoning, including both legal analysis and legal synthesis. One can dissect a case and then construct an improved way of treating similar cases. In the thrust-and-parry classroom setting, teacher and student think through a case and its rights and wrongs. The method prepares the student for the practice of law, rather than transmitting theoretical wisdom about the law.

Since 1910 or so, the case method has been less grandiosely conceived than during the Langdell era. This turn of events, in retrospect, was inevitable.[2] The principles did not prove to be as uniform across courts or time as had at first been thought, because precedent cases revealed incompatible and sometimes rival legal theories. The method was also isolationist in the context of the modern university: It made law a specialty without connections to other professions, and it undercut interdisciplinary investigation.

The enduring value of legal casebooks rests in the way they teach students to distinguish the nature of principles and evidence at work in the case. By examining cases, students learn which courts are considered adept at legal reasoning, how to assemble facts, and where the weight of the evidence lies. They are then enabled to transfer that weight elsewhere in new cases. It is widely (although not uniformly[3]) agreed that this type of study offers substantial benefits in the training of lawyers, whatever its pitfalls and shortcomings.

THE CASE METHOD IN BUSINESS

Historical Development

When the case method at the Harvard Law School enjoyed its peak of influence, it spawned a new infant across campus at the Harvard Business School, which opened its doors in 1908. The first dean of the school, Edwin F. Gay, decided that courses on commercial law would use only the case method, whereas other courses would use it in conjunction with lectures and reports. Dean Gay stated that "the example of the Harvard Law School," greatly prized in academic business circles, was responsible for this decision.[4] Cases and reports were introduced gradually into business policy and marketing courses. Because the faculty was acclimated to lecturing, Gay had to push hard for more extensive use of the case system, although he never used the method in his own economic history courses.

The method began to flourish throughout the curriculum under Dean Wallace B. Donham, who assumed the office in 1919. His training in law proved instrumental, as the following account by a later dean of the business school, Donald K. David, makes clear:

> Dean Donham's training in the law and his own wide business experience gave him the conviction that the case method was the sound approach for instruction. . . . Dean Donham recognized that the development of the case system for teaching business would be a slow and expensive process. The law schools had the decisions of the courts, the medical schools had hospital cases and clinical records, and the scientific schools had their laboratories and records of experiments. In contrast, there were nowhere any records of the process of making business decisions. Therefore the development of the case system in the Business School had to take the slow and hard way; . . . those who gathered cases had to go out to the businesses themselves to record the actual situations.[5]

Following Langdell's example, Donham pushed his faculty to develop casebooks. Faculty began to collect materials for cases through systematic and comprehensive searches and from sources in government, business research, and journalism. Although these searches were at first limited to industrial management, the school persuaded people in different areas of business to provide accounts of their practices and experiences. This research was called *fieldwork* and was done on field trips.[6] There was no attempt to present either good or bad, successful or unsuccessful practices. Rather, the intent was to present the typical and significant problems faced by business administrators. During the period from 1920 to 1940, over $2 million was spent on case development. Dean Donham had achieved the same level of commitment to the case method as had Langdell. Under him, Harvard (and subsequently many other business schools) became case-centered. This orientation reversed previous presumptions about the classroom: The curriculum became discussion-oriented, rather than lecture-oriented.

The insights, analytical judgments, and arguments of the students became so important in some classrooms that professors became facilitators rather than instructors. This outcome did not mean—and does not today mean—that instructors need less preparation time for case-method teaching. The case method is widely thought to involve a more detailed level of preparation than lecturing, demanding more in-class knowledge from student and teacher alike. (Of course, once the case has been taught on several occasions, preparation time decreases for instructors.)

It has never been expected that the case method in business schools could achieve the status of a science or that the cases would be treated in a uniform way. The more typical view has emphasized a broad, commonsense perspective:

> The case method is so varied, so diverse, so adaptable to the nature of the individual course and to the personality of the individual instructor, that no single person can portray it accurately. Indeed, the only discernible common thread . . . is the emphasis on student participation in the educational process . . .—assessing the facts, making the analysis, weighing the considerations, and reaching a decision.[7]

Under this model, the cases collected for courses are chosen with two criteria in mind: (1) The case requires reflection and decision making under circumstances of complexity, and (2) the case will incite vigorous classroom discussion. As the first criterion suggests, cases that involve dilemmas are preferred. As both the first and the second suggest, a case that promotes recounting of information rather than reflective involvement is unacceptable. Accordingly, the presuppositions of business school professors often stand in sharp contrast to those of law professors. Cases in business are not used primarily to illustrate principles or rules. The fundamental idea is to develop a capacity to grasp problems and to reason effectively toward their solutions.

The innovations required for a case-based curriculum generated controversy, and even hostility, at the business school. At stake was the future of two clashing educational philosophies. On the one hand, there is the process of distilling knowledge through lecturing—an efficient manner of transmitting material and one that is comfortable to many students. On the other hand, education can be viewed as a medium that equips the student to confront an environment under constant change and innovation, and in which decisions must be made. To adapt a distinction of Gilbert Ryle's, the difference in training and educational philosophy is rooted in the distinction between knowing *that* and knowing *how*.[8] The purpose of the case method in business has long been to train students in how to think and act in complex and shifting business environments. The pioneers who pushed hardest for the case method knew that facts and general principles were sacrificed in order to sharpen the capacities for thought and decision making. Thus, one might know nothing about what probability theory is but a great deal about how to think under circumstances of probable outcomes.

The Essence of the Case Method

Despite the previously noted warnings about diversity in approaches to cases, there is a certain essence to the technique of the case method as practiced in business schools. This is accurately recounted in a classic article on the case method by Charles I. Gragg:

> A case typically is a record of a business issue which *actually* has been faced by business executives, together with surrounding facts, opinions, and prejudices upon which executive decisions had to depend. These real and particularized cases are presented to students for considered analysis, open discussion, and final decision as to the type of actions which should be taken. Day by day the number of individual business situations thus brought before the students grows and forms a backlog for observing coherent patterns and drawing out general principles. In other words, students are not given theories or hypotheses to criticize. Rather, they are given specific facts, the raw materials, out of which decisions have to be reached in life and from which they can realistically and usefully draw conclusions. . . .
>
> There is no single, demonstrable right answer to a business problem. For the student or businessman it cannot be a matter of peeking in the back of books to see if he has arrived at the right solution. . . .
>
> The instructor's role is ... to provoke argumentative thinking, to guide discussion, ... and if he chooses, to take a final position on the viewpoints which have been threshed out before him. ... But *authoritarian* use of the cases perverts the unique characteristics of the system. The opportunity which this system provides the students of reaching responsible judgments on the basis of an original analysis of the facts is sacrificed.[9]

One conviction underlying this pedagogical viewpoint is that students have typically been trained in universities as if they were children. The lecture-based university assumes that students are unable to think until they have been given a thought apparatus. Decision making is considered an adult function into which students will gradually grow. Those who initiated the case method believed that a school of business has as one of its premiere functions "to achieve the transition from what may be described as a childlike dependence on parents and teachers to a state of what may be called dependable self-reliance."[10] The case method was envisioned as the cornerstone of this shift and advance in pedagogy. Many of its practitioners still hold similar views.[11]

No assumption is made in this method that there is a right answer to any problem that is presented, but only that there are more or less successful ways of handling problems. Just as a medical student must learn not only to diagnose a patient's problem but also to exert a clinical judgment about its alleviation, a student who properly uses the case method not only must understand a problem situation in business but also must construct a recommendation for its resolution.[12] Many cases in this volume unfold so that they demand such resolution from discussants. "Drug Testing at College International Publishers," "An Accountant's Small-Time Trading," and "Rumpole's Revenge, or Women in Catering" are three examples.

However, the larger business community has never been convinced that this method should be the sole—or even chief—mode of instruction. Many companies believe that business is too diverse and requires detailed knowledge unobtainable from case studies alone. For example, CBS decided to sell its ownership of Fawcett Books and the Popular Library. It had not done well in the mass market paperback book industry with these subsidiaries. When it came time to assign blame for failure, the case method received much of the criticism. "Fawcett and Popular were ruined by Harvard MBAs," said Patrick O'Connor, who had moved from Fawcett to Pinnacle Books. He added, "Book publishing is a unique business; it can't be done with case studies."[13]

Good Management and Problem Avoidance. Many moral problems and dilemmas found in this volume could have been avoided or minimized through more skillful management. For example, good management has probably not been present when persons face dilemmas about whether to blow the whistle on corporate wrongdoing. In this chapter, the cases of "An Explosive Problem at Gigantic Motors" and "The Reluctant Security Guard" feature this issue of whistle-blowing. They stimulate reflection on whether, by whom, and when the whistle should be blown. Studying cases to determine which steps management could have taken to avoid ever reaching this point can be beneficial, as can reflecting on procedures that might have deflected or defused a problem.

Often cases should be examined in terms of alternative strategies and actions. Usually such a rich array of alternatives is available that it is not feasible to reach agreement on a single best solution, but such agreement need not be the purpose of case analysis. Learning how to spot and manage problems is no less important. Disagreements may even produce constructive discussions about why some beliefs and principles ought to be reevaluated and readjusted.

Two Concepts of the Case Method

The analysis to this point suggests a critical difference between case analysis in law and in business. Cases in law are based on the reasoning of judges. A court's reasoned opinion is the *form* of the case, the facts the *matter*. In any attempt to extract evidence or other useful parallels from the case, the facts alone are sterile and substitutable. But in business, the cases have no such form. There is no reasoned opinion or precedent case to be studied for its controlling principles and weight of evidence. The cases themselves are nothing but the facts; and one cannot expect from a study of the facts that principles can be generalized. There are no principles and no predictability because there is no set reasoning and no common law. To this extent, legal methods are peculiar to law and cannot be transferred to other professional school contexts.

Thus there are at least two concepts of the case method. Let us call these two methods the *problem-based* case method and the *authority-based* case method. The problem-based case method is the governing ideal in business, although it is now widely used by teachers of ethics. This method focuses critical thinking on a problem. It stimulates reflection on appropriate actions and policies, and the problems provoke decision making on both personal and social levels. In using this method, there is (usually) no ultimate authority, and disagreements are expected to abound.

The authority-based case method contrasts noticeably. Here facts are purely instrumental; the judge's reasoning about the facts is the central feature. Students learn how judges think, and they must master this thinking—not the social or moral problems presented by the case. The problem-based method can be used to examine these same cases, but to employ a problem-based approach is to abandon the authority-based approach. In the latter, predictability in transferring the reasoning from one case to another is a virtue, because what one seeks to learn in using the authority-based method is what will happen in the courts.

The Case Method in Philosophy and Ethics

The philosopher R. B. Perry once tendered the following reflection on education in the humanities:

> [I]n subjects such as philosophy and literature, in which it is likewise respectable to entertain different opinions, teachers hesitate to teach their students how to choose among them, and hesitate themselves to choose. But thought is applied to action through *decision*. Giving students ideas without enabling them to draw conclusions is like giving them sharpened tools without teaching them what to do with them.[14]

Until recently, this perspective had never been connected in philosophy to the case method or to professional practice in fields such as business. Much work done in philosophy is oriented toward a problem-based approach to learning, but the idea of honing the ability to make decisions through case analysis has not traditionally been a part of the curriculum.

This hiatus is modestly surprising. Socrates notoriously practiced some aspects of the case method with consummate skill. He taught moral philosophy by using a method in which he served as a kind of midwife by eliciting from the student reflection, insight, understanding, and both theoretical and practical judgment. He never lectured about ethics, but rather engaged the student in a dialogue that often eventuated in discovery and mutual decision making. His method started with a profession of ignorance (not theory) and proceeded to pointed questions that eventuated in proposed principles or universal definitions. He tested the latter by hypotheses, then modified and tested them further until theoretical insight into principles or definitions was achieved. The term "Socratic method" is today sometimes used synonymously with "case method," because both methods use conversational exchanges to address a particular problem or decision needing investigation and resolution.

Another tradition in the use of cases dates from Aristotle, who discussed the role of practical wisdom and practical judgment in directing human activities. The goal of ethics, he maintained, is to engage in practical reasoning. He depicted a person of practical wisdom as one who envisions what should be done in particular circumstances, using a capacity of prudence and intelligence that he thought distinguishable from intellectual abstraction and cleverness. Such a person has the deliberative excellence essential to achieving the proper ends of practice through choice.

Centuries later, Immanuel Kant discussed the study of cases and examples in sharpening a student's capacity for practical judgment. Kant did not rely as centrally as Aristotle on the person of good practical judgment, but Kant did maintain that the study of case examples is an effective means of training students in practical decision making.

The case method has also had an interesting history in philosophical and theological traditions now commonly referred to as *casuistry.* This tradition is skeptical of rules and principles: One can make actual moral judgments of agents and actions only when one has an intimate understanding of particular situations and a history of similar cases. Apart from an acquaintance with both a situation and a case history, such as case histories in the courts that contain authoritative decisions, one is in no position to resolve moral problems. Until there is a case history rich enough that a cultural unit is able to agree that it is normatively adequate, moral reasoning cannot be applied to new cases within that cultural unit.[15] Just as the courts could not function without case law, we could not be moral reasoners without a similar case history that for us is authoritative.[16]

Recently in philosophy there has been a revival of interest in casuistry as a constructive moral methodology, and, more generally, there has been a stirring of interest in the use of case studies. Many philosophers now insist that their departments should address moral and social problems through both abstract theory and concrete decision making based on attention to particulars. Some have maintained that "case studies are employed most effectively when they can readily be used to draw out broader ethical principles and moral rules ... [so as] to draw the attention of students to the common elements in a variety of cases, and to the implicit problems of ethical theory to which they may point."[17]

One use of cases in both philosophy and business is less as a *source* of generalizations than as a *test* of generalizations. By this criterion, cases help to sharpen and refine theoretical claims, especially by highlighting the uses, inadequacies, and limitations of theories. Cases illustrate the application of ethical notions, rather than act as a medium from which they can be extracted. Also, cases illustrate principles at work, and they exhibit how informed judgments are expressed. Case analysis, then, brings a general principle, proposal, or procedure under scrutiny to see how well it applies to one or more particular circumstances. A related maneuver is the use of cases as counterexamples to proposed principles or policies. For example, various features in the case of "Confidential Accounts at Swiss Bank Corporation" in this volume could be used to test proposed policies of confidentiality of financial information in virtually any banking or brokerage environment. Similarly, "Commissions at Brock Mason Brokerage" could be used to test one's conceptual and moral accounts of conflict of interest.

A somewhat grander vision of case analysis is found in John Rawls's proposal that in developing a normative ethical theory, it is appropriate to start with the broadest set of our considered moral judgments about a subject such as justice and then to erect principles that reflect our judgments. These principles can then be pruned and adjusted by testing cases against them. Suppose, for example, that we select problems of deceptive advertising and corporate failure to be environmentally responsibile for examination. Some widely accepted principles of right action might be construed, as Rawls puts it, "provisionally as fixed points," but also as "liable to revision."[18] Paradigm cases of what we all agree are right courses of action might be listed and examined, and we could then undertake a search for principles consistent with our judgments about these paradigm cases. These principles could be tested by reference to other paradigm cases, and other considered judgments could be found in similar cases, to see whether they yield counterintuitive or conflicting results. The purpose of this process is to bring ethical theories and principles into a coherent unity with our considered judgments about particular cases. Presumably, the more complex and far-reaching the cases that force revisions, the richer the resultant theory will be.

One point of using a more theoretical orientation to cases is that the case method in business can become an unrewarding exposure to the unreflective prejudices of others unless shaped by some moral framework. Discussion and reflection may lack critical distance from cultural blindness, rash analogy, and mere popular opinion. How is the user of cases to identify unjust practices, predisposing bias, and prejudicial use of analogy in order to avoid one-sided judgments?[19] For example, studying the facts in the case of "Lockheed Martin's Acquisition of Comsat" might only immerse one in the current system of lobbying and campaign contributions without achieving any distance from the prejudices or blindness of the system. As valuable as cases are, they cannot be expected to transmit real moral understanding through a recounting of facts unless supplemented by some more general framework or theory.

"The 'Facts' of the Case"

The majority of cases in this volume are factual; most use actual names rather than fictitious ones. What is reported about Napster's commitments and policies, Absolut's marketing of Vodka, AT&T's affirmative action policies, the role of IBM's management in handling its employees, and Nike's use of "commercial speech" are presumably the facts of the case. It is prudent, however, to have reservations about this notion. Events at IBM or Nike may not have transpired exactly as reported here, for several reasons.

First, analysis of the notion of a fact has proved to be an elusive task. A fact is typically analyzed as an empirically confirmable or falsifiable statement that describes some event or object. These factual statements are either true or false. A moral value, by contrast, is an evaluative statement or judgment concerning what is or is not good, right, or virtuous. Evaluative statements appraise and assess events, whereas factual statements describe some concrete aspect of the event and do not appraise or assess. Unfortunately, the ideal of value-neutral facts often dissipates at the level of reports of facts. For example, eyewitnesses in criminal trials often report facts differently; journalists often provide substantially different accounts of a press conference; and scientists use different theories that guide them to see the facts differently from other scientists.

Second, the facts as presented are always selected for a purpose. From an infinity of events in a given day, the nightly national news is condensed to less than thirty minutes. Such selectivity does not itself entail a distorting bias and may be an intelligent and a revealing structuring of an otherwise massive array of events and relationships. The tobacco advertising case in this volume ("Banning Cigarette Advertising") is an example of a long history that requires careful selection from a vast store of accumulated information. Whole volumes and thousands of newspaper articles have been written on some of the cases in this text (e.g., see "Arthur Andersen's Dual Role at Enron"), and yet these volumes and articles themselves omit aspects of what occurred. The cases in this volume have been carefully scrutinized to minimize the problem of bias, but the cautious reader should remember the likelihood that different individuals will describe and evaluate circumstances differently.

This reminder is particularly applicable when companies and individuals are named. The pictures of management in the cases of Mitsubishi Motors and Arthur Andersen, for example, are not favorable, but we lack many facts about what transpired at those companies over a multiyear period. What is emphasized in the case descriptions in this volume may be deemphasized or even ignored in other accounts. There is no neutral mirror of history. Human actors can do no more than interpret the actions of others, without escaping the possibility of bias or incompleteness that such interpretation necessarily entails. A useful rule of thumb is to try to set aside the identities of individuals and companies while *assuming* that the facts are correct. One can then more easily criticize decisions and strategies.

Third, corporations have often been treated harshly by journalists. As a result, many corporations have become leery of turning their records over to journalists or giving informative interviews. At present, there is something of a cold war between the two groups. Journalists tend to view corporations as inherently secretive and as presenting facts with a one-directional spin. Those in management, in turn, often regard journalists as biased and sensationalistic distorters of the truth who tend to see the world in terms of conflicting forces. They view reporters as unqualified for the range of issues their newspapers commission them to study; and they remind us that a single reporter may be assigned to cover (in a remarkably short period of time) such diverse matters as new products, embezzlement schemes, plant relocations, labor relations, securities, investments, price hikes, company growth, CEO salaries, and profits.

This is not the place to arbitrate such distrustful conflicts, but it is pertinent to note that the press is frequently an unavoidable source of certain information about cases (see, e.g., the cases of "Pornography's Many Markets and Distributors," "Nike's Defense of Its Vietnamese Factories," and "Lockheed Martin's Acquisition of Comsat"). In other cases, a corporation may likewise be an indispensable source (see, e.g., "How Reserve Mining Became Cleveland-Cliffs," "The NYSEG Corporate Responsibility Program," and "Confidential Accounts at Swiss Bank Corporation"). The fact that these sources are essential but sometimes uncheckable provides one more reason to place some distance between the facts of the case and the actual circumstances from which they arose. "The facts as reported" or "the facts as they have thus far emerged" are more apt descriptions.

There is a final reason to exercise caution about the facts of the case. Those who study cases almost invariably want more facts. They believe that if only more facts were known, dilemmas and uncertainties would disappear. (Good examples of the felt need for more information are "H. B. Fuller in Honduras: Street Children and Substance Abuse," "Drug Testing at College International Publishers," and "AIDS, Patents, and Access to Pharmaceuticals.") A temptation is to doctor the case by adding hypothetical facts, usually prefaced by someone saying, "But what if ...?" These retreats to new or different facts are understandable reactions, but it is generally best to suppress them in the analysis and discussion of the cases in this volume, which have been selected precisely because they present difficult problems that must be handled in circumstances of incomplete information. Part of the process of case analysis is to confront the problems as presented, not to alter the circumstances or shelve the problems on grounds of insufficient facts. Moreover, presenting more facts often does not dissolve the problem; it may only increase the situation's complexity, an outcome that in turn compounds the challenges inherent in case analysis.

This observation does not imply that it is never useful to modify the conditions and then think through problems under new conditions. To the contrary, this method of modifying the facts can be valuable, and skillful teachers use it with success. Furthermore, these warnings are not intended to discredit the careful reader who looks for pertinent missing facts. However, persons in business must make decisions every day on the basis of incomplete and uncertain information, and the reader should study cases under similar conditions of uncertainty. To do otherwise would be to distort "the 'facts' of the case."

NOTES

1. Langdell's first casebook, *Contracts*, is treated in Lawrence M. Friedman, *A History of American Law* (New York: Simon & Schuster, 1973), pp. 531f. The general account of the case method in this section is indebted to this source, and also to G. Edward White, *Tort Law in America: An Intellectual History* (New York: Oxford University Press, 1980).

2. See White, *Tort Law in America,* esp. pp. 154ff.
3. For a sharp criticism of the method and its milieu in the training of lawyers, see Michael J. Kelly, *The Scandal of American Legal Education* (Baltimore: University of Maryland School of Law, 1979).
4. Melvin T. Copeland, "The Genesis of the Case Method in Business Instruction," in M. P. McNair, ed., *The Case Method at the Harvard Business School* (New York: McGraw-Hill, 1954), p. 25.
5. Donald K. David, "Foreword," in McNair, ed., *The Case Method,* p. 11.
6. Copeland, "The Genesis of the Case Method," in McNair, ed., *The Case Method,* p. 32.
7. McNair, "Editor's Preface," in McNair, ed., *The Case Method,* p. 11.
8. Gilbert Ryle, "Knowing How and Knowing That," *Proceedings of the Aristotelian Society* 46 (1945–1946), pp. 1–16.
9. Charles I. Gragg, "Because Wisdom Can't Be Told," *Harvard Alumni Bulletin* (1940), as reprinted in McNair, ed., *The Case Method,* pp. 6–7, 11–13 (italics added).
10. *Ibid.,* p. 8.
11. For useful pedagogical material, see Louis B. Barnes, C. Christensen, and Abby Hansen, *Teaching and the Case Method* (Cambridge, MA: Harvard Business School Publishing, 2001); and Charles M. Vance, *Mastering Management Education* (Thousand Oaks, CA: Sage Publications, 1993).
12. For readily available and useful material on the case method in business schools, see Darden Business School available from dardencases@virginia.edu (as posted 2003); see Professor James G. Clawson's "Case Method" (UVA-PHA-0032), "Managing Discussions" (UVA-PHA-0049), "Mapping Case Pedagogy" (UVA-PHA-0035). See also the Harvard Business School, at its web site; search under "case method" for a diverse body of materials.
13. John F. Berry, "CBS Decides It Wants Out of the Paperback Business," *The Washington Post,* February 7, 1982, pp. G1, G4.
14. R. B. Perry, *The Citizen Decides: A Guide to Responsible Thinking in Time of Crisis* (Bloomington: Indiana University Press, 1951), Chapter 6.
15. Albert R. Jonsen and Stephen Toulmin, *The Abuse of Casuistry: A History of Moral Reasoning* (Berkeley: University of California Press, 1988); and Jonsen, "Casuistry," in P. Werhane and R. Freeman, eds., *Encyclopedic Dictionary of Business Ethics* (Malden, MA: Blackwell Publishers, 1997). This casuistical tradition was prominent among Jesuits in the seventeenth century when it came under attack by Blaise Pascal in his *Provincial Letters.* The negative characterization of casuistry found in contemporary ethics dates from Pascal's attack. On this intellectual background, see Edmund Leites, ed., *Conscience and Casuistry in Early Modern Europe* (Cambridge: Cambridge University Press, 1988).
16. John Arras, "Principles and Particularity: The Role of Cases in Bioethics," *Indiana Law Journal* 69 (1994), pp. 983–1014.
17. Daniel Callahan and Sissela Bok, *The Teaching of Ethics in Higher Education* (Hastings-on-Hudson, NY: Hastings Center, 1980), p. 69.
18. John Rawls, *A Theory of Justice* (Cambridge, MA: Harvard University Press, revised edition, 1999, esp. pp. 17ff, 40–45, 508–09). See also Rawls's comments on reflective equilibrium in his *Political Liberalism* (New York: Columbia University Press, 1996), esp. pp. 8, 381, 384, and 399; and Norman Daniels, *Justice and Justification: Reflective Equilibrium in Theory and Practice* (New York: Cambridge University Press, 1996).
19. See Cass Sunstein, "On Analogical Reasoning," *Harvard Law Review* 106 (1993), pp. 741–91, esp. 767–78; Loretta M. Kopelman, "Case Method and Casuistry: The Problem of Bias," *Theoretical Medicine* 15 (1994), pp. 21–37.

CASE STUDIES IN BUSINESS, SOCIETY, AND ETHICS

CHAPTER ONE

Employees and the Workplace

Peer Review of Grievances at Shamrock-Diamond Corporation

The Shamrock-Diamond Corporation was founded by an entrepreneur in 1895 as a manufacturer of cutting, drilling, and grinding instruments. By 1912, the company had begun to build overseas plants. Then, as the oil industry grew, Shamrock-Diamond expanded further. In 1965, sales exceeded $300 million for the first time, and the corporation's status progressed from privately held to publicly held. Today it consists of 72 distinct firms employing 18,600 workers at 96 plant sites in 15 countries. The company specializes in cutting tools, drilling equipment, grinding machines, sealants, and safety products.

Mr. Mario Pellegrino has been chief executive officer of this corporation for twelve years. The company has been profitable and has increased its dividends and workforce every year that it has been under his direction. For the past week, Pellegrino has been preparing a presentation and proposal for a meeting of his board of directors. After he calls the meeting to order, he gives his explanation about an additional agenda item. Although the agenda for the meeting had been mailed, the new item was not listed. Pellegrino considered the matter to be too touchy, and he selected this occasion to approach the board with his views. He does not expect these views to be fully shared by board members.

Pellegrino begins his presentation to the board as follows:

> You know that we have always been keen on a high standard of ethics in this corporation. Over the years we have developed separate codes of ethics to govern problems of "questionable payments" abroad, acceptable advertising of our products, and nondiscrimination in employment. These proposals put us out front in the 1980s, and we are still ahead of other American corporations.
>
> Two years ago, as some of you know, I took part of my vacation and attended a two-week seminar on "Ethics and the Business Corporation" at Dartmouth College. To my surprise, the focus of the discussion among the participants in this seminar was on em-

ployee discontent and the responsibilities of management to ame-liorate this discontent. I discovered that only a tiny minority of American corporations have institutionalized ethics programs di-rected at employee-management relationships. These programs in-clude ethics committees and management development programs that have ethics units in their curricula. Many corporations, of course, have so-called "open-door grievance" policies, but these are intimidating to employees and rarely eventuate in truly objective grievance hearings.

One idea that has met with increasing acceptance but also in-creasing resistance is the use of Peer Review Panels to resolve em-ployees' complaints and grievances. This idea was constantly dis-cussed at Dartmouth, and I was deeply impressed with the idea while I was there.

Pellegrino pauses to measure the reaction from his board, which is com-posed of successful businesspersons, none of whom had previously reflected much on these issues of management-employee relationships. He then pro-ceeds to explain that upon returning from the Dartmouth seminar, he immedi-ately set up a meeting with his Council of Managers at a large plant site in Worcester, Massachusetts, for the purpose of implementing a small-scale, two-year test period for peer review of grievances at the plant.

Under his insistent guidance, the managers agreed to the experiment. During the planning stages, they reached the conclusion that one of the poten-tial advantages of having a more explicit personnel policy was that formal rules would protect good managers and good employees alike. Before they began to implement their ideas, the managers established explicit standards for firing, merit evaluation, retirement, and participative management by workers. The first decision they reached was that they would no longer permit a manager to fire an employee without having a stated reason or without informing the em-ployee of his or her right to an independent hearing.

Working closely with some of the most influential managers, Pellegrino implemented his—and now their—ideas for peer review of grievance cases. They appointed four peer employees and three managers to hear each case and ruled that the conclusions of this group were absolutely binding, with no fur-ther appeal possible for a losing party. They also devised an intentionally infor-mal arrangement for hearing the complaint and reviewing the evidence. No representation by lawyers was permitted for any party, and the hearings were conducted in a room with only eight chairs arranged in a circle. The manager, the grievant, and individual witnesses were each called into the room sepa-rately. Coffee was served during the interview, and the discussion proceeded on the model of a conversation among friends. Complete confidentiality was as-sured to all parties, the only exception being that confidentiality could not be assured in the event of a subpoena.

The first case that came before the group involved a five-year, female employee who had received only modest raises for three straight years, whereas comparable male colleagues had received raises that were almost twice as large. The employee had prepared a massive pile of exhibits to show that the manager had a history of downgrading women and upgrading men. Upon review, it was established to the satisfaction of all seven members of the committee that the manager did have a history of favoring men, at least for promotions and raises. Although the manager at first insisted on his objectivity and fairness, he came to see that his record did not support his claim. The employee was given her full raise, retroactive for three years, and her performance ratings were upgraded. The manager promised to reform his processes of review.

Everyone was buoyed by the success of this first case. Even the manager praised the fairness of the process. But as time wore on, the managers had become less satisfied with the experimental procedure. Over the full two-year period, management decisions were upheld in 59 percent of the cases, but managers came to view this statistic as more a failure than a success. Most management victories were won in cases in which employees under their supervision were desperate and had no real opportunity to win. Moreover, virtually every manager had been overruled in a case in which he or she was certain that an unfair decision had been reached through the peer review process. The managers had lost 86 percent of the cases in which they had fired an employee. These employees were typically reinstated under the same manager's supervision, leading to hostility and tension. The reinstated employees disliked working under someone whose authority they had undermined through the grievance process.

Managers came to believe that a system of four peers and three managers was unbalanced and unfair. They felt embarrassed by many of the decisions and believed that their authority was undermined by a procedure that could overturn any of their decisions at any time. Most concluded that they had been asked by the company to be supervisors but that the authority that permitted them to supervise was denied by the peer review system. They were now leery of firing any employee, no matter how poor the person's performance. Almost anything was preferable, they thought, to another grievance hearing. The plant manager who had most closely monitored the hearings admitted that after the end of the two-year experiment, the morale of the managers was at an all-time low.

Pellegrino is fully aware of this disappointing history as he stands before his board. He has repeatedly interviewed the managers at the plant, 85 percent of whom would like to see either the peer review process dismantled or its composition changed so that managers are in the majority. Pellegrino disagrees. He wants to make the process more objective by adding one outside member to the committee, a person from neither labor nor management. Although his managers are highly skeptical of this "third-party solution," as they called it, Pellegrino is firm in his convictions. He now concludes his presentation to the board with the following statement of what are for him heartfelt views:

> Business firms have typically been organized hierarchically, with production line employees at the bottom and the CEO at the top and the interests of the stockholders given supremacy. However,

there are now many reasons to challenge these arrangements. Employees want to make an essential contribution rather than serve as means to the end of profit. They want decent salaries and job security, and they also want appreciation from supervisors, a sense of accomplishment, and fair opportunities to display their talents. Many employees are also interested in participating in the future of the company, defining the public responsibilities of the corporation, and evaluating the role and quality of management.

Although it will be expensive, I want to give our employees all these opportunities. If we can implement this plan for grievance hearings and peer review in all our plants, I am confident we will be a much happier family. I also believe that the corporation as a whole will be better off. We will be more attractive to potential employees, our plants will be built on trust, unions will find no reason to organize our labor forces, and costly lawsuits by employees will not arise.

I want to assure you that if we do successfully implement this program, I will be back asking for more in the way of programs to protect the employment rights of our employees. These policies will cover maximum-hour workweeks, rights against discharge and discipline, privacy rights, severance pay, and standards for pensions. I simply want you to know now what the implications are of your approval of this plan.

At this point Pellegrino turns to his board and asks the members to approve his plan without modification and without further experimental testing at other plants. He notes, however, that there may be room for compromise, despite his strong preference that the package be implemented as a whole.

NOTES

1. http://www.dol.gov/asp/programs/drugs/workingpartners/dot.htm.
2. *Law & Policy Reporter,* 1997 (Lexus-Nexis Academic Universe Document).
3. *Report of the House Subcommittee on National Security, International Affairs, and Criminal Justice.* Second Session. June 27, 1996. Washington, DC: U.S. Government Printing Office, 1997.
4. Jeffrey Rosen, *The Unwanted Gaze* (New York: Random House, 2000).
5. As reported by OraSure Technologies, study performed by LabOne, Inc., "Oral Fluid Testing for Drugs of Abuse: Positive Prevalence Rates . . . ," *Journal of Analytical Toxicology* (Nov./Dec. 2002)

Awkward Advances at *Your Old House* Magazine

At the office of the successful architecture magazine *Your Old House*, two employees—Dominique Franck and Ellsworth Tooley—find themselves avoiding each other. Life at the office is unhappy when they meet. The manager of personnel, Howard Cork is caught up in this awkward situation.

DOMINIQUE FRANCK

Dominique Franck is a senior account representative in the advertising department of *Your Old House*. She supervises junior account representatives who directly contact potential advertisers to sell advertising space. She and Peter Keating, the other senior account representative, are each responsible for half the staff, although her half consistently outperforms Keating's. Both report directly to Henry Cameron, the manager of the advertising department. Recently, Dominique was excited to learn that Cameron will soon be promoted to the magazine's editorial board. Since by any performance standard, her results are greatly superior to Keating's, Dominique feels sure that she is destined to replace Cameron.

Dominique thinks of herself as a self-assured person with a strong desire to succeed in the male-dominated publishing industry. Dominique behaves in what she considers a professional manner at all times. Everyone recognizes that she is a hard worker, typically putting in many hours beyond the forty per week required officially by her position. She sees herself as demanding but never unfair to her subordinates—a combination that she believes accounts for her staff's superior bottom-line performance. Dominique feels some regret that this posture prevents her from developing the kind of workplace friendships that some others develop, but she sees this loss as part of the price she must pay to make it as a woman manager. Dominique keeps a strict separation between her social and her professional lives, and she would never even consider pursuing a personal relationship with any coworker.

This case was prepared by John Hasnas and revised by Tom L. Beauchamp. Not to be duplicated without permission of the holder of the copyright, © 2003 by John Hasnas, George Mason University Law School.

ELLSWORTH TOOLEY

Dominique gets along fairly well with everyone at the magazine except Ellsworth Tooley, one of the senior editors. Ellsworth has both editorial and managerial responsibilities. As an editor, he decides which articles will be printed in the magazine and makes editorial recommendations regarding them. As a senior editor, Ellsworth is also a member of the editorial board, which makes the most important managerial decisions for the magazine. The board is composed of the nine men (no women, as yet) who are senior managers or editors. It has responsibility for selecting those who are to be hired into or promoted to managerial positions.

Ellsworth, now age fifty-two, was born in Lubbock, Texas. His family was extremely poor, and Ellsworth always had to work as a boy, but he managed to put himself through college, getting a B.A. in English at Texas Tech. Following graduation, he married his college sweetheart, got a position as a reporter for *The Dallas Morning News*, and began his career. By 1984, Ellsworth had worked his way up to a high editorial position with *The Dallas Morning News*. At that time, he left Dallas to join the staff of *Your Old House*, then a new magazine. Ellsworth was quite happy with his position, and things had gone well for years until his wife died eighteen months ago. After a very rough six or seven months, during which he saw a psychologist for depression, Ellsworth began to put his life back together and rededicated himself to his work, in large part to compensate for the considerable emptiness in his personal life.

Ellsworth thinks of himself as a skilled professional, but one who has never forgotten the importance of a friendly demeanor that his Texas upbringing impressed upon him. Accordingly, Ellsworth tries hard to maintain an informal and a friendly manner with his coworkers and subordinates. He will often chat with the male employees about sports or politics. He also tries to make small talk with the female employees, although he finds this effort more difficult, since his age, upbringing, and life experience have left Ellsworth largely ignorant of the subjects that are today of interest to women.

Ellsworth has a habit of attempting to greet all coworkers with a complimentary comment in an effort to overcome the intimidating effect that his high-level position can have on lower-level employees. Even when Ellsworth doesn't know their names, he will greet an employee with a comment such as "Nice suit, son" or "Looking good today, dear."

FRICTION BETWEEN DOMINIQUE AND ELLSWORTH

Dominique has long considered Ellsworth to be a typical "male chauvinist pig." Ellsworth habitually engages in behaviors that Dominique finds offensive and demeaning to the women who work at the magazine. She despises the way he addresses the women on the staff as "Honey" or "Dear"—and refers to them collectively (in conversations with other men) as the magazine's "Fillies." In addition, he far too often greets them with some comment about their appearance such as "Nice dress. I don't know how I'll keep my mind on my work while you're around."

Ellsworth is unaware that several women in the office view him as Dominique does. He believes that he gets along fairly well with everyone at the magazine except Dominique—who, he now realizes, abhors him. In his opinion, she could accurately be described as uptight, arrogant, cold, aloof, and demanding. He has heard repeatedly from the reps that she is driving them unmercifully hard, while hardly ever dispensing a "Nice job" or "Well done." Ellsworth believes that her bottom-line results have been gained at the expense of a happy workforce, even a grumpy one. This treatment does not represent the managerial style that he deems most appropriate for an organization like *Your Old House.*

Five months ago, Dominique and Ellsworth had a serious run-in. After a private meeting in his office concerning the advertising budget, Ellsworth asked Dominique to go out to dinner with him. It was during his loneliest period, and he was desperate for female company and a social life. On that particular day, he couldn't stand the thought of going home again to an empty house. Dominique told him that since he was a superior of hers, and one whose judgment could have an effect on her future career, she thought it would be inappropriate and that she had a personal policy of never dating coworkers. Rather than accept her refusal, Ellsworth responded by saying, "Oh, loosen up, Dominique. People go out with coworkers all the time. Let your hair down. I guarantee you that you won't be disappointed."

Dominique found this response to be both condescending and offensive, possibly even threatening. Still, she retained her calm and said, "Mr. Tooley, you are putting me in a very awkward situation. I don't think it would be a good idea, and I'd appreciate it if you would drop the subject." Although shaking at the time, Dominique thought she had acquitted herself well under the circumstances. For his part, Ellsworth interpreted what she said to mean that she would like to go out with him but was concerned with the appearance of impropriety. He did understand that she found it an awkward situation and that she would rather not go out.

A few days following this encounter, Dominique overheard two of the female secretaries discussing Ellsworth at lunch. Upon inquiring, she learned that he had propositioned these two single women and thereby had profoundly upset both of them. The final straw for Dominique came the following week when she encountered Ellsworth at the water fountain. Ellsworth, who was passing by at the time, said, "Have you reconsidered my proposal of last week? I would really like to get to know you better."

From the look on her face, Ellsworth realized that he had made a second terrible error in judgment. He knew, after reflecting on the first time he had asked Dominique out, that he was seeking an escape from his loneliness and

rate behavior in Japan and that Japanese plant managers in the United States were simply attempting to integrate American male workers fully into a "Japanese" industrial and corporate culture in order to promote harmony, loyalty, productivity, and good morale.

Another cultural factor cited as a source of problems is the tradition of loyalty of Japanese employees to their employer. Employees cited long-standing efforts to instill and to foster such attitudes at all levels of management in the Illinois plant, in order to counter the American tradition or custom of confrontation between management and union employees. In this instance, the cultural strategy may have backfired by encouraging managers to respond unsympathetically and defensively to the filing of complaints about sexual harassment. A computer programmer at the plant explained that there was little that sympathetic bystanders could do to protect women from abuse. He testified that Japanese management informed people who complained of inappropriate behavior that "the nail that sticks up gets beaten down."[6]

Press reports in Japan have been very different from American press reports. The majority opinion in Japan seems to be that this entire affair has been overblown and that the cultural criticisms represent simply another instance of "Japan bashing" in the United States. However, many Japanese citizens, including younger workers and females, take a different view. A young female management trainee at a rival Japanese automaker who had also studied in the United States expressed disdain for the behavior of Mitsubishi workers and for the defensive response of the Japanese press. The issues, she felt, were generational and gender-based, not cultural.[7]

II

Mitsubishi Motors Vice President and General Counsel, Gary Schultz, issued a statement to the press in response to the formal filing of the EEOC suit, stating that "discrimination of any kind will never [be]—and has never been—tolerated at this plant." Though he criticized the filing of the suit as politically motivated (during an election year), Schultz later admitted that the company had itself documented eighty-nine incidents of sexual harassment over the past ten years—a rate (he hastened to add) far below that claimed in the current litigation.[8]

Following the announcement of formal charges, the plant management sent a letter to its employees maintaining that the company "cannot allow allegations of political and monetary motivation to dampen our morale and efforts."[9] At the suggestion of Sheila Randolph, a procurement branch manager, the company organized a rally for workers near the Chicago regional office of the EEOC. Schultz himself made an announcement to employees in a company-wide meeting:

> "We've got to win the media by parading thousands-strong in Chicago. . . . [The suit makes the company look like] a band of sex

maniacs. . . . We can't tell you what to do because if we do it comes across as so biased that it losses its effect. . . . You are all clever people. . . . I ask you to think of things that might help us get through this. . . . I want to see a backlash."[10]

Nearly 3,000 workers attended the Chicago rally. The company shut down production at the Illinois plant for a day, paid employees their full salary, and provided lunch and round-trip transportation, chartering altogether some fifty-nine busses to transport volunteer participants to Chicago. One worker explained at the rally, "We're here because right now we're worried about our jobs, and that the publicity will hurt our products."[11]

The sign-up sheets for the rally that were posted in advance throughout the plant indicated those employees who supported the plant and singled out those who did not. Those who chose not to participate in the rally were expected to work their normal plant shift and were required to submit written explanations for this choice to their supervisors. The company also set up phone banks in the plant and encouraged workers to telephone their congressional representatives, the White House, and representatives of the media (on company time and at company expense) in order to defend the integrity of the company. Anna Rogers, a technical coordinator in the plant, was quoted as having described the EEOC suit as "just a blatant case of slander."[12]

Some employees subsequently reported that the company-sponsored responses to the pending suit created an extremely tense working environment within the plant. Many women who had not initially complained of harassment stated that, at this time, they were pressured to support the plant publicly and that the pressure inflamed gender-based hostilities in the plant. Several residents of the town of Normal spoke out in favor of the plant and against the veracity of the women plaintiffs. Local female restaurant employees interviewed by a reporter from *The Washington Post* described the EEOC's action as "a bucket of hogwash," claiming that the male auto workers' actions were "all in good fun."[13]

Not all executives in the Mitsubishi international conglomerate (or *keiretsu*), however, agreed with the strategies pursued by the Mitsubishi Motors division. "I think it's a terrible idea. It sounds like pressuring someone rather than going through the judicial process," said James Brumm, the General Counsel at Mitsubishi International Corporation, a New York-based trading company. Another public relations official in the conglomerate added this: "I'm totally mystified. I'm not so concerned about being branded the discrimination company any more, but being branded the incompetence company."[14]

III

In addition to the aggressive response to the EEOC, Mitsubishi Motors pursued legal counteraction against twenty-eight female workers who independently filed a private sexual harassment suit. The company's lawyers asked for the plaintiffs' gynecological and psychological records. "One of the plaintiffs has a pattern of promiscuous sexual behavior involving male workers at the plant," said Roy David, a lawyer for Mitsubishi.[15] For several weeks following the formal filing of charges, the company steadfastly refused to cooperate with the EEOC on its investigation of the sexual harassment allegations. The company maintained that it would like to settle the case promptly but not on the government's terms.

Abruptly, on July 16, 1996, the management at Mitsubishi Motors decided to change the direction of its strategy. Officials announced that they would begin "a comprehensive training program on sexual harassment for all of the more than 4,000 employees at the plant, beginning with managers. Senior executives will participate annually in a two-day workshop entitled 'Men and Women as Colleagues,'" the company reported. The company also announced that it had retained former U.S. labor secretary Lynn Martin to review its policies and make recommendations for needed changes. In addition, Mitsubishi announced that it would hire an employee to serve as ombudsman to collect and adjudicate complaints concerning sexual and racial discrimination and that it would start a vigorous program to increase the number of its car dealerships owned by women and minorities. Tsuneo Ohinouye, Mitsubishi's chairman and CEO, called a news conference to announce the innovations and stated that he hoped to settle the EEOC lawsuit in the near future.

EEOC Chairman Gilbert F. Casellas responded by praising Mitsubishi's efforts to improve the Illinois workplace through such training but also warned that the company's actions "in no way affect the EEOC's ongoing litigation against Mitsubishi." An attorney representing the women who had filed a separate lawsuit against the company criticized the new program as "window dressing," noting that the company had thus far done nothing to compensate the women who had experienced severe sexual harassment.[16]

IV

The suit brought by female employees was settled in 1997 for about $10 million. However, the suit brought by the EEOC in 1996 continued beyond this point. In an attempt to satisfy the EEOC, Mitsubishi took a number of steps to reduce the potential recurrence of sexually discriminatory incidents, particularly in response to an extensive body of recommendations made by Lynn Martin and consultants whom she had appointed to review the situation.

The company proposed a set of workplace changes that included restructuring equal employment opportunity functions, comprehensive training in sexual harassment prevention through a new required course on the subject, systematic inspection of job descriptions and job assignments to check for racial and sexual bias, more sensitivity in work hours to the demands of child-rearing, new and improved leadership in the human resources department, scaling salaries higher for managers who demonstrate an ability to handle sexual harassment charges, creating new positions that facilitate communication among company employees and management, and setting up a team from outside the company to monitor progress in the company on an ongoing basis.

Martin's group of consultants recommended thirty-four changes in its final report, all accepted by management. These systemic changes came as the culmination of recommendations by Martin's three-person staff, who had spent two years at Mitsubishi, at a cost of $2 million. According to Steven Hofman, a labor consultant who coordinated the Martin review, this new system will "send the clear message, through action as well as policy, that inappropriate behavior is not tolerated" in this company. Martin herself expressed the opinion that sexual harassment occurs in innumerable plants in the United States, that cultural stereotyping had falsely (in this case) pointed to Japanese culture as at the root of the problem, and that Mitsubishi had taken the unusual step of grappling aggressively and seriously with the problem and moving forward. The company claimed that, with Martin's assistance, it had achieved a "model workplace."[17] Japanese officials were reported in the Japanese press as being optimistic that these changes, when implemented, would pave the way for a settlement with the EEOC.

Within a year of Martin's recommendations, Mitsubishi settled the case with the EEOC. The court's Consent Decree, entered June 23, 1998, provided for payment of $34 million to the victims of sexual harassment at Mitsubishi's facility in Normal, Illinois, for wide-ranging injunctive relief, and for the creation of a blue-ribbon panel of monitors to track Mitsubishi's efforts to comply with the Decree.[18] In September 2000, three monitors submitted their second annual report under the Consent Decree, stating that "Mitsubishi is in compliance with the Decree, has sexual harassment in the plant firmly under control, and has made commendable progress in improving its systems for preventing such behavior and dealing with it appropriately when it occurs."[19] However, the report also cautioned that continued vigilance would be required: "The challenge for [Mitsubishi] now is to institutionalize these systems [for preventing and dealing with sexual harassment] so that when the Decree expires a year from now, the company can continue the significant progress it has made."[20]

The final report released on May 23, 2001, reiterated the successes that Mitsubishi had achieved, with a corollary warning against falling into complacency. The EEOC stated that it was encouraged by the final report and had become convinced that the policies that the litigation had prompted had made and would continue to make a "huge and positive difference in the daily work life of many women." The EEOC was convinced that an active and ongoing system of monitoring by outside reviewers had been effective (two members of the three-member panel board were women). The EEOC soon thereafter declared victory and closed its investigation of Mitsubishi. It agreed with the company that many positive changes had been made and that continuing efforts were under way to maintain a proper workplace environment.[21]

However, several commentators have pointed to the difficulty of changing the long-standing corporate culture of a company in a few months—or even a few years—especially when the problems of sexual harassment were as pervasive as the evidence indicates they were at the Mitsubishi plant. In interviews conducted by *The New York Times* in 2000, current and former Mitsubishi workers claimed that sexual harassment remains a serious problem despite the policies enacted by Mitsubishi to change the situation.[22] Many female workers declined to discuss the issue, and few workers were willing to go on the record about their experiences at the plant. Other workers, predominantly male, complained to *Times* reporters about a double standard, asserting that the company ignores all provocative behavior by women and minorities, while assiduously guarding against such behavior by white males.

NOTES

1. Korsten Downey Grimsley, "EEOC Says Hundreds of Women Harassed at Auto Plant," *The Washington Post,* 10 April 1996, p. A13.
2. "EEOC Sues Mitsubishi Unit for Harassment," *The Wall Street Journal,* April 10, 1996, p. B1.
3. "Why Men Stay Silent: Fear of Retaliation Fostered Abusive Atmosphere, Mitsubishi Workers Say," *The Washington Post,* May 26, 1996, p. H7.
4. *Ibid.,* p. H1.
5. *Ibid.,* p. H7.
6. *Ibid.,* p. H7.
7. Privileged correspondence, discussing the news reports and public reaction to the U.S. Mitsubishi case in Japan; name withheld by request.
8. *The Washington Post,* April 10, 1996, p. A13.
9. "Fighting Back: A Mitsubishi U.S. Unit Is Taking a Hard Line in Harassment Battle," *The Wall Street Journal,* April 22, 1996, p. A1.
10. *Ibid.*
11. "Mitsubishi Workers March on EEOC," *The Washington Post,* April 23, 1996, p. A9.
12. "Mitsubishi Organizes Rallies to Protest Sex-Harassment Suit," *The Wall Street Journal,* April 18, 1996, p. B12.
13. "Auto Plant Sexual Harassment Case Divides Community," *The Washington Post,* April 24, 1996, p. A17.
14. "Fighting Back: A Mitsubishi U.S. Unit Is Taking a Hard Line in Harassment Battle," *The Wall Street Journal,* April 22, 1996, p. A1.
15. "Lawsuit Distracts Mitsubishi Motors from Repair Effort," *The Wall Street Journal,* April 29, 1996, p. A19.
16. "Mitsubishi Takes Steps to Reshape Workplace," *The Washington Post,* July 17, 1996, pp. D1, D8.
17. *Newsday* (Nassau and Suffolk Edition), February 13, 1997, p. A75; "Mitsubishi Fields Plan to Fight Sexual Harassment," *Associated Press* release, February 13, 1997; "Model Workplace Plan Unveiled for Mitsubishi Motors Manufacturing," *Japan Economic Institute Report,* No. 7 (February 21, 1997). See also http://www.jei.org/Archive/JEIR97/9707w4.html
18. EEOC, Chicago District Office, U.S. Equal Employment Opportunity Commission Press Release: "Monitors Say Mitsubishi in Compliance with EEOC Consent Decree; Sexual Harassment 'Firmly Under Control' at U.S. Plant," September 6, 2000; See, further, EEOC, U.S. Equal Employment Opportunity Commission Press Release: "EEOC Responds to Final Report of Mitsubishi Consent Decree Monitors," May 23, 2001.
19. "U.S. Equal Employment Opportunity Commission Press Release," September 2, 2000.
20. *Ibid.*
21. EEOC Chicago District Office, U.S. Equal Employment Opportunity Commission Press Release: "EEOC Responds to Final Report of Mitsubishi Consent Decree Monitors," May 23, 2001.
22. Reed Abelson, "Can Respect Be Mandated? Maybe Not Here," *The New York Times,* September 10, 2000, Section 3, p. 1

The Reluctant
Security Guard

David Tuff, age twenty-four, is a security guard who was on the payroll for seventeen months at the Blue Mountain Company in Minneapolis, Minnesota. Blue Mountain manages and operates retail shopping malls in several midwestern states. The company has a security services division that trains and supplies mall security guards, including those for the Village Square Mall where Tuff was until recently employed.

Minnesota state and local laws require that security officers be licensed and approved by the county police department. Security officers are required to obey the police unit's rules. Tuff completed the required training, passed the security guard compulsory examination, and was issued a license. He consistently carried out his guard duties conscientiously. Previously a four-year military policeman in the U.S. Marine Corps, Tuff was praised by his commanding officer for both his service and his integrity.

Part of his job training at Blue Mountain required that Tuff learn the procedures found in the *Security Officer's Manual*, which uses military regulations as a model. Two sections of this manual are worded as follows:

Section V, subsection D.

> Should a serious accident or crime, including all felonies, occur on the premises of the licensee, it shall be the responsibility of the licensee to notify the appropriate police department immediately. Failure to do so is a violation of the provisions of this manual.

Furthermore, the manual permits the following action if the provisions are violated:

Section XI—disciplinary and deportment

A. General
1. The Private Security Coordinator may reprimand a licensee as hereinafter provided. In cases of suspension or revocation, the licensee shall immediately surrender his identification card and badge to the County Police Department. . . .

B. Cause for Disciplinary Action
   13. Any violation of any regulation or rule found in this manual is cause for disciplinary action.

The reverse side of a security officer's license bears these statements:

Obey The Rules And Regulations Promulgated By The Superintendent Of Police.
   We will obey all lawful orders and rules and regulations pertaining to security officers promulgated by the superintendent of police of the county or any officer placed by him over me.

Given this language, Tuff believed that his license could be revoked or suspended for *any* failure to report illegal behavior such as drunk driving and selling narcotics. He had sworn to uphold these regulations at the end of his training and had signed a statement acknowledging that he knew a police officer could ask for his badge if a conflict should arise.

Fourteen months after Tuff joined the company, Blue Mountain issued new rules of procedure outlining certain assigned duties of its security guards. These rules required security officers "to order and escort intoxicated persons, including persons driving under the influence of alcohol, off its parking lots and onto the public roads." The rules did not instruct security officers either to arrest the drivers or to contact or alert the police.

Tuff immediately spoke out in opposition to the company's new policy. Over the ensuing months, he expressed his dissatisfaction to every company officer he could locate. He complained to his superiors, sometimes several times a day, that he was being asked to set a drunk out on the road who might later kill an innocent person. Tuff described to these supervisors several imaginary but very realistic scenarios in which a drunk clearly violated the law just after being escorted off one of the mall parking lots. He depicted bone-chilling circumstances in which it was known that drunk drivers when escorted away were in no condition to drive and then later hit and killed a pedestrian.

His immediate supervisor, Director of Security Manuel Hernandez, told him that if any such situation arose, he should contact the on-duty supervisor in charge, who would make the decision. Hernandez noted that most drunks do not weave down the road and hit someone. Tuff was not satisfied and used mildly abusive language in denouncing the rules. He was not abusive to Hernandez, who had been his friend, but Hernandez became upset and told Tuff that his complaints irritated his supervisors and that they could tolerate only so much of his rude behavior. Hernandez also cautioned him that he should worry less about his license and more about his paycheck. Neither man put any complaint in writing. Tuff never received a written warning or reprimand from any company official. He repeated many times that he considered the policy to be illegal, violative of the rules he had sworn to uphold, and dangerous to the maintenance of his license. Neither his supervisor nor the company manager agreed with his interpretation. They encouraged him to continue his job as usual, but under the new rules.

Tuff then contacted a volunteer organization working to prevent drunk driving. At first he simply sought the interpretation of a lawyer at the organization concerning whether the policy was legal and whether his license was in jeopardy, but later he voiced a specific complaint about the Blue Mountain policy. Tuff's supervisors were then approached, on the basis of this complaint, by representatives of the volunteer organization, which expressed strong opposition to Blue Mountain's policy for security guards and its rules regarding the treatment of drunk drivers. The organization's representatives stated that they agreed with Tuff that the policy violated the rules that security guards had sworn to uphold and that the policy was dangerous to the maintenance of the licenses of the guards.

In the following weeks, Tuff discussed the company policy with several other concerned security guards employed by Blue Mountain. He met with security officers Fred Grant and Robert Ladd at a restaurant after work. They discussed the company procedure and its conflict with their licensing requirements and sworn commitments. They considered going, as a group, to the local newspaper with their grievances over the company policy.

Instead, Tuff, on his own initiative, contacted a local television news station and a local newspaper. He talked to four reporters about several drunk driving incidents at Blue Mountain parking lots. The reporters pursued Tuff's stories by talking to company officials about the policy. The reporters were subsequently able to prove to their editors' satisfaction that Tuff's complaints to the media were not given in reckless disregard of the truth and were, in fact, truthful.

Hernandez called Tuff into his office to discuss these disclosures to the TV news team and the newspaper. Hernandez asked Tuff to sign a document acknowledging that he had spoken with news reporters concerning Blue Mountain company policies, but he refused to sign. Hernandez reminded him of a company policy prohibiting an employee from talking to the media about company policies. This policy is mentioned on a list of company rules distributed to all employees that states that violation of the rules could result in dismissal or in disciplinary procedures. Tuff knew the company rule but did not consider his revelations a violation, because he had not spoken with the press *on company time.*

Hernandez considered Tuff's interpretation of the rule's scope ridiculous. He consulted with the company's Council of Managers that afternoon. Every manager agreed that Tuff's interpretation of the rule showed a blatant disregard for company policy and that Tuff's excuse was an ad hoc rationalization. They also agreed that Tuff had shown himself to be a complainer and a man of poor judgment, qualities that rendered him unsuitable to be a Blue Mountain security guard. The discussion of this problem at the meeting took little more than ten minutes. Council members instructed Hernandez to give Tuff a few days' leave to reflect on the situation. Hernandez duly reported this conclusion to Tuff, who then departed for his home. The number of days of leave he should take was not specified, but both men agreed in an amicable though tense meeting that they would be in touch.

CHAPTER TWO

Customers, Clients, and Consultants

KCRC's Incentives for Advertisers

San Francisco radio station KCRC is owned by ACME Investments, a large company with many subsidiary interests. KCRC broadcasts a classic rock format popular with the city's twenty-five to forty-nine age group, which accounts for about 50 percent of the metropolitan population. In operation since 1986, KCRC currently leads in the Arbitron Radio national ratings for the classic rock category. Approximately twenty-five radio stations in the same division directly compete with KCRC.

Radio stations generate income by selling advertising air time. The radio industry competes directly with newspaper and television syndicates for advertising clients, and rival local radio stations compete for the available advertising dollars. San Francisco Bay area radio stations earned approximately $240 million in advertising revenues in 2002. Advertisers must allocate their funds among the competing radio, television, print, and billboard markets; radio garners only about 9 percent of all media advertising dollars. (A single large newspaper often receives over $400 million in advertising revenues in a single year.)

To maintain station profitability in the competitive advertising market, KCRC station manager and part owner, Scott Reed, together with ACME's top management, created an "incentive" program for advertisers. They and many others in the business call it a "value-added incentive." ACME designed the plan to ameliorate the annual first-quarter revenues slump (known in the industry as "soft time"), during which there is extensive air-time availability. They wanted to use value-added incentives to attract the top advertisers; and they had seen it used successfully by national networks and leading firms in the broadcasting and telecommunications industry (and in some journals in the industry). The successes had been most impressive.

Under the KCRC plan, clients who spent $36,000 in "new" money in first-quarter advertising would receive a free, all-expenses-paid (and tax-free) cruise for two to Cozumel, Mexico, with travel to, and tickets for, the Super Bowl on the return trip. "New" money meant that *existing* clients had to in-

This case was prepared by Tom L. Beauchamp, with research assistance from John Hannula and Megan Hughes, and revisions by John Cuddihy, Katy Cancro, and Jeff Greene. It is entirely based on fact, but names have been changed to protect the sources of the information. Not to be duplicated without permission of the holder of the copyright, © 1992, 1996, 2003 by Tom L. Beauchamp.

crease current advertising by $36,000, and *new* clients had to spend $36,000 to be eligible. The first quarter ran from December 17, 2001, to April 15, 2002 (to include the pre-Christmas advertising period as an incentive to provide additional benefit for advertisers). Each client received air time during the quarter for the $36,000. The trip cost KCRC $8,500 per client (each "client" being a couple).

As the incentive plan evolved, Scott became concerned for two reasons. First, he believed that some clients were purchasing unneeded and perhaps unwanted air time just to obtain the vacation. The businesses that participated in the incentive program were usually small and family-owned, with the owner doubling as the business's financial manager. Scott wondered whether the cruise offer led the owners to make unsound business judgments that were based on personal or family reasons, rather than business reasons. Upon "earning" the incentive cruise, one diamond merchant stated flatly that the station's plan was the only factor in his decision to purchase the additional air time.

Second, Scott thought the plan might function to lower KCRC's overall profit margin. More cost-effective options and better business incentives, such as decreased advertising rates, could have been used instead to attract the same business. ACME had employed Scott to increase station profits, but he worried that perhaps the Super Bowl cruise was not the best possible strategy with which to achieve the station's financial goals. The incentive program, from his perspective, ran the risk of undercutting *profits* with its considerable expenditure on clients, even though *revenue* would increase. Although Scott's regional vice president at ACME and his staff adamantly disagreed with him, there seemed to be no way to demonstrate who was more likely to be correct.

One client, Ray Manta, raised a special concern. He was employed by a new publishing company owned by the largest bookstore chain in the United States. When approached about the cruise trip, he reported to Scott that "I can't accept anything as a gift, because my employer has strict rules against both gifts and kickbacks." However, three hours later, Ray was back on the phone with Scott. He wanted to know whether the station considered the incentive plan a *gift.* Scott informed him that the station viewed the offer as a *bonus,* not as a gift. Ray still felt that under the rules of his parent company, he could not accept such a bonus. He did believe, however, that if he paid for the cost of the trip out of his personal funds, he would not be violating company rules. Ray had discussed the trip with his wife, who was enthusiastic about the prospect.

After further reflection, Ray called Scott and said, "I know the actual cost to you can't be $8,500, so can you tell me the real cost?" Scott's actual costs were in fact $8,500, but he knew that Ray was tempted by the carrot. He said he would check the "real costs" and get back to him. Scott called a travel agent and confirmed that some much less elegant and shorter cruise and Super Bowl trips were being marketed at $3,400.

Scott then went to Ray's office. With a wink, Ray asked, "What are the real costs?" With a wink back, Scott queried, "What do you think they are?" Ray said, "Oh, I imagine $3,200 is about right." Scott, with mock surprise, quickly to really raunchy stuff—just hard-core porn. . . . I thought: What are we doing? We don't have topless waitresses in the restaurant."[14]

It took Omni several years to implement family programing in its hotel rooms because the companies that provide pay-per-view service to hotels are often reluctant to exclude adult films from their offerings, fearing a resulting loss in profits.[15] After months of negotiation, LodgeNet agreed to provide Omni Hotels with a cable system that excluded pornographic fare. Although many hotels argue that customer demand dictates the services they provide, including in-room adult entertainment, Omni claims to have found that its customers support the company's decision to exclude adult movies from its entertainment offerings. The company has received more than 50,000 letters in support of its new policy since its implementation.[16]

General Motors is—as of this writing—a significant distributor of legal pornographic movies through DirecTV, which is owned by the GM subsidiary Hughes Electronics. Through DirecTV, GM provided service to 9 million homes in the United States in 2000,[17] and in the same year DirecTV users spent an estimated $200 million on pay-per-view adult films.[18] In October 2001, General Motors agreed to sell Hughes Electronics, including DirecTV, to EchoStar Communications for approximately $26 billion.[19] However, there was no indication that the sale of DirecTV was prompted by any concerns about the content of the programming available on the cable system.

AT&T also distributes adult movies through its digital cable system. In 2001, AT&T earned more than $62 billion in annual revenues and provided cable services to 16 million homes in the United States.[20] In December 2001, AT&T, like General Motors, arranged to sell AT&T Broadband to the rival cable company Comcast for $47 billion in stock and $25 billion in assumed debt.[21] However, there is no indication that the sale was prompted by concerns about the content of the programming offered by the cable system.

According to the company's website and its on-screen program guides, DirecTV offers adult programming to its viewers through pay-per-view channels such as Vivid TV, the Hot Network, and the Hot Zone. The website also describes the system of parental controls that are available to customers free of charge. Parents may choose to restrict any number of channels or may restrict programs above a particular rating. Parents may also set a spending limit on pay-per-view channels. These controls do not prevent parents from viewing restricted programs because a PIN number allows them to bypass the controls.[22]

AT&T Broadband's cable system also distributes adult films through pay-per-view channels, including the Hot Network.[23] According to the AT&T website, parents can control access to these movies by blocking particular movies or programs or by blocking programs with particular ratings. Parents can also set a limit on the amount of money that may be spent on pay-per-view each month or can prevent adult titles from being shown on the screen.[24]

For mainstream companies, the motivation for involvement in the distribution of pornography is similar to that cited by Marriott and Hilton within the context of the hotel industry. Customer demand and higher profits drive mainstream cable companies into the distribution of pornography. Adult pay-per-view features are more profitable for cable companies than less explicit films. Cable companies such as DirecTV or AT&T Broadband typically receive 80 percent of the revenue that flows from adult pay-per-view movies, whereas they usually receive only 50 percent or less of the revenue that flows from mainstream Hollywood films.[25] In addition, adult videos are priced higher for the consumer—often double or triple the cost of mainstream films. Though the costs involved in making adult videos is less, customers are willing to pay more to view them.

In a 2000 letter, Daniel Sommers, President and CEO of AT&T Broadband, responded to the concerns of consumers who do not approve of the adult content offered on the AT&T Broadband pay-per-view system. He said, "We're upgrading our Broadband systems in response to customer demand for more choice and better value in cable service. . . . We think this combination of choice and control is the most appropriate method of distributing for an adult pay-per-view channel such as The Hot Network. . . . This service is available only to those customers who seek it out, individually order it, pay a fee for it, and choose to watch it in the privacy of their homes."[26] The letter points out that The Hot Network is also featured on other cable networks, suggesting that AT&T Broadband offers this programming in order to compete with other companies.

Some critics have expressed concerns that when mainstream companies such as AT&T and General Motors become involved in the adult film business, films that were once on the margins of entertainment may become more acceptable in society at large. When the cochairman of the Religious Alliance Against Pornography, Cardinal William Keeler, met with AT&T Chairman Michael Armstrong in the spring of 2001, he told Armstrong, "When a company like AT&T, which has won the hearts and allegiance of so many, gets into this business, it's a way of legitimating it, saying it's OK, it's alright. That's the 'Good Housekeeping Seal of Approval', and we don't want to see it put on this kind of business."[27]

Other critics of the pornography industry claim that adult films represent the exploitation of women and the decay of family values. These critics range from religious leaders who argue that pornography in any form is sinful, to antipornography proponents who claim that "pornography is degrading to women and sets them back to a time when they were looked upon as mere sex objects and nothing more."[28] Antipornography feminists also point to a correlation between pornography and sexual crimes, arguing that the "facts are clear. Sex and violent crime offenders have a critical link to pornography. These sex offenders had a high exposure to pornography as adolescents, and it carries on with them during their lifetime."[29]

There are several social investment mutual funds that attract investors with an antipornography stance. Either these funds decline to own stock in any company that distributes or produces pornography, or they use ownership of such stock to attempt to bring about change within the company. For example, *it's not my job to determine our sales policy. Isn't that part of your marketing strategy? I thought our policy was that all product inquiries should be passed on to the sales department and that the decisions would be made there. Don't you check the background of these people, Ellen? I thought everyone knew that Sequa was in trouble.*

Ellen: *OK, let's calm down a little. Obviously, we have a little confusion here. No, Rachel, I don't sign off on every sale. I haven't had time to investigate every contact that Mitchell is following up. But of course there are some users I would be really uncomfortable about our releasing our product to. Mitchell, maybe you and I need to get together to agree what our policy should be and whom we would and would not like to be working with.*

Siegler: *Hold on, I've never really said this before, but if we are getting into the business of working only with people that we like, then I've got some problems with Celltechron. They are using private funding to do research in areas prohibited by federally funded research, including the creation of embryos. I am strongly opposed to my programming skills being used for experiments that are just unethical. Don't I get a say in what our customer policy is?*

Leheny: *Never mind the people you object to, Siegler. There's a whole bunch of sales that we are proposing where we have no idea what our software will be used for. I've been talking to labs in China, Russia, and The Netherlands. All they will tell me is that they are doing leading-edge genetic research. They could be doing all sorts of dreadful things that we might think are immoral, and yet we would never know.*

There's a principle here. We are making software that allows people to experiment with the fundamental code of life. We have a duty to make sure that the people we sell to are not using our product for evil purposes. You wouldn't market whips to a torture regime, would you?

Mitchell: *Look, I don't know what you want me to do here. I wish I'd never opened my mouth. Of course I wouldn't sell to crazy, evil people, but what is our basis for accepting customers—that they are goody-goodies? Look at our biggest customer of all, HealthPharma. It's one of the biggest and most respected pharmaceutical firms in the world. But last year they got caught overcharging Medicare by $10 million. Does that make them unethical? Does that mean we shouldn't do business with them? Come on, guys! We are just starting up this business. We have a bit of a market lead, but we have several competitors just a few steps behind us, who would just love us to start rejecting business. And what will Accelerix say if we start to slow down? They've just been parading us to the stock-market analysts as the exemplar of the new growth strategy. They are trying to pave the way for an IPO for us in twelve months. Investors don't like uncertainty; we have to sort this out now. Ellen, I need help. You need to give me some guidelines here.*

Ellen: *Look, everyone has got a little overexcited here. Sorry, it's my fault. I should have closed this conversation down earlier. We need to have a structured debate about this. We need to come up with a plan that we are all comfortable with and that allows us to grow the business. Let's arrange a brainstorming meeting for tomorrow. I encourage you all to think about this stuff tonight and concentrate on coming up with some concrete proposals on how we deal with whether or how we should limit who we do business with.*

NEXT DAY'S MEETING

Ellen still didn't know what she felt about the issues. As a rule she liked to have as few policies as possible and to encourage debate and personal initiative within her team. However, maybe these issues were so high-risk that a strong policy would be the only solution. On the other hand, wouldn't a policy get continuously out-of-date with the rate of technological progress in biotech? Also, she had to think of a way that both these issues and issues like them could be discussed within the team without the conversation degenerating into name-calling or cynicism. Ellen opened the notebook she used to prepare for team meetings and wrote "Proposal for managing Protoshape-3d end-use dilemmas" at the top.

Confidential Accounts at Swiss Bank Corporation

Alan Adler is an investment adviser in Zurich, Switzerland. Educated at the London School of Economics, he established his practice in Zurich because he saw an international market for wealthy clients who prefer to keep their financial transactions in Switzerland's confidential and sophisticated financial network. Alan trades in international currency, bonds, and stocks for his clients, each of whom keeps at least $1.5 million in his or her personal account. Most of his clients are from Germany, the United States, and Canada, with some from Great Britain and South Africa. He has no clients from Switzerland but often trades in Swiss currency.

Alan prefers the extraordinary freedom with which investment counselors can deal with their clients in Switzerland, and he has always liked being able to assure his clients of *absolute* confidentiality. He maintains client records by number rather than name. When he started out in the business, he recommended that customers use only "numbered accounts" in their banks. These accounts are stripped of name identifiers. However, these accounts were banned by law in 1993. Still, in this tradition, Alan makes his annual reports to clients by their numbers only, and his clients use only their numbers in correspondence. Alan keeps the decoding system for names and numbers in a Swiss Bank Corporation (SBC) safe-deposit box. He does not file a report with the government and is not legally required to do so.

The Swiss Bank Corporation has always been crucial to Alan's client relationships. All clients keep their money and securities in their own names in SBC accounts, but Alan has obtained written authorization from each client allowing him to use the client's money in the account to buy stocks, bonds, or foreign currency, which are then placed in their accounts. Although all transactions are at his discretion, Alan cannot himself *withdraw* funds from a client's bank account. Alan receives no fees per transaction. His fees come only from a percentage of the annual net *gains* that he makes for his clients. He bills annually for these fees, which are usually wired directly to his account. Trust—and trust alone—bonds him to his clients. He does not, and would never, legally contest nonpayment.

This case was prepared by Tom L. Beauchamp and revised by Jeff Greene and Ahmed Humayun. Not to be duplicated without permission of the holder of the copyright, © 1992, 1996, 2003 by Tom L. Beauchamp.

Alan has become concerned in recent years about the extent to which his promises of confidentiality to clients can be sustained. Swiss banks have clearly shifted grounded from their previously secretive policies. The Swiss government has become more interested in prosecuting local tax abuses, and foreign governments have been pressing for additional revisions in financial regulations. Jean-Paul Chapuis, once the Swiss Bankers' Association's managing director, has said, "There is no guarantee of secrecy if you are dishonest." As the bankers view their situation, Swiss banks can no longer remain aloof from international financial restrictions because their expanded operations have made them vulnerable to international pressures. Local law (not Swiss law) applies in the countries in which Swiss bank branches conduct their business.

Alan has long handed or mailed to his customers a booklet entitled *Profile,* published by the Swiss Bank Corporation as an annual report and explanation of bank services. He has urged his customers to read the section entitled "Switzerland's Advantages as a Financial Centre," which guarantees a "safeguarding of privacy." Two of the sections are these:

7. Tax Morality

Switzerland is one of the few countries in which voters can directly determine how heavy their tax burden should be. This prevents prohibitive tax rates and is an important precondition for tax morality. The principle of self-assessment is yet another reflection of the special relationship between the Swiss and their government. The safeguarding of privacy vis-a-vis the tax authorities is guaranteed by banking secrecy.

The state concentrates its efforts on combatting the abuse of this relationship. In recent years, the measures to hinder tax evasion and tax flight have been substantially strengthened. Parliament, and secondarily the people, may amend existing fiscal disadvantages (Stamp Duty Act, double taxation of corporate earnings) at any time within the framework provided for statutory revisions.

8. Responsibility of the Individual

In contrast to countries with a centralist political structure, Switzerland places great emphasis on the individual citizen's responsibility for himself. The State's role is to guarantee the impartial administration of justice as well as an environment propitious to economic activity.

Until recently, Alan simply asked his clients to read these sections and told them that his data and the bank's data were strictly secret, protected by a pledge of confidentiality. However, recent events have convinced him that the Swiss government and banks are modifying their methods of cooperating with foreign requests. His concerns first began many years ago when the government froze the Swiss bank assets of two former foreign dictators, Ferdinand Marcos and Jean-Claude Duvalier, at the request, respectively, of the Filipino and Haitian governments. Previously, Swiss banks had consistently refused to confirm even whether they held a deposed ruler's account. The U.S. government had tried for nearly twenty years to locate suspected Nazis' bank accounts, but it could not penetrate Swiss confidentiality regulations.

Recently, Swiss banks have changed directions and cooperated with the U.S. Securities and Exchange Commission in prosecuting even such matters as persons suspected of insider trading and other relatively "minor" offenses. In a worrisome development for Alan, the Bank Leu Limited divulged the name and records of one U.S. customer in return for immunity from prosecution for the bank. The Swiss government shortly thereafter announced that it was helping the U.S. government investigate three cases of tax fraud. Later, Swiss government officials (for the first time) outlawed money laundering, and shortly thereafter the government announced that it would ease its formerly strict rules on secrecy in banking and would investigate alleged money laundering. The Swiss Parliament then began formal debate on appropriate legislation.

In 1993, the "numbered accounts" were declared illegal, and in 1994, Switzerland's lower house of Parliament approved legislation that allowed banks to report suspected illegal activities without fear of breaking bank secrecy laws. In 1995, some innovative uses of Swiss law permitted victims of criminal activity to recover lost funds from the bank accounts of those who had defrauded or swindled the victims. Some concern has been expressed by Swiss government officials that these developments carry matters too far and challenge the foundations of banking secrecy laws and individual sovereignty.

Two U.S. court cases have badly shaken Alan's confidence. In a Tampa, Florida, case, U.S. District Court Judge Ben Krentzman threatened two Swiss lawyers with contempt citations unless they ceased to resist efforts to obtain financial information about U.S. criminal suspects with Swiss bank accounts. The contempt threat successfully intimidated the lawyers into stopping a legal maneuver to defend their client. In the second U.S. case, federal Judge Milton Pollack threatened Banco della Svizzera Italiana—a Swiss bank—with a daily $50,000 fine unless it disclosed the identities of traders in the common stock of St. Joe Minerals. Faced with the seizure of its U.S. assets, the bank "persuaded" one of its customers to waive his secrecy rights and then identified him. Alan now realizes that the Swiss government, under international pressure, especially from the United States, will help prosecute bank clients involved in illegal financial transactions, money laundering, and many transactions that it formerly allowed under the umbrella of legitimate secrecy.

Disconcerted by these developments, Alan requested further information from the Swiss Bank Corporation. He learned that the SBC's most recent edition of the *Profile* booklet had been revised, with the sections concerning banking secrecy omitted. Another SBC booklet published by the bank entitled *Secrecy in Swiss Banking* explained banking policies in new and, he thought, unnerving detail. The bank affirmed the premium placed on individual liberty and privacy in Switzerland, but it forthrightly recognized that banking secrecy is not absolute. Alan read a section entitled "Limitation of Banking Secrecy under Swiss Law":

Where stipulated in the law, banks are required to furnish to public authorities pertinent information on clients' accounts. Such disclosures are mandatory in actions involving inheritance, bankruptcy and debt collection as well as in all criminal cases, but not in ordinary tax matters. . . .

Switzerland is party to many bilateral and multilateral conventions for legal assistance with other countries. Where such treaties exist, Swiss authorities assist foreign countries in criminal cases under conditions provided by these treaties. To be prosecuted as a crime, however, the alleged offense must always be considered a crime under Swiss law, too.

Alan concluded that the legal shelter of secrecy in Switzerland still rivaled any world competitor—for example, the Bahamas' banking system—but nonetheless was shrinking in scope and reliability. Although Swiss banks remain at the top of the global private banking market, he thought, the assault on client confidentiality now seemed sure to have a profound impact on the nature of his business—particularly since international pressures on Switzerland were continuing for increased disclosure.

The foundation of banking secrecy in Switzerland has historically been enshrined in article 47 of the Swiss Banking Act, which provides for criminal sanctions (imprisonment for no longer than six months or a fine of not more than 50,000 Swiss francs) against anyone who divulges confidential information of which he or she has become aware in a capacity as an officer or employee of a bank (and against anyone who tries to induce others to violate professional confidentiality). Recent legislation suggests a subtle but significant shift from giving bankers the "right" to report suspicious transactions to rendering bankers "obligated" to make such reports. Moreover, bankers who have reason to believe that a transaction has the potential to be criminal in nature must now clarify the specific nature of the problematic transaction with customers or be held accountable later on.

Alan, like most other Swiss investment counselors, has finally begun to appreciate the significance of these changes. In 1999, a friend of Alan's was involved in a case in which Swiss magistrates (acting on a request initiated by the Nigerian government) froze about $620 million of Nigerian assets allegedly embezzled by the late dictator Sani Abacha. After an inquiry, the federal banking commission sanctioned twelve banks for their handling of this money. This action proved to be only the first instance of what has since been called the "naming and shaming" policy in which the government publicly reprimands offending banks and sanctions them for transgressions that violate Swiss law.

In the year 2000, two banks, UBS and Credit Suisse, announced a voluntary due-diligence code largely motivated by anti-money-laundering laws that had been enforced in Switzerland since 1998. Under this code, banks would have to check the identities of account holders, and suspicious transactions would have to be reported to authorities without notifying customers. Moreover, accounts would be frozen if a magistrate so ordered in the course of a criminal investigation. Although these provisions were already required by law, to a modest degree, the voluntary acceptance of a personal due-diligence code that seemed to frustrate traditional banking confidentiality has proven to be a powerful symbolic step in Switzerland. Moreover, the European Union has since been urging an expanded provision for information exchange regarding financial information, ostensibly for the purpose of a more united and stable Europe. Although Swiss banks continue to resist these EU demands, the trend to openness in European banking became very apparent between 2001 and 2003.

In light of all these developments, Alan wonders what responsibilities he has to his customers to alert them to the momentous changes in the Swiss system. Some of his customers probably do not know about the dramatic nature of the changes that have been made in the last seven or eight years. Should he warn them of new risks? How could he state the current situation without being alarmist? Alan has never known—and does not want to know—whether his customers report the status of their accounts to their respective governments. However, he has personally given his customers a guarantee of secrecy and confidentiality. He would never violate that confidentiality himself. Yet his safe-deposit box does contain his clients' names, addresses, and account numbers; and he could always be pulled into a legal investigation.

Alan sits down before his word processor and begins to draft a letter to inform his clients of the various developments. But when he reads his words on the screen, the changes that he is announcing sound ominous, as if the clients' names and accounts might not be secret at all. He decides to try another draft tomorrow to see whether his words sound less alarming. Then, his eyes land on a story in today's newspaper. According to this story, a private detective in New York was successfully hired by the Kuwaiti government to trace the hidden assets of the now-departed Iraqi dictator Saddam Hussein. This investigator had managed in just a few days to use giant computerized databases and private contacts to trace Hussein's hidden wealth to over forty "secret" bank accounts throughout the world. As he reads the details of this story, Alan finds that he has even less of an idea of what to say in his letter to his clients.

Commissions at Brock Mason Brokerage

James Tithe is the manager of a large branch office of a major midwestern brokerage firm, Brock Mason Farre Titmouse. He manages forty brokers in his office. Mr. Tithe formerly worked for Shearson-Lehman/American Express, but when that firm was turned into Smith Barney (later Salomon Smith Barney), he disliked his new manager and left for Brock Mason. He has enjoyed the new challenge at Brock Mason, which is an aggressive firm interested primarily in higher-risk investments with the potential for greater return to both client and broker. At Shearson his clients had been predominantly interested in CDs, unit investment trusts, government bond portfolios, and municipal bonds, which he found boring and routine forms of investment aimed at people at or near retirement age. He also now likes the fact that commissions are higher on the items he is training his brokers to sell at Brock Mason.

Although he became bored at Shearson, James had been comfortable with and appreciative of the complete discretion that this firm had given him to recommend a range of investments to his clients. He had been free to consult at length with his clients and then to sell what seemed most appropriate in light of their objectives. This same array of conventional investment possibilities (many with relatively low commissions) is still available to him and to his brokers at Brock Mason, but the firm has an explicit strategy of trying to sell growth stocks recommended by Brock Mason analysts first and all other items second. The reason for this strategy is higher commissions together with a belief that recommendations are usually better informed and more timely when backed by a recent report from an expert, in-house analyst.

James accepts this viewpoint, but he has been bothered for some time by certain facts about the aggressive side of his firm. As is common in the brokerage industry, the largest commissions are paid on the riskier and more complicated forms of investment. In theory, the reason is that these investments are more difficult to sell to clients and have the potential for greater returns. However, James has become convinced that most investors have only a poor idea of the risks that they are assuming and of how much more they are paying brokers for these items, some of which return more than 8 percent to brokers. Moreover, James has been taught at Brock Mason not to train his brokers to spend a lot of time talking to clients (as he had done at Shearson), because time is money. James is certain that his brokers often sell the riskier and more complicated forms of investment even when that particular investment is not in the best interest of the client. Although Brock Mason, like all other brokerage firms, advertises a full range of products and free financial planning by experts, all salespersons dislike financial planning per se because it takes a large amount of time and carries zero commission. In effect, they do financial planning only if a client insists on it and is willing to come into the office, where it is easier to *sell* during the process of planning.

James has long appreciated that there is an inherent conflict of interest in the brokerage world: Although the broker is presumed to have a fiduciary responsibility to make recommendations on the basis of the financial best interest of the client, the broker is also a salesperson who makes a living by selling securities and is obligated to attempt to maximize profits for the brokerage house. The unspoken broker's rule, seldom advantageous to the client, is "The more trades made, the better." Commissions are thus an ever-present temptation for brokers, even though they are obligated to present alternatives objectively and discerningly.

Many clients today ask James's brokers about mutual funds, which have grown increasingly popular. Brock Mason has a diverse array of house mutual funds that are less risky forms of investment for most clients; and the firm also markets some very safe mutual funds from well-known outside suppliers, including Nuveen Funds, Alliance Funds, Pimco Funds, MFS Funds, Pioneer Funds, Dreyfus Funds, and Franklin Templeton Funds. Moreover, the Brock Mason Equity-Income Fund has one of the best records in the industry. This fund is very profitable both from Brock Mason's perspective and from that of its brokers. The National Association of Securities Dealers (NASD) allows a firm to charge up to 8.5 percent commission or load on a mutual fund; Brock Mason has been able to charge the full 8.5 percent because of the success of this fund (and despite the fact that the entire senior staff of this fund recently resigned and went to another brokerage firm, a transition that Brock Mason has not mentioned to it clients). As an extra incentive, an additional percentage of the commission on an initial investment is returned to a broker if he or she can convince the client to reinvest the dividends automatically rather than have them sent by check in the mail. Brock Mason also offers a fully paid vacation in Hawaii for the five brokers who annually sell the largest number of shares of stock.

Brock Mason, like most other brokerage firms, suffered financially as a result of the stock-market slump from 2000 through 2002. Business declined 24 percent, and Brock Mason encountered difficulty in paying for the sophisticated electronic equipment that sits on each broker's desk. James's superiors pressured him to persuade his brokers to market even more aggressively. James has not resisted this pressure, because he sees that his brokers work hard, and he does not think that they are overly compensated. James's own take-home earnings last year came to $198,000, an amount 35 percent more than he had ever earned at Shearson. A friend of his began his own financial planning firm last year and retains 100 percent of his commissions, netting him $275,000 in his first year. His friend rejected the idea that he charge either a flat fee or a percentage of profits in lieu of commissions for his recommendations and services. In his judgment, flat fees would have cost him more than 30 percent of his earnings.

Securities firms are required by law to disclose all commissions to clients. However, James and his brokers are aware that mutual funds, unit investment trusts, and the like are usually easier to sell than straight stock and bond purchases, because the statistics on fees are buried in a pile of information in a prospectus that most clients do not read prior to a purchase; indeed, the prospectus is often mailed many days after the purchase, and there is no report prior to the transaction, or ever, of a dollar figure for the commission. Brokers are not required to disclose commissions orally to clients and rarely do; moreover, few clients ask what the commission is. James has been instructed to tell his brokers to avoid all mention of commissions unless the subject is explicitly raised by the client.

The Securities and Exchange Commission (SEC) does not require a broker to obtain a written consent from a client prior to a purchase. The SEC does occasionally determine that a markup is so high at a brokerage house that the commission amounts to fraud. It is here that James has drawn his personal "moral line," as he calls it. His rule is that only if the SEC considers a markup or type of sale to be fraudulent will he discourage his brokers from marketing the associated item.

Despite this rule, James has additional *personal* guidelines that prevent him from using various marketing strategies. For example, he will not *own* any of the stocks that he personally recommends to his brokers for their clients. This guideline has caused him some pangs of uncertainty, because it is common for brokers to own what they sell and for them to believe that the investment is a good one. James used to own virtually everything that he really *believed* in selling (by contrast to what supervisors and analysts *recommended* that he sell), but in 2001, James had read several stories about stock analysts who owned stocks, recommended those stocks in their reports, and then cashed in their profits as soon as the stock went up. Some of the recommendations were rigged to raise prices, but in other cases it appeared that analysts lacked objectivity in their reports precisely because they already owned the stock of the companies on which they were reporting.

The problem had become sufficiently acute in the industry that Merrill Lynch and Credit Suisse First Boston had (in mid-2001) banned their analysts from owning stock in companies they cover; and Goldman Sachs Group Inc. and Morgan Stanley Dean Witter began requiring that all equity analysts *disclose* whether they own the stocks they are covering. James was proud of himself for his insight that he and his brokers had the opportunity to piggyback on the recommendations in their analysts' reports (which brokers always see before their clients do) and then cash in, just as the analysts themselves could cash in. James had decided that this easy money was too easy.

James had also thought of a better system that he would like to see put in place: Analysts and brokers, he thinks, should be able to own everything they recommend, but they should be required to hold their ownings for at least a year after (first) recommending them. James had ventured onto this idea because a friend of his at the firm Piper Jaffray (U.S. Bancorp) had told him that analysts there are allowed to own stocks in companies they recommend but that they must then hold the stocks for at least ninety days. James liked this rule but thought ninety days too short a period of time. He also thought that analysts and brokers should not be allowed to sell a stock, in any amount, if their firm currently had a "buy" recommendation on that stock (in effect, trading against their own recommendations).

If his proposals were followed, James thought, analysts and brokers would really have to believe in the stock and could not make easy money. James liked the old Morgan Stanley Dean Witter television ad: "We make money the old-fashioned way; we earn it." James thought that his system would be far more honest than the present one, but he was anxious at the thought of recommending this system to his supervisor, who was sure to laugh and say "Sure!" He knew that his boss would say this because he knew the mentality of the brokerage industry. He had heard two "principles" mentioned for years, as if they were unrevisable axioms of the brokerage world. The first principle is "If a practice is rotten, ban it; don't reform the system by requiring people either to own what they recommend or to take commissions only on their profits." The second principle is "Always erect a Chinese wall between the research work of analysts and investment recommendations." Both principles have an obvious appeal at some level, but both of them bother James. He has never figured out how to work these principles coherently into his own personal guidelines.

James is now wondering more than ever about the prudence, completeness, and coherence of his personal guidelines. He has been around long enough to see some unfortunate circumstances—they are *unfortunate* but not *unfair*, in his judgment—in which unwary clients bought unsuitable products from brokers and had to live with the consequences. Recently, one of his brokers steered a 55-year-old unemployed widow with a total account of $480,000 (inherited upon the death of her husband) into the following diversification: 25 percent in a U.S. government bond fund, 25 percent in dividend-paying stocks, 25 percent in corporate bonds yielding 7.8 percent, and 25 percent in the Brock Mason Equity-Income Fund. But the woman did not understand at the time of purchase how low the dividends on the stocks and the mutual fund would be. She has far less annual income than she had anticipated. Now she feels that she must sell the stock at a loss and purchase a high-dividend-paying instrument. She blames the broker for misassessing her situation and putting her into investments that are unsuitable for a person of her age and means. She has threatened a lawsuit to attempt to "recover money lost due to unethical behavior." Being a Canadian citizen, she has already filed a complaint with the Investment Dealers Association of Canada.

James and the woman's broker have been shaken by this client's vigorous protest and display of a sense of being wronged. As a result, James decided to take the case to the weekly staff meeting held on Wednesday mornings, which all brokers attend. There was a lively discussion of the best form of diversification and return for the widow. But James's attempt to introduce and discuss problems of conflict of interest in the brokerage industry during this session fell completely flat. His brokers were not interested and could not see the problem. They argued that the brokerage industry is a free market arrangement between a broker and a client who knows that fees are charged. Disclosure rules, they maintained, are well established, even if particular percentages or fees are sometimes hidden in the fine print. They viewed themselves as honest salespersons making a living through a forthright and fair system.

James walked away from this meeting thinking that neither the widow nor the broker had been prudent in making decisions that met her specific needs, but again he viewed the outcome as unfortunate rather than unfair. He had to agree with his brokers. No client, after all, is forced either to deal with the firm or to make any purchase.

Consulting for Jones and Jones Pharmaceutical

Ricardo D'Amato is a high-salaried executive who for four years has been on the payroll of a large U.S.-based pharmaceutical company, the Jones and Jones Company. Located at the European headquarters in Sweden, D'Amato, an American, is in charge of certifying that new products are ready for the approval and registration process and for subsequent marketing. His office is responsible for sending new products to the relevant government authorities in all European countries, each of which has an organization similar to the U.S. Food and Drug Administration (FDA), where drugs are tested for safety and effectiveness.

Although D'Amato's relations with his peers have been without significant strain, he now finds himself enmeshed in controversy and crisis. He has refused to authorize a $15,000 payment on a contract the company has with a consultant in Switzerland. The contract calls for the company to pay the specified fee to a distinguished pharmacologist, Dr. Helmut Koenig, for giving advice on how to obtain approval from the Swiss regulatory authorities. Dr. Koenig is uniquely qualified for this work because he is employed by the Swiss Drug Regulatory Agency, the agency that is responsible for approving all drug products for marketing in Switzerland.

Sitting on D'Amato's desk is an internal memo written by the most powerful vice president at Jones and Jones, who arranged and then signed the contract with Dr. Koenig. The memo has a section on credentials that says, "Dr. Koenig is a vital influence and creator of opinion in the approval of drug applications in Switzerland." D'Amato was alarmed when he discovered Dr. Koenig's position of government influence and his precise contractual arrangement with Jones and Jones. D'Amato believes that it is unethical to make such payments to a person who is currently involved with the approval of five to ten pending product registrations for Jones and Jones. Indeed, he thinks that it is unethical even to discuss drug applications with him in a manner that could influence his opinion. He has written both his superiors and Dr. Koenig to this effect.

In particular, Dr. Koenig is involved with the application for Lotriprox, a drug that those who have tested it for the company believe to be more effective

This case was prepared by Tom L. Beauchamp and Kelley MacDougall. Not to be duplicated without permission of the holder of the copyright, © 1992, 1996, 2003 by Tom L. Beauchamp.

in the treatment of psoriasis than its main competitors. Jones and Jones has submitted the original application for approval of this drug twice; the Swiss Drug Regulatory Agency rejected both attempts. On each occasion the agency said there was a lack of evidence of the drug's effectiveness. The agency also complained about the quality of the research performed to show effectiveness. It said there were missing data points, unexplainable changes in the middle of clinical trials, and inadequate controls to prove the conclusions reached by researchers. Also, it said that, from the trial design, one could not determine whether the apparent improvement in skin condition was attributable to Lotriprox or not.

This reaction made no sense at all to D'Amato, who is himself an expert in drugs for psoriasis. By American standards, he thought, this is a fantastic clinical trial and a fabulous drug. He is therefore unsure exactly what the problem is. In this respect, he sees that someone like Dr. Koenig could provide sound advice about how to proceed with Swiss authorities. Moreover, he knows that all of his superiors at Jones and Jones view the receipt of Swiss approval as vital because regulatory agencies in other European countries often follow the Swiss lead because of the scrupulous care taken by Swiss authorities.

Although D'Amato is an American, most of his fellow executives in Sweden come from European countries. Almost all of his colleagues have given him their opinion on the matter: They uniformly concur that the practice of hiring regulators as consultants is a common and accepted practice in Switzerland and that it should not be challenged. Also, they point out, correctly, that other companies that market similar products have been hiring these consultants for years. In addition, they deny that this practice involves the use of devious or special influence to get applications approved, and they emphasize Dr. Koenig's ability to properly advise pharmaceutical companies on how to proceed.

Dr. Koenig has responded in a terse letter directly to D'Amato that he knows as well as anyone else how to keep his consulting work separate from his work at the regulatory agency. He notes in the letter that he has many times been in this position and that there are clear advantages in his dual role that can be enjoyed by both the company and the regulatory agency. For example, he is able to keep on top of every aspect of a drug and of the approval system. He points out that the reason Jones and Jones has not previously obtained approval for Lotriprox is the company's "terrible testing" of the drug, which is within his professional domain.

D'Amato does not accept these arguments. He has the reverse view: The science is good, and the ethics of hiring Koenig is bad. He views his colleagues as offering rationalizations conveniently "justified" by a corrupt system. However, he has tried to make it clear to those with whom he has discussed his views that he is not disputing how the Swiss consulting process actually works. His concern is with the acceptance of these practices by his company, Jones and Jones. He sees the contract with Dr. Koenig as a willing and devious violation of practices that are unacceptable in the United States—and in his company, which is, after all, American. He knows that the U.S. Food and Drug Administration would never tolerate such an arrangement, and he sees it as intolerable himself. The problem is that no one else in the European office sees the situation as he does.

Three weeks ago, on his own authority and without anyone's advice or approval, D'Amato wrote the Intercantonal Office of Medicaments in Switzerland to ask for an investigation of the questions of ethics that were on his mind and for a clarification of the Swiss system. To his surprise, he received a courteous, respectful, detailed, and carefully crafted response. The investigators said that they found that Jones and Jones pharmaceutical products and the products of many other companies have been approved for marketing after the hiring of well-placed consultants, and they found no indication that these approvals were made under fraudulent circumstances. Unless D'Amato could submit additional evidence to the contrary, the investigators concluded that there was no reason why an educated and experienced adviser could not separately render his or her services to an outside company. In fact, they advised him that it makes good practical sense for Jones and Jones to obtain evaluations from European experts prior to submitting products for approval. As they see it, this process facilitates the production of a safer and more effective product, and it spares both the company and the regulatory agency time that would otherwise be wasted considering inferior products.

D'Amato is unpersuaded. He maintains that Dr. Koenig is locked in an untenable conflict of interest. D'Amato is convinced that under the Swiss system, any corporation of sufficient size and financial backing could wield unfair advantage over less powerful companies. To him, the conflict of interest and unfair advantage are so obvious that no reasonable and sensitive person could miss them.

D'Amato's supervisor, Raymond Freymaster, has now intervened in a process that he believes cannot be allowed to stalemate any longer. He has told D'Amato that the contract with Dr. Koenig is proper and therefore that the amount owed on the contract must be paid. Freymaster has increased the pressure by saying that if D'Amato does not authorize payment within ten days, he will be fired, and Freymaster will then authorize the payment himself. D'Amato now sees no way to maintain both his integrity and his job. Meanwhile, his colleagues have strongly advised him that his sense of integrity is fostered by a very American set of values.

Arthur Andersen's Dual Role at Enron

In November 2001, it became known that at least since 1997, Enron Corporation had been keeping debts off its books and had overstated profits by $400 million in its financial reports. These reports had been approved by its auditor, Arthur Andersen Inc., whose responsibility it was to make sure that the financial statements released by Enron were accurate. These statements had encouraged both investors and thousands of Enron employees to buy Enron stock. Soon after the discovery that profits had been misrepresented, Andersen admitted that it had incorrectly audited some statements, and on January 15, 2002, the accounting firm also admitted that some of its employees had destroyed documents related to the Enron investigation. Meanwhile, Enron filed for bankruptcy protection, following the disappearance of $68 billion of its market value.

Public outcry over the unexpected demise of Enron and its effect on thousands of investors prompted calls for a thorough investigation of Enron and Andersen in order to determine the reasons for the collapse. One of the first problems discovered by the initial investigation was the shredding of documents by Andersen employees in a Houston office on October 23, 2001, soon after the Securities and Exchange Commission (SEC) announced that it was beginning an investigation of Enron's accounting irregularities. Andersen admitted on January 15, 2002, that its auditors destroyed these documents. Critics viewed this illegal destruction of vital information as demonstrating that Andersen had something to hide—in particular, that Andersen had acquiesced in Enron's deceptive accounting practices.

A report prepared by Enron's (newly appointed) board of directors claimed that "virtually all" of the accounting misrepresentations perpetuated by Enron were "determined with extensive participation and structuring advice from Andersen."[1] Known as the Powers Report, this study was prepared by William Powers, dean of the University of Texas School of Law, and William McLucas, former enforcement director of the Securities and Exchange Commission. The Powers Report concluded that "The evidence available to us suggests that Andersen did not fulfill its professional responsibilities in connection with its audit of Enron's financial statements, or its obligation to

This case was written by Ahmed Humayun and Tom L. Beauchamp. Not to be duplicated without permission of the holder of the copyright, © 2003 by Tom L. Beauchamp.

bring to the attention of Enron's board . . . concerns about Enron's internal controls over the related-party transactions."[2] According to this report, Andersen extensively participated in the implementation of Enron's elaborate accounting practices.

Andersen had provided several services to Enron, and the two firms had a long-standing professional relationship. Andersen provided both *auditing* and *consulting* services to Enron. Its *auditing* service had two components. The first involved preparing quarterly and other relevant financial statements and ensuring that Enron had adequate accounting systems that could detect fraud and irregularities. The second involved officially certifying the financial statements produced by Enron and ensuring that the company complied with the law. Andersen's *consulting* arm provided advice to Enron on how to present those figures in the form of profitable investments.

Critics have claimed that Andersen's misdemeanors were the natural consequence of conflicts of interest inherent in the multifaceted professional relationship it had formed with Enron. There are allegedly three kinds of conflicts. One kind arises from performing both outside and inside auditing functions. Andersen was responsible for setting up the accounting systems that produced annual financial reports and for evaluating the financial reports that resulted from its own approved systems. In its function as an *outside* auditor, Andersen was essentially putting the seal of approval on its own system and judging how well it had implemented that system. In order to detect any fraud or irregularities in Enron's financial statements, Andersen would have had to accept at least some complicity in any problem that its own systems created.

The second kind of conflict of interest involves the dual responsibilities of auditing and consulting functions provided to Enron by Andersen. Specifically, the question is whether an accounting firm should calculate quarterly or annual financial reports for a client—performing an auditing function—and then provide advice about how to manipulate those figures in order to yield profitable results. Andersen's success as a consultant would be gauged by general indicators of economic strength as expressed by Enron's financial statements. Critics argue that accounting firms placed in this position are tempted to coordinate their accounting functions with their consulting functions, and hence to present the results of its auditing service in as favorable a light as possible.

Much of the controversy spawned by Andersen's relationship to Enron has centered on the coziness of auditing and consulting services, but even more basic questions have been raised about whether accounting firms need more distance from management than they have traditionally had. The third alleged conflict of interest deals with this question of independence. What does it take to provide an impartial validation that financial reports do in fact represent the true state of the business? Accounting firms are *hired, paid,* and *fired* by management. Since the accounting firm provides the service and management chooses to purchase the service, management can at any point terminate the service. Many critics maintain that the deepest problem is not with consulting services per se, but with the system that allows management (rather than government or oversight by professions) to choose and reward those who inspect their company. Critics point out that the system allows for only minimal public reporting by auditors. From this perspective, the debate over separating auditing from consulting should center on whether auditors and/or consultants have adequate independence from management.

After the stock market crash of 1929, the U.S. government gave the job of auditing financial statements of public companies to the accounting industry. Ever since, the accounting industry has maintained that it does not need external regulation, either by governments or professional associations, because it can put in place mechanisms that prevent fraud. Its theory is that accounting firms are the logical choice for "regulatory oversight."

Critics of Andersen (and of the accounting industry generally) are skeptical of this theory. They point out that Andersen had a long history of abusing accounting standards and that the existing system failed to unmask Andersen's failures. They assert that the large financial payments to Andersen from Enron and Andersen's close relationship with Enron affected the professional judgment of both, encouraging them to push, and ultimately to bend and break, accounting rules.

In a case that unfolded in the Courts at approximately the same time as the Enron debacle, Andersen signed off on the books for a church foundation, the Baptist Foundation of Arizona. This foundation was a nonprofit company that offered high interest rates on retirement funds but that hid large debts and losses. Arizona authorities discovered that the "foundation" was, in fact, a Ponzi scheme that used incoming money from new investors to pay the old investors. Andersen, which approved the foundation's financial statements from 1984 through 1987 stated that it had been intentionally deceived by the foundation. It claimed to have performed honest and conscientious audits, but lawyers for defrauded clients asserted that Andersen failed to take steps that any sound auditing firm would take and failed to follow a number of leads presented by its own tax staff. In June 2001, Andersen paid the largest civil penalty in SEC history for an accounting firm ($7 million) for approving audits for Waste Management.

Despite these questions arising out of the Andersen-Enron scandal, large accounting firms today strongly resist the thesis that the current system causes a loss of objectivity and independence—or a conflict of interest. These firms consider Andersen an aberration. They maintain that no data about the industry indicate that any kind of conflict of interest, whether related to the dual responsibilities of auditing and consulting, or to adequate independence from management, has presented a widespread problem. They acknowledge that the Big 5 accounting firms in the United States earn about three-and-a-half times as much in advisory or consulting work as in auditing fees, but they see these figures as reflecting the industry as it stands today, not as reflecting wrongdoing or moral problems. Moreover, these firms point out that much of the consulting work has little to do with risky financing or potential executive manipulation. For example, much of the consultation work for companies involves making company policies conform to regulatory standards. Some of these activities are legally required of auditors. Other work includes consulting about federal and state taxes and helping to create audit committees composed of company directors. The purpose of the latter committees is to ensure that audits are independent and unbiased.

From this perspective, good consulting actually promotes auditor independence and oversight. The financial information that needs to be recorded, processed, and then displayed to the public and used for future investments is easier and more efficiently prepared by one firm with a familiarity with its client's business and accounting systems. The accounting industry maintains that over time, knowledgeable accountants should be able both to improve the accounting systems and to provide better financial advice for firms. This arrangement is also cheaper than having separate firms carry out consulting and auditing functions, because firms providing both services will offer evaluations and recommendations at an overall cheaper cost. This is the traditional, and still prevailing, point of view in the accounting industry.

Shortly after the collapse of Enron, the Big 5 accounting firms released a statement that announced their intention to strengthen financial reporting and auditing standards. They reiterated their basic belief in the adequacy of self-regulation, concluding that "self-regulation is right for investors, the profession, and the financial markets." But critics are unconvinced. Accounting's main regulatory body, the Public Oversight Board (POB), was created in the 1970s in response to a rash of audit failures at public companies that had shaken public confidence. However, the POB has no enforcement powers, and its investigative activities are limited to instances of egregious failures of accounting standards after the fact. The POB has also not developed extensive regulations for the new problems facing the accounting industry, such as deciding whether there is an untenable conflict of interest between auditing and consulting or the more general problem of how to maintain accounting independence from clientele management. The lesson to be drawn from recent history, critics assert, is that the POB has failed in practice and that self-regulation will not prevent abuses like those encountered in the Enron-Andersen case.

Despite the different positions on the various conflicts of interest and their implications, there is general agreement that the accounting industry of today has moved away from its main function of auditing public and private companies. For every $1.00 that large firms earn from audit services, they now earn an estimated $2.69 from nonaudit work, according to a survey by the U.S. Securities and Exchange Commission.[3] Any alleged conflict of interest between consulting and auditing, then, is unlikely to go away as *accounting* companies expand their *consulting* operations.

NOTES

1. Greg Farrell and Jayne O'Donnell, "Enron Board Jumps into Blame Game," *USA Today,* February 4, 2002, p. 1B.
2. http://money.cnn.com/2002/02/02/companies/enron_report
3. Joshua Chaffin and Michael Peel, "Big Five Uncomfortable in the Spotlight," *The Financial Times,* March 5, 2002, p. 28.

CHAPTER THREE

Stakeholder Interests and Government Interests

Napster's Free Market in Intellectual Property

In November 1999, a small start-up company named Napster launched a revolutionary concept in Internet software. The company was to provide a forum free of all charges for individuals to share music files in the individual's possession with other Internet users from around the world. Napster was founded on the principle that it would charge no fees for its service, which allowed for the uninhibited transfer of files. Napster was founded by two brothers, John Fanning and his eighteen-year-old younger brother Shawn, who wrote the program code for Napster. The forum they created made use of the uploading of music files, making them available for use by others—and the downloading of music files, making the files available for use on one's own (personal) computer. The music files being traded made use of a file format known as MPEG-3—MP3, for short.

In establishing this system, Napster made it clear that no permanent online music library was created; all file-sharing would be person-to-person—that is, from one individual to another individual. Therefore, the only library available through Napster would be those music selections being shared (uploaded) by Napster users. In signing on for the service, users were required to agree to the terms of service, stating that *no copyrighted material could be uploaded or downloaded* over Napster.

The original Napster software user agreement stated that "copying or distributing unauthorized MP3 files may violate United States and foreign copyright laws. Compliance with the copyright law remains your responsibility."[1] MP3 files are created through a process of pulling files off a compact disc and saving them in the easily accessible MP3 format. From the outset, Napster CEO Eileen Richardson announced that the company was in talks with the Recording Industry Association of America (RIAA), a lobby of the largest groups in the industry. "We're committed to working with them. We're going to follow all the laws to the letter, including the Digital Millennium Copyright Act. . . . [Napster is] much more about community. We are not interested in people doing anything illegal."[2] There was initial enthusiasm about this view from some sectors of the music industry. For example, Marc Geiger, manager of ArtistDirect, an online marketing venture for major artists, declared, "I love it. [Napster] is totally community-oriented and a 'pass the music' [play]. It argues totally for the subscription model we have been yapping about."[3]

However, Napster raised questions from the beginning about the role of copyright law on the Internet. Could the freedom of the web completely bypass central tenets of law established in the noncyber world? Napster released its 2.0 beta version—essentially, a test phase—toward the end of 1999.[4] On December 6, 1999, the RIAA—including A&M Records and fourteen other record companies—announced that it was bringing a suit against Napster for copyright infringement.[5] The RIAA declared that Napster, while forcing users to accept the terms of agreement, was primarily used for illegal purposes. From this perspective, it was facilitating copyright violations against its own stated commitments. The RIAA argued that the majority of MP3 files were illegal copies of professionally produced and recorded albums; consequently, the majority of users were violating the Napster terms of agreement and copyright law. Lydia Pelliccia, an RIAA spokeswoman, said, "We spent many days sampling the Napster community, and found that virtually all file traffic is unauthorized" (that is, not authorized by copyright owners).[6]

The initial response from Napster CEO Richardson was one of astonishment: "For chrissakes we're still in beta. . . . We are freaking four months old."[7] Richardson reaffirmed this commitment elsewhere: "There's no chance that if an artist doesn't want their music on the Internet, that we want to put it there. Absolutely, positively not."[8] Before litigation began, a number of attorneys felt that Napster could win a favorable decision. Arnold Lutzker, a partner in the Lutzker & Lutzker law firm in Washington, D.C., argued that Napster could claim that the software has legal purposes, and called the RIAA's suit a 'stretch.'[9]

This claim was based on the perspective that it would be difficult to prove Napster liable for the actions of its users. Others looked at the situation pragmatically. "This is a really awful move on [the RIAA's] part," said audio consultant David Weekly. "If what they're trying to do is prevent programs like Napster from coming out, they gave every teenage hacker the incentive to write their own. . . . If executives have in the back closet similar distribution programs like Napster, what are the best hackers in the world working on?" This concern would increase as time moved on.[10]

The action against Napster was not the first taken by the RIAA for the use of illegal MP3s. Prior to its suit against Napster, the RIAA had complained about a University of South Carolina student who was making illegal MP3s available from his computer. Following that case, seventy-one students at Carnegie Mellon University were disciplined for using illegal MP3s when the RIAA sent the school letters threatening a lawsuit.[11]

The RIAA lawsuit went to the U.S. District Court for the Northern District of California in the summer of 2000, where the Association made its argument that Napster knowingly allowed and contributed to the infringement of copyright law. The case revealed the magnitude of Napster's influence: According to Napster's own documents, there would be approximately seventy-five million Napster users by the end of 2000. At one point, Napster claimed its service was growing by 200 percent a month.[12] Napster's own internal documents revealed an ambition to "take over, or at least threaten, plaintiff's role in the promotion and distribution of music."[13]

Nonetheless, Napster argued that the majority of its files came from unknown and unestablished artists who freely and knowingly shared their music to gain exposure. Additionally, Napster focused on the community aspects of its services provided through its chat room.[14] The company argued that the chat rooms were a powerful marketing tool for new artists, although the RIAA argued that the music of unsigned artists was only a front for Napster's real appeal in proliferating the copyrighted songs of well-known artists. Napster also made an appeal to several precedent-setting court cases. It claimed on the basis of *Vault Corp. v. Quaid Software* that "even one substantial non-infringing use precludes contributory liability." In other words, if Napster were to have one use that did not violate copyright law (such as the distribution of the work of new artists), it could not be held accountable for other, infringing uses. The district court never addressed this argument, but it did state that it was not bound by the *Vault Corp.* decision. Napster also argued that it is an internet service provider (ISP) and, under the decision in *Religious Technology Center* v. *Netcom On-Line Communication Services*, could not be held liable for the activities of its users.[15]

On July 26, 2000—with a slight modification on August 10, 2000—Napster received an injunction to suspend its services. The injunction prohibited Napster from "engaging in, or facilitating others in copying, downloading, uploading, transmitting, or distributing plaintiffs' copyrighted musical compositions and sound recordings, protected by either federal or state law, without the express permission of the owner."[16] This injunction covered only copyrighted files, not other functions such as chat rooms and music files of noncopyrighted material.[17] Napster filed with a federal appeals court and received an emergency stay of the injunction, so that its services could be continued during the appeal.

Meanwhile, some artists were taking matters into their own hands. The band *Metallica* and rap star Dr. Dre both filed lawsuits against Napster. The filing of *Metallica*'s court papers became a media event when drummer Lars Ulrich and the band's attorney personally delivered thousands of pages of paper documents, in thirteen boxes. They claimed to have identified over 300,000 Napster users who downloaded *Metallica* files.[18] Napster later disabled users who were verified as having downloaded *Metallica* files, although it noted that Metallica did not object to all types of file-sharing of their music, stating that "Metallica makes no claim of copyright infringement with respect to recordings of their songs made by fans at Metallica live concerts."[19]

The actions being taken in court (and on college campuses) led to broader considerations: Was downloading a copyrighted file from Napster the same as shoplifting a CD single from a music store? Is it morally unjustified for two owners of two CDs to swap files from those CDs? If two students can swap their CDs, why can they not swap files from those CDs? Does the fact that purchased and owned material is copyrighted make any difference as to whether it can be copied and swapped between individuals?

Opinions on such questions were mixed in publications on these subjects. James Post, a Boston University professor who teaches business ethics, asked fifty of his students if downloading MP3s could be equated with theft. Most said that they would copy songs and whole albums "without a second thought" about the ethics of their actions.[20] Many saw Napster as a "quiet rebellion" and tried to "strike a blow for what they see as freedom" through their downloading.[21] On the other side of the issue were those who equated downloading with theft.

The RIAA dealt with the "swap meet" analogy in the district court, arguing that under a previous federal decision—*Fonovisa, Inc. v. Cherry Auction, Inc.* (where a swap meet was held accountable for independent vendors who sold counterfeit recordings)—that "Napster is essentially an Internet swap meet . . . in many ways indistinguishable from the [defendant] in *Fonovisa.*"[22] Still others argued that Napster should be a starting point for a new dialogue in the growing conflict between free-Internet supporters and industries that are based on copyright law. Some also wondered whether there was a privacy issue at stake when institutions such as universities monitored all the files in student computers to determine whether, through the university's internet services, there had been an illegal downloading of music files.

Meanwhile, the litigation continued on several fronts. The 9th Circuit Court of Appeals reviewed whether the injunction placed on Napster by the district court created an unnecessary financial hardship on the company during its transition to a legal and an accepted format in which it would charge for its services and pay a reasonable rate for copyrighted materials. The court noted that "the district court's conclusion that plantiffs have presented a prima facie case of direct infringement by Napster users is not presently appealed by Napster."[23] It reached its decision on February 12, 2001, refusing to lift the district court's injunction against Napster. The court found that "Napster, by its conduct, knowingly encourages and assists the infringement of plaintiffs['] copyrights and that "it is apparent from the record that Napster has knowledge, both actual and constructive, of direct infringement."[24] The appeals court affirmed the district court's conclusion that Napster has the ability and responsibility to supervise the conduct of its users. Nonetheless, the Appeals Court did modify the form of the injunction against Napster's services (to take effect on March 5, 2001). The appeals court found that the original injunction was too broad, requiring the elimination of *all* of what was then labeled illegal activity from Napster's system. The appeals court determined that Napster should be required only to demonstrate a reasonable effort in eliminating such illegal uses.[25] Napster was also ordered to reach an agreement with the RIAA and the other bands that had filed suit.

Napster struggled for months to negotiate with the music industry, including a $1 billion, five-year offer just days before the injunction took effect on March 5.[26] The offer was rejected, but later, in June 2001, Napster appeared to have reached a deal with the RIAA. It announced on June 5 that it had signed a deal with MusicNet, a copyright clearinghouse, that included Warner Music Group, EMI Records, and Bertelsmann AG—three of the largest companies in the industry. The deal would take effect on the condition that Napster could prove that it had the capacity to halt the illegal trading of copyrighted music.[27]

However, on July 11, 2001, in a swift and an unanticipated move, the district court issued another injunction against Napster. It maintained that Napster was not making substantial progress in reforming its system and in reaching agreement with the music industry.[28] The court called Napster's efforts a "disgrace" because it was not exercising its ability to effectively screen out filename variants (the listing of songs and artists under slightly changed names, for example, "Mitallica" instead of "Metallica") to the court's satisfaction. Napster appealed this severely modified injunction, on grounds that it would do lasting and irreparable harm to Napster's business. The injunction did in fact turn out to be a crushing blow to Napster, because many users began to sign on with other online music sources such as KaZaA and Morpheus.[29]

Ironically, the modified injunction occurred the day before Napster resolved its lawsuits with *Metallica* and *Dr Dre*. Both out-of-court agreements were reached on the condition that Napster would continue to refine its filtering technology to prevent the sharing of illegal files.[30] Sources also said that cash settlements were part of both deals, although the amounts were undisclosed.[31] Both lawsuits were dropped.

In the summer of 2001, Napster finally concluded a mutually acceptable agreement with the RIAA. The terms included Napster's payment of $26 million to the associated parties for past damages and $10 million toward future royalties.[32] By the end of 2001, Napster had also begun to reach agreements in Europe. On November 5, 2001, Napster signed a multiyear licensing deal with Vitaminic SpA, Europe's leading "digital platform" for the proliferation of electronic forms of music, allowing Napster's music to be shared over Vitaminic's networks, and putting Vitaminic's giant cache of music at the disposal of Napster.[33] Later in the year, it signed a licensing deal with 150 independent European music labels.

As the litigation continued, several observers outside the courtroom made arguments on behalf of Napster. Some argued that Napster actually boosted record sales by providing free samples for consumers. Circumstantial evidence for this connection was a peak in record sales during the year of Napster's debut and a decline in sales the year that it ceased operation.[34] This same argument had previously been used by Napster in its court cases involving its "Fader Report." The district court rejected the value of this data and questioned the methodology of the research. The appeals court then accepted the lower court's ruling on the report. Other commentators pointed to the loss of a powerful venue of exposure for up-and-coming artists.

Throughout the course of litigation, artists and industry experts remained split in opinions about Napster. Many took a view notably similar to that of Metallica and Dr. Dre. As rapper Sean Puffy Combs (a.k.a., Puff Daddy) put it, "I couldn't believe it when I found out that this Napster was linking thousands of people to the new Notorious B.I.G. album, *Born Again*, a week before it even hit the streets."[35] Scott Stapp, lead singer of the rock band Creed, commented that "When my music is given away, as taboo as it is for me to say, it is stealing. My music is like my home. Napster is sneaking in the back door and robbing me blind."

However, other artists were more ambivalent about, and some even supportive of, Napster. Throughout the court hearings, numerous artists and artist associations filed amicus curiae (friend of the court) briefs and declarations in support of Napster. Among these were Chuck D., leader and cofounder of Public Enemy; Erik Gilbert, Vice President and General Manager of 75 Ark Entertainment; and Jim Guenirot, owner of Time Bomb Records and manager of The Offspring.[36]

For its part, Napster declared that it would appeal to Congress for clarification of federal copyright law. This course had already been anticipated by a few members of Congress. In particular, after the Court of Appeals refused to relieve the injunction against Napster, Senator Orrin Hatch, then chairman of the Senate Judiciary Committee, declared that he would hold hearings over the future of Internet commerce generally and of Napster specifically. "I guess my feeling about this Ninth Circuit decision is a gnawing concern that this legal victory for the record labels may prove pyrrhic and short-sighted from a policy perspective," Hatch said in a speech on the Senate floor.[37] Although Hatch agreed with the court's decision, he argued that by cracking down too hard on this highly centralized company, the decision would lead users to other, less easily regulated trading sources. His prediction turned out to be correct.

The Napster saga has led to a significant modification of the music industry. It has led to agreements between the industry and other MP3 forums, such as MP3.com and MSN Music. It has brought about lawsuits against Morpheus, KaZaA and Grokster, three MP3 forums that debuted during Napster's absence in the early months of 2001.[38] Some argued, after the rulings against Napster, that although those rulings—and the continued pursuit to shut down online music trading forums—may be in line with the law, stopping the spread of illegal music-file trading is, in the end, impossible. Others suggest that evidence for this statement is found in the sustained proliferation of Napster copycats. Other sites, such as Morpheus, use a "decentralized" form of music distribution, meaning that not all file transfer is directed through a single website (as was the case with Napster).[39] The result is an exponentially more difficult challenge for the music industry to ensure the enforcement of the conclusions reached in the Napster litigation.

Napster faced an uncertain future in early 2002. The company was still restricted by a court order that prohibited any further operations until copyrighted works were protected on its website. The company struggled to survive and to develop a system that would comply with the law. In June 2002, Napster filed for bankruptcy protection in a Delaware court, reporting less than $10 million in assets and over $100 million in debt.[40] The company then received outside purchase offers by a dozen or so media companies. In November 2002, Napster was purchased for approximately $5.3 million by software company

Roxio, which assumed none of Napster's pending liabilities.[41] Roxio began to lay plans for a revival of Napster, perhaps using very different software.

The various companies that survived Napster's downfall continue to rely on technology that makes it difficult to detect file sharing. The later systems are built on so-called peer-to-peer programs. They have withstood several court tests. However, early in 2003, a California federal judge approved a lawsuit against KaZaA, whose parent company (Sharman Networks) maintains headquarters in Australia.[42] Since the company conducts much of its business in the United States (with approximately 21 million U.S. users), it is subject to American copyright laws. On January 22, 2003, U.S. District Judge John Bates ordered the online division of Verizon Communications (an Internet Service provider) to release (to the RIAA) the identity of one of its customers who downloaded up to 600 songs a day from KaZaA. Using this method, the courts are able to identify peer-to-peer users. Since KaZaA has been downloaded more than 100 million times, the potential for lawsuits, investigations, and back payments is substantial.[43] At the same time, this system of identification raises new issues about digital privacy.

The downloading of copyrighted works has become a problem beyond the music industry. On February 28, 2002, in a hearing before the U.S. Senate Committee on Commerce, Science, and Transportation, an expert testified on behalf of the Walt Disney Co. that more than 350,000 "illegal pirate movies" are downloaded from the Internet every day.[44] Napster copycats all build on the idea of a free-music forum, while leaving unresolved the deep issues of fairness in an industry lacking a clear understanding of where free exchange ends and piracy begins.

NOTES

1. Jennifer Sullivan, "Napster: Music Is for Sharing," *Wired Digital*, November 1, 1999.
2. *Ibid.*
3. *Ibid.*
4. *Ibid.*
5. Brian Hiatt, "RIAA Sues Napster, Claiming 'Music Piracy,'" *Sonicnet.com*, December 8, 1999.
6. Jennifer Sullivan, "RIAA Suing Upstart Startup," *Wired Digital*, November 15, 1999.
7. *Ibid.*
8. Brian Hiatt, "RIAA Sues Napster, Claiming 'Music Piracy,'" *Sonicnet.com*, December 8, 1999.
9. *Ibid.*
10. *Ibid.*
11. *Ibid.*
12. *A&M Records, Inc. v. Napster, Inc.* 114 F. Supp. 2d 896, at 902.
13. *Ibid.*, at 903.
14. *Ibid.*, at 907–8.
15. *A&M Records, Inc. v. Napster, Inc.* 114 F. Supp. 2d 896, at 904, 916–19.
16. *Ibid.*, at 927.
17. *Ibid.*, at 917.
18. Napster Press Release, "Response to Metallica Action, Publicity Stunt," May 3, 2000.

19. Napster Press Release, "Heavy Metal Heavyweights K.O. Fans," May 10, 2000.
20. Megan Tench, "Moral Divide Over Napster Copying Music via Internet Service Seen as Theft to Some, OK to Others," *The Boston Globe*, February 24, 2001.
21. *Ibid.*
22. *A&M Records, Inc.* v. *Napster, Inc.* 114 F. Sup. 2d 896, at 919–20.
23. *A&M Records, Inc.* v. *Napster, Inc.* 239 F. 3d 1004, at 1013.
24. *Ibid.*, at 1020.
25. *Ibid.*, at 1023–24.
26. John Healey and P. J. Huffstutter, "Napster Offers Record Labels $1-Billion Deal," *The Los Angeles Times*, February 21, 2001.
27. Christopher Stern, "Napster Signs Deal to Offer Music From Record Giants," *The Washington Post*, June 6, 2001.
28. John Healey, "Napster Acts to Relaunch Song Service," *The Los Angeles Times*, July 13, 2001.
29. *Ibid.*
30. Napster Press Release, "Napster and Metallica Reach Accord," July 12, 2001; *Napster Press Release*, "Napster and Dr. Dre Reach Accord," July 12, 2001.
31. Benny Evangelista, "Musicians Settle Napster Suits," *The San Francisco Chronicle*, July 13, 2001.
32. Napster Press Release, "Napster, Songwriters and Music Publishers Reach Landmark Accord for Proposed Settlement and Licensing Agreement," September 24, 2001.
33. Napster Press Release, "Vitaminic Licenses Vast Music Repertoire to Napster," November 5, 2001.
34. E.g., Joel Selvin, "Did Napster Help Boost Record Sales?" *The San Francisco Chronicle*, August 5, 2001.
35. Brian Hiatt, "RIAA Sues Napster, Claiming 'Music Piracy,'" *Sonicnet.com*, December 8, 1999.
36. *http://www.napster.com/pressroom/legal.html* for listing.
37. "Senate to Hold Hearings Over Napster Ruling," *Cnn.com*, February 15, 2001.
38. "Record Industry Sues Morpheus and Other Decentralized File-Sharing Services," *Sonicnet. com* (November 2001).
39. Matt Richtel, "Judge Orders Napster to Police Trading," *The New York Times*, March 7, 2001.
40. "Napster Files for Bankruptcy," BBC News, Monday, June 3, 2002: http://news.bbc.co.uk/1/hi/business/2023201.stm
41. CNN Money (November 27, 2002): http://money.cnn.com/2002/11/27/news/deals/napster/index.htm
42. CNN.com Technology, "KaZaA File-Swapping Lawsuit Gets OK" (January 13, 2003): http://www.cnn.com/2003/TECH/internet/01/13/music.trial.ap/index.html
43. Jonathan Krim, "Recording Firms Win Copyright Ruling," *The Washington Post*, January 22, 2003, p. E1.
44. Reuters, "Eisner Seeks Federal Role in Halt in Digital Piracy," *Findlaw.com*, March 2, 2002.

Violent Music: Sony, Slayer, and Self-Regulation

On July 22, 1995, sixteen-year-old Royce Casey, fourteen-year-old Joseph Fiorella, and sixteen-year-old Jacob Delashmutt had a well-planned course of action: Offer a virgin sacrifice to Satan and perform necrophiliac rituals with the body. On that date, the three boys called fifteen-year-old Elyse Pahler, a local girl who had at times been in trouble with drugs, and invited her to a eucalyptus grove just outside San Luis Obispo, California, roughly a half mile from her parents' home, to smoke marijuana. After smoking, Delashmutt stepped behind Elyse and slipped his belt over her neck in a choke hold; Fiorella stabbed a six-inch hunting knife into her neck and then passed the weapon for the others to use. They then stomped her neck and dragged her corpse into the middle of the eucalyptus grove. According to court records, the three boys gave conflicting accounts of whether they had sex with the corpse, but police and prosecutors reported that they did have sex.[1]

One of the boys testified that the murder took place to seek satanic help in ensuring the success of the boys' heavy metal trio, which was named Hatred. Fiorella, though, stated that it was less clear cut. Before pleading guilty to the murder of Elyse Pahler, Fiorella told authorities that he and the other two would often stay up several nights in a row, taking drugs and listening to the music of the "death metal" band named Slayer. "[The music] gets inside your head. . . . It's almost embarrassing that I was so influenced by the music," said Fiorella.[2]

The music of Slayer has a large following, and the band is regarded as an icon of heavy metal. The band released its first album in 1983, celebrated its ten-year anniversary in 1991, and by 2001 was recognized as among the most popular metal bands of the previous decade. Yet its lyrics have caused as much controversy as popularity. One of the most discussed examples has been the album *Reign in Blood*, which contains numerous references to Josef Mengele, the Nazi doctor who conducted human experiments in death camps.[3]

The murder of Elyse Pahler sparked a new wave of argument over the influence of controversial and violent lyrics, such as those produced by Slayer, on young people. Over time, many lawsuits have been brought against the producers of violent entertainment, and all have been thrown out in the United States on First Amendment grounds. The parents of Elyse Pahler, David and Lisanne Pahler, took a different approach in seeking reparation for the death of their daughter. In a lawsuit filed in 1996 and funded by the law firm Milberg Weiss Bershad Hynes & Lerach—the same firm that (successfully) sued R. J. Reynolds Tobacco for marketing "Joe Camel" to children—the parents sued Slayer and its Sony-affiliated label American Recordings for *marketing* and *selling* harmful materials (that is, Slayer's music) to minors.[4] The lawyers asserted that "The *distribution* and *marketing* of this obscene and harmful material to adolescent males constituted aiding and abetting of the criminal acts described in this complaint. . . . None of the vicious crimes against Elyse Marie Pahler would have occurred without the *intentional marketing strategy* of the 'death metal' band 'Slayer.'"[5]

The lawyers introduced their case with this line of argument:

> This is a case about public health. It is about big business, putting profits over safety. In violation of California law, Slayer and the Business Defendants marketed Slayer's product containing indecent and harmful matter to children. This action seeks to remedy these unlawful and unfair marketing practices. This action does not seek to in any way prohibit Slayer's right or ability to write, perform or otherwise express their views, any more than do the age restrictions associated with Playboy Magazines, or "X" and "R" rated movies. This is a case about harm, not taste.[6]

> After an extensive study of Slayer's lyrics, the lawsuit notes that the band's "albums and lyric books" contain 126 instances of profanity, and that each of the band's albums "has an average of 16 such expletives—words that cannot be commercially aired to minors."[7] In addition, the lawsuit notes that "Virtually every song describes violence against women, including the rape, torture, stalking and beating of women."[8]

The lawsuit cites American Recordings, Rick Rubin (a producer for Slayer), Columbia Records, Sony Music, and CBS, among others. The lawyers argue that "To ensure such profits, the Business Defendants 'commercialize' the music by involving themselves in the writing and production of the music."[9] By focusing on the marketing aspect of the case, the Pahlers and their lawyers intended to sidestep First Amendment issues and focus on the idea that explicit music can be deliberately and successfully targeted to malleable, easily influenced audiences.

Strong advocates of free speech rejected the validity of this contention. "We're getting to the point if we let these cases go forward, that someone can say 'Shaft' glorifies vigilantism. There is a really serious danger [that creators will decide] to not make a movie or not write a book," said Peter Eliasberg, a lawyer in Los Angeles for the American Civil Liberties Union.[10] The band Slayer also vigorously rejected the validity of the lawsuit. In a July 1998 interview with *Guitar World* magazine, Paul Bostaph, drummer for Slayer stated, "They're trying to blame the whole thing on us. That's such [expletive]. If you're gonna do something stupid like that, you should get in trouble for it." He went on to criticize the murder, noting that "Pahler's killers did not even accurately follow the necrophilia sacrifice rituals" detailed in Slayer's songs.[11] In a separate 1998 interview, lead vocalist Tom Araya said, "We're part-time evil. If we were really evil, we would be doing everything we're writing about," and a long-time publicist, Chris Ferraro, said, "They're the nicest people. . . . It's a matter of opinion how you take in the music, but I think it's fiction, period. They're nice, conservative people, believe it or not."[12] Finally, Superior Court Judge Jeffrey Burke rejected the argument of the lawsuit by dismissing (in October 2001) the case on free-speech grounds. He also found no liability on the part of Slayer or its label. He agreed that Slayer's music was protected on First Amendment grounds, regardless of the marketing arguments made by the Pahlers and their attorneys.[13]

Though the legal argument was thus dismissed, the arguments about marketing explicit content to young audiences reappeared in a series of studies performed by the Federal Trade Commission (FTC) in September 2000, with two follow-ups in April 2001 and December 2001. The original study documented how R-rated movies, music with "explicit lyrics labeling," and mature-rated video games frequently fall into the hands of children and teenagers, and how those industries intentionally target an under-eighteen audience. The December 2001 follow-up contained statistics about the marketing of explicit music. In examining the marketing plans for explicit recordings, submitted by the major recording companies of the RIAA to the FTC, the Commission found that two of those plans directly aimed to promote recordings at high schools; that another referred to promotions in "teen magazines"; and that, though one plan targeted only a young adult (eighteen through thirty-four) audience, the remainder of the submitted marketing strategies "detailed plans to place advertising in media that would reach an audience with a majority or substantial percentage of children under 17."[14]

The same marketing plans also routinely used print advertising in magazines with a substantial teen audience. Of the fourteen explicit recordings outlined in those plans, eight discussed placing ads in magazines with a "majority or substantial teen audience."[15] From June through September 2001, the Commission reviewed issues of eight magazines with a "majority or substantial readership under 18" and found that each of the five major recording companies, which corporately compose the RIAA, had placed ads for explicit recordings in at least two of the following magazines: *Metal Edge, Right On!, Teen, Teen People, Thrasher,* and *YM.*[16] In another investigation, the Commission, over an eight-week period, monitored advertising for explicit recordings in thirty-one popular teen television programs. As the Commission stated its results, "A review of first-airing data showed that all five major music recording companies advertised their explicit content recordings on popular teen shows such as *Total Request Live, Direct Effect,* and *106th and Park.*"[17]

The previous FTC reports had revealed even wider ad placement in primarily under-eighteen forums and had accused the RIAA of a lack of formal commitment to self-regulate the industry in the areas studied by its reports—in particular, advertising placement and content. In this respect, the findings of the December 2001 follow-up were the most favorable for the industry to date.[18] However, the FTC report and follow-ups continued to fuel the ongoing debate in Congress regarding the regulation of the entertainment industry. These debates date from long-standing moral objections to the industry on the part of some congresspersons. The September 2000 FTC report had been called for by President Bill Clinton, Senator Joseph Lieberman, Senator John McCain, and Senator Sam Brownback, and the subsequent follow-ups had been conducted at the request of the Senate Commerce Committee.

After the release of the initial FTC report, Senator McCain had inquired as to whether targeting children with adult-rated violent movies, music, or games would constitute a violation of Section 5 of the Federal Trade Commission Act prohibiting "deceptive" and "unfair" advertising.[19] Although the Commission believed that many constitutional and legal barriers to regulation of the industry existed, it outlined several theories under which industry actions could be defined as "deceptive" under the FTC Act. One goal was to stop the advertising or marketing of explicit-content music (and R-rated films and mature-rated games) aimed at children.[20] The FTC recognized the obvious difficulties of enforcing this standard,[21] and no action came of these recommendations.[22] It recommended that Congress continue to "promote substantially improved, voluntary, self-regulatory efforts."[23]

In the spring and summer of 2001, Senator Lieberman, a longtime critic of the entertainment industry, pushed an entertainment marketing bill to "direct the Federal Trade Commission to regulate the music, movie and television industries as it does other businesses that engage in false and deceptive advertising."[24] The issue of targeting youth with explicit materials was at the heart of this bill's construction; the bill's verbatim purpose was "To prohibit the targeted marketing to minors of adult-rated media as an unfair or deceptive practice."[25] The House counterpart to the bill, introduced by Representative Steve Israel, used identical language.[26] The two bills focused almost exclusively on restricting the targeting of youth with explicit materials by redefining the meaning of "unfair" and "deceptive." However, the bills never found adequate support in Congress and quietly were shelved.

Recording labels continue to defend self-regulation. Industry officials have proposed that warning labels be placed on CDs according to an age-based system, although there is no age-restricted purchase of those products. Hilary Rosen, president of the RIAA, has noted that in a "spot check" of more than 200 recordings from May to November 2001, warning labels were visible on all recordings, as opposed to the relative obscurity of such information on recordings the year previous. Ms. Rosen also noted that earlier in 2001, 24 percent of full-page music advertisements carried warnings; by November 2001, the percentage had climbed to 97 percent.[27]

Supporters of industry self-regulation found encouraging news in the FTC's December 2001 follow-up report. Despite its previous reprimands, the Commission found several areas of improvement in self-regulation when compared with both the September 2000 report and its April 2001 follow-up. The FTC reported that (1) the RIAA now recommends that industry members place clear parental advisories in all television and radio advertising, street marketing samplers, and music giveaways; (2) song lyrics are often posted on the artists' websites or on songfile.com; (3) the RIAA and the National Association of Recording Merchandisers (NARM) have formed a Parental Advisory Implementation Task Force to assist music companies in meeting existing program guidelines; and (4) the RIAA has founded parentalguide.org, a website to further educate parents on the role of explicit content advisory labels.[28]

The FTC released another follow-up report in June 2002. Though improvements were noted in the movie and video-game industries, officials criticized the lack of improvement in the music industry. Little improvement was seen in advertising in magazines and on the television,[29] although BMC Music did announce that it would begin placing advisory stickers on explicit-content albums.

Despite the apparent improvement of industry self-regulation by disclosure, many questions continue to be raised about whether these entirely voluntary efforts are adequate to keep potentially harmful music out of the hands of young persons like Royce Casey, Joseph Fiorella, and Jacob Delashmutt. In April 2001, Senator Lieberman introduced a bill that would permit the FTC to limit the marketing of explicit entertainment directed at youths.[30] Though he subsequently withdrew this bill, regulation of youth marketing continues to be a source of conflict between lawmakers and industry executives.

NOTES

1. Sharon Waxman, "Did 'Death Metal' Music Incite Murder?; Lawsuit Against Band, Distributors Could Overcome First Amendment Hurdle," *The Washington Post* (January 23, 2001), p. E1.
2. Chuck Philips, "Murder Case Spotlights Marketing of Violent Lyrics," *Los Angeles Times* (January 21, 2001), p. C1.
3. Sharon Waxman, "Did 'Death Metal' Music Incite Murder?; Lawsuit Against Band, Distributors Could Overcome First Amendment Hurdle," *The Washington Post* (January 23, 2001), p. E1.
4. *Ibid.*
5. *Ibid* (emphasis added).
6. *David Pahler, et al. v. Slayer, et al.* Superior Ct., California, County of San Luis Obispo, Case no. CV-79356, at 2.
7. *Ibid.*, at 5.
8. *Ibid.*, at 5–6.
9. *Ibid.*, at 3.
10. *Ibid.*
11. Chuck Philips, "Murder Case Spotlights Marketing of Violent Lyrics," *The Los Angeles Times* (January 21, 2001), p. C1.

12. Saron Waxman, "Did 'Death Metal' Incite Murder?" *The Washington Post* (January 23, 2001), p. E1.
13. Chuck Philips, "Suit Over Metal Band's Lyrics Is Dismissed," *Los Angeles Times* (October 31, 2001), p. 3.2.
14. Federal Trade Commission, *Marketing Violent Entertainment to Children: A One-Year Follow-Up Review of Industry Practices in the Motion Picture, Music Recording, and Electronic Game Industries* (December 5, 2001), p. 15.
15. *Ibid.*, p. 16.
16. *Ibid.*
17. *Ibid.*, pp. 15–16.
18. See: Federal Trade Commission, *Marketing Violent Entertainment to Children: A Review of Self-Regulation and Industry Practices in the Motion Picture, Music Recording, and Electronic Game Industries*, September 11, 2000; *Marketing Violent Entertainment to Children: A Six-Month Follow-Up Review of Industry Practices in the Motion Picture, Music Recording, and Electronic Game Industries: A Report to Congress*, April 24, 2001.
19. Statement of Senator John McCain during the Hearing on Marketing Violence to Children, September 13, 2000; Federal Trade Commission, "FTC Calls for Continued Congressional Oversight of Self-Regulatory Efforts by Entertainment Industry; Cites Significant Legal Obstacles to Law Enforcement Action," November 21, 2000.
20. Federal Trade Comission, letter to Senator John McCain, November 20, 2000, pp. 2–3.
21. *Ibid.*
22. *Ibid.*, p. 5.
23. *Ibid.*, pp. 6–7.
24. Ken Maguire, "Lieberman Renews Efforts on Entertainment Marketing Bill," The Associated Press (June 21, 2001).
25. S. 792, p. 1.
26. H.R. 2246, p. 1.
27. Laura M. Holson, "U.S. Is Said to Criticize Music Industry on Marketing," *The New York Times* (December 4, 2001), p. A17.
28. *Ibid.*, pp. 17–18.
29. FTC, "*Marketing Violent Entertainment to Children: A Twenty-One Month Follow-Up Review of Industry Practices in the Motion Picture, Music Recording, and Electronic Game Industries*" (June 2002).
30. See Bill Summary & Status, *http://thomas.loc.gov*, S.792; *Ibid.*, H.R. 2246. (Introduced on April 26, 2001.)

An Accountant's Small-Time Trading

Donald Davidson is a young accountant who recently went into practice for himself. He literally placed a Certified Public Accountant (CPA) shingle on a mantel post outside a basement office that he rented in a reconstructed part of downtown Frederick, Maryland. He chose this location because of its low overhead, which was all he could afford as he got his practice under way. Although in Frederick he has only two clients, Washington, D.C., with its inexhaustible need for accountants, is only forty miles away. Donald made a number of contacts in Washington during a previous job that he briefly held at an accounting firm. Donald's father is a lawyer/accountant with a solid practice in Washington and is positioned to send business Donald's way.

In fact, his father has already sent him one important client, Mr. Warner Wolff, the president of the medium-sized First National Bank of Beltsville, located in the Maryland suburbs of Washington. Donald has been working on Wolff's personal accounts, including his income taxes and two Pension Accounts for himself and his wife that he has created through a consulting business managed by his wife. Donald, who has often talked with Mr. Wolff about the bank's plans and programs, hopes there might be some contract work to be done for the bank in the future.

One day while going over books of the pension accounts, Donald noticed that Mr. Wolff had sold the entire diversified portfolio of stocks in his wife's pension account for a value of just over $249,000. Mr. Wolff had then bought $248,982 of stock in the First National Bank of Beltsville for his wife's pension account. Upon seeing the record of these trades, Donald jokingly commented to Mr. Wolff that he must have supreme confidence in his managerial abilities to put all of his wife's pension money in the stock of his own bank.

Mr. Wolff, a sober and forthright person, took Donald's comment as a serious inquiry into the reason for the trades and gave a serious answer: "Although it won't be announced for three months and is top secret," he said, "we have signed a merger agreement with the largest bank in Maryland, and our stock price should rise dramatically on the announcement date." Donald was

This case was prepared by Tom L. Beauchamp. The case of Donald Davidson is based on a factual history, but names, locations, and dates have been changed. Not to be duplicated without permission of the holder of the copyright, © 1992, 1996, 2003 by Tom L. Beauchamp.

surprised at being let in on the secret, but he presumed that Mr. Wolff took the disclosure to be protected by normal accountant/client confidentiality. He thought nothing more of it and concluded his work on the records.

However, on the drive home, he began to mull over his client's timely purchase and saw that the same opportunity is available to him. He has no cash to invest, but he has an IRA (individual retirement account) worth $10,000. The bank certificate of deposit in which he has invested his IRA will be coming due in three weeks, and he will need to reinvest this money. Why not, he thought, put all $10,000 in the stock of the First National Bank of Beltsville?

As a student at the Wharton School, Donald studied insider trading and the regulations governing it that were issued by the Securities and Exchange Commission. He vaguely remembered that the principle behind the SEC regulations is that it is illegal to trade on nonpublic, financially useful information that has been misappropriated or secured by a breach of fiduciary duty. Donald now felt a need to bone up on his rusty understanding. He consulted a textbook that he had studied as a student and read the following description:

> The practice of insider trading has long been banned in the United States. The Securities and Exchange Commission (SEC) has actively sought rules against such trading since the enactment of the Securities Exchange Act of 1934. Under the terms of this law, a trader is forbidden to use information obtained on the inside to buy or sell securities or to pass the information on to others so that they may benefit. In the important precedent case of *S.E.C. v. Texas Gulf Sulphur,* a court held, "Anyone in possession of material inside information must either disclose it to the investing public, or, if he is disabled from disclosing it in order to protect a corporate confidence, or [if] he chooses not to, must abstain from trading in or recommending the securities concerned while such inside information remains undisclosed."
>
> Insider trading has proven difficult to define. An "inside trader" is someone who trades in the stock of a corporation based upon material nonpublic information he has obtained by virtue of his relationship with the corporation. Some believe that the information should be relevant to the price and to the purchase of the stock. For example, one might have confidential information that could not be disclosed and yet would not likely affect the stock's price even if it were known. The SEC has said that the nonpublic information must be *misappropriated* by the trader, but a definition of the term "misappropriate" has likewise proven difficult.
>
> There is considerable moral ambiguity surrounding insider trading. The SEC believes that the insider trading laws serve a moral purpose: preserving the fairness and integrity of the nation's securities market. Investors who have nonpublic inside information are thought to be unfairly advantaged. The underlying principles of

these laws are that all investors in a free market should have equal access to relevant information, that securities markets must operate on faith and trust, and that insider trading undermines public confidence in the marketplace. The United States Supreme Court has stressed a different moral purpose. The Court has held that an inside trader is one who violates a fiduciary duty to retain confidential information; insider trading is, therefore, like stealing from an employer. Insider trading is also believed to obstruct the market in capital formation.

Other authorities do not consider insider trading unfair. Several scholars have argued that permitting insider trades would make the securities market more efficient. The activity of the traders would be spotted and the market would respond more quickly to essential information. Ben R. Murphy, a partner in a merchant banking firm in Dallas, argues as follows: "My theory is that if we didn't have [insider trading laws] the market would eventually discount all the leaks and rumors and become more efficient. People would have to take a risk on believing the rumors or not." It is noteworthy that over $50 billion of securities trades daily on American exchanges, and no one is prepared to argue that even as much as 1 percent involves insider trading or any form of illegal transactions.

Jonathan Macey, Professor of Law at Emory University, has argued that a person who locates undervalued shares in a company through inside information can provide a valuable service to the market by the discovery, whether insider trading occurs or not. But in order to encourage such discovery the person or institution must be allowed to profit. This is basically what stock analysts do; they all try to get information not yet public before their rivals do in order to reward clients who pay for their activities. The amateur investing public has no chance against such professional knowledge and can only hope that the market price already reflects insider information. Macey concludes that "a complete ban on trading by those with confidential information about a company would be disastrous to the efficiency of the capital markets. If such a rule were enforced, nobody would have an incentive to engage in a search for undervalued firms, stock prices would not accurately reflect company values, and, perhaps worst of all, investment capital would not flow to its most highly valued users. Thus, we would all be better off if the SEC would de-escalate its war on insider trading."

After reading this textbook summary, Donald took a walk to his local library. There he located some October 2000 rules that had been adopted by the SEC. These rules had been passed to make it easier to prosecute insider trading cases. His eyes fell on Rule 10b5-1. This rule provides that a person is liable for insider trading if he or she "was aware of the material nonpublic information when the person made the purchase or sale." According to this rule, a prosecutor does not have to show that the trader actually *used* the nonpublic information as the basis of the sale, only that the trader was *aware of* the information.

As Donald read further, he quickly came to appreciate that federal securities laws regulating insider trading had developed gradually and in a somewhat loose manner from both the SEC and judicial decisions. Donald thought to himself that terms like "misappropriated" and "material nonpublic information" were vague and would likely be handled in a highly subjective way or on a case-by-case basis. He did not think that he personally would be engaging in a breach of fiduciary duty by trading in the bank stock, because he had no relevant fiduciary duty. As he saw it, he had a fiduciary duty not to disclose the secret that his client had revealed, but disclosure was not his intent. In his judgment, he no more obtained the information through a breach of fiduciary duty than does a bartender who overhears information at the bar about a merger of two companies. Donald asked himself, "What fiduciary duty could possibly require me not to buy this stock? Moreover, even if it is material nonpublic information, I did not get it as an insider; indeed, I do not have any really *inside* information, and I am hardly an inside trader. For all I know, Mr. Wolff's deal may be more tentative than he says or may even collapse."

These thoughts followed from Donald's inference, based on what he had read, that the Justice Department construed insider trading to apply exclusively to an *insider* with a fiduciary duty to a corporation not to use confidential information obtained in their relationship. He could not see that he had any such corporate connection. Insiders were almost always Wall Street professionals. He also knew that in one of the few cases to reach the U.S. Supreme Court, the Court had dismissed charges of insider trading against a printer who had traded stocks on the basis of the reading of confidential information he had been given to print. The Court held that the printer had no legal obligation not to use the confidential information in this manner. Donald saw himself as in much the same situation as the printer.

While he was at the library, Donald read up on some famous insider trading cases. The ones that now stuck in his mind were three sensationalized cases that had at one time received considerable public attention, each in a quite different circumstance. The first case involved a reporter, R. Foster Winans of *The Wall Street Journal*, who had taken advantage of his position as a reporter to obtain information that positioned him to make trading gains (this he had not done very effectively) and had also enabled him to pass on the information to his friends and associates (who did very effectively make quick and lucrative trades). Winans was a Wall Street reporter but still was an "outsider" from a Wall Street perspective. These excesses of a youthful journalist did not seem to Donald to directly address any serious problem of insider trading.

He was more troubled by the case of Dennis Levine, a managing director who specialized in mergers and acquisitions at Drexel Burnham Lambert. Levine had been arrested and successfully prosecuted for trading the securities of fifty-four companies on insider information in order to earn over $12.6 million. Levine was one of Wall Street's most successful figures and had taken home $3 million in salary and bonuses during a single year. Levine's walk on the wrong side of Wall Street evidently began on a trip to the Bahamas, where he deposited funds at secret branches of a Swiss bank. Using code names, he ultimately set up two dummy Panamanian corporations that traded through the Bahamian/Swiss bank. He engaged in a continuous pattern of trading that netted him the $12.6 million. The SEC launched an investigation after noting a pattern of suspiciously well-timed stock trading at the Swiss Bank's U.S. trading accounts.

Donald was irritated by a third case, which he found very distant from his own situation. In the celebrated investigation of the Enron scandal in 2002, court filings showed that Enron executives repeatedly sold the company's stock as they foresaw the firm's increasingly grim prospects. Many executives profited in the millions of dollars even as they learned from inside information of dramatic corporate losses. For example, just as Enron Broadband was losing millions of dollars, its head, Ken Rice, made $72 million in stock sales carried out systematically from 1998 through late 2001. Similarly, Enron's CEO, Ken Lay, had sold his stock for roughly $101 million on virtually every business day during the worst period of sales, while telling his employees that the quarterly earnings outlook for this period was "great." This case angered Donald, but he also saw little applicability to his own circumstance.

In reading these stories, Donald could see that the SEC had become convinced that insider trading is rampant and difficult to detect. The SEC was now closely investigating the fact that the stock of a takeover target almost always jumps in price immediately before a takeover offer is announced to the public. For example, when General Electric acquired RCA, the stock had jumped a dramatic sixteen points immediately prior to the public announcement. The SEC's massive investigation of this case and related ones made it clear that the agency is dedicated to policing efforts in the attempt to contain insider trading.

SEC prohibitions have applied traditionally only to persons with a regular connection to the operation of the nation's securities markets. But in pursuing its recent cases, the SEC discovered that insider trading was not confined to corporate insiders. It determined that many Wall Street "outsiders" were actively involved. In discussing this problem, *Business Week* boldly reported that

> Executives do it. Bankers do it. Accountants, secretaries, and messengers do it. And so do printers, cabdrivers, waiters, housewives, hairdressers—and mistresses. Some do it on their own. Others work in rings with connections as far away as Switzerland and Hong Kong. But they all work the shadowy side of Wall Street by trading on inside information to make money in the stock market.

Donald could see that he definitely fit this characterization, and he certainly had obtained his information in confidence; but, again he could not see that he was violating that confidence or that he had either directly or indirectly stolen his information. Donald was buoyed to read a quotation taken from the investment journal *Barron's*, which maintained that the SEC is "riding roughshod over due process of law" and drying up the free flow of information and harming the interest of those it is sworn to protect. The *Barron's* article adamantly insisted that some persons who had been found guilty of insider-trading violations had done no legal wrong and that the SEC had twisted the idea of "misappropriation" of information to the breaking point in getting convictions. In the Winans's case, said *Barron's,* the only wrong done was the moral wrong of violating *The Wall Street Journal's* rules of ethics. But this was just a matter of journalism ethics, not business ethics, as far as Donald could see.

Donald had been an accountant long enough to know that government rules, especially Internal Revenue Service rules, had multiple interpretations and borderline case situations. He recognized that he might be in a borderline situation morally, but he could not see that he would be violating any clear legal principle by purchasing the bank stock. After considerable thought, he decided that he would buy the stock in three weeks, unless he saw new reasons not to do so. However, he felt uneasy about his decision. He was not too worried about the law. Donald's two deepest concerns were his IRA and his integrity.

Lockheed Martin's Acquisition of Comsat

Lockheed Martin is the largest defense contractor in the world. Lockheed, along with its competitors, has contributed to various federal election campaigns and has invested heavily in lobbying with the goal of sustaining, improving, or expanding its business activities with help from the government. A key component of the success the company has been achieved through financial contributions and political lobbying. In particular, political action committees (PACs, as defined later) and informational services have been utilized.

THE ACQUISITION OF COMSAT

Long respected for its solid economic performance, Lockheed Martin has struggled to maintain this reputation in recent years. In December 1998, Lockheed announced that there would be an unexpected shortfall in the company's fourth-quarter earnings. Early in 1999, it was determined that earnings were 23 percent below the prior year's, and it was estimated at the time that the 1999 earnings would also be weak. Even before these financial disclosures were made, Lockheed had decided to secure new growth areas outside defense, especially in global telecommunications. Peter Aseritis, an industry analyst with CSFB Securities, noted at the time that "Lockheed wants to be a much bigger player in a much faster-growing and more profitable business [i.e., telecommunications] than their core defense business."[1]

This strategy led Lockheed to seek to acquire Comsat—formerly a quasi-government satellite company created by the Communications Satellite Act of 1962—to be the U. S. participant in an international satellite network of communications. Over a thirty-eight-year history, Comsat served as a global provider of satellite and digital networking services, products, and technology. It was the driving force in the creation of INTELSAT, an international satellite organization that grew to have 143 member countries and signatories. Lock-

This case was prepared by Tom L. Beauchamp and Ahmed Humayun, and revised by Joseph Folio. Not to be duplicated without permission of the holder of the copyright, © 2003 by Tom L. Beauchamp.

heed sought to obtain Comsat's exclusive rights to international satellite communications, which would make Lockheed the sole provider to other American corporations on the INTELSAT system.

Lockheed faced political and legal problems in the attempt to acquire Comsat. Among other provisions of the 1962 charter by Congress was a stipulation that no single investor could own a majority stake in INTELSAT. Legislators had been concerned that ownership of and access to Comsat and INTELSAT by one company would give monopoly power to that company. Despite this barrier, the estimates that Comsat would more than triple Lockheed's revenues from telecommunications and make it the leading player in the market motivated Lockheed executives to attempt to persuade the government to allow it to acquire 100 percent of Comsat.

Lockheed's competitors in the telecommunications market vigorously opposed such a move. These firms included Boeing, Motorola, AT&T, General Electric, NBC, and MCI Worldcom. They wanted to renegotiate long-term contracts with Comsat and to have their own guaranteed access. If these competitors had their way, Lockheed's acquisition of any *part* of Comsat would not allow the company to have *total control* over Comsat. Many other interest groups opposed the sale of Comsat on grounds that it would lead to an increase rather than a reduction in international phone rates.

In September 1998, the chief operating officer of Lockheed Martin Global Telecommunications, Brian Dailey (and other executives), met with Representative Thomas J. Bliley, Jr. (R-Va.), then chairman of the House Commerce Committee. Bliley had a history of opposition to special advantages and government support for Comsat. He wanted it to operate as a true commercial competitor. Lockheed hoped that Bliley's desire to ensure unfettered competition would go as far as releasing Comsat from its government ties but not so far as to block the proposed merger. Bliley was noncommittal but noted in this meeting that Lockheed would simply have to persuade members of the Senate that Comsat's charter should be changed.

Lockheed took precisely this course, scheduling meetings with as many senators as possible. Late in 1999, Senator Conrad Burns (R-Mont.) arranged legislation that would allow Lockheed to acquire Comsat. In addition, Lockheed sought an amendment to the House appropriations bill that would remove the provision that required no one investor to have a majority stake in Comsat. When these lobbying efforts failed, Senator Trent Lott (R-Miss.) and House Speaker J. Dennis Hastert (R-Ill.) stepped in and pledged that a satellite reform conference committee would produce Comsat legislation in upcoming months. If it passed, this legislation would enable Lockheed to meet its deadline for closing the Comsat purchase.

In February 2000, agreement was reached on a Satellite Privatization Bill by Chairman Bliley, Senator Conrad Burns, and Representative Edward J. Markey (D-Mass.). These members of Congress announced that they had agreed to produce legislation that (1) mandates pro-competitive privatization of INTELSAT (and Inmarsat), (2) ends Comsat's monopoly over INTELSAT access in the United States, (3) ends various privileges and immunities for IN-

TELSAT and Comsat; and—critical for Lockheed—(4) eliminates the ownership cap on Comsat. These members of Congress argued that this arrangement would bring lower prices for consumers, create more jobs for workers, privatize in a pro-competitive manner, end monopoly status for Comsat, create more opportunities for overseas business ventures, and breed innovation and technological change in the telecommunications industry. Congressman Markey expressed deep appreciation to Chairman Bliley for his leadership in advancing a "more competitive international satellite blueprint for the country; I also want to applaud his efforts in crafting today's agreement with Lockheed Martin and commend as well Senator Conrad Burns for his work on the Senate side."[2] Ultimately the favorable legislation was passed, and Lockheed became sole owner of Comsat.

INFLUENCING LEGISLATION

Lockheed had exerted its formidable influence to pass this legislation, but it deserves notice that other firms with resources and connections were doing much the same thing at the same time, namely, trying to influence structure of the Comsat legislation in their favor. In this respect, there was competition— on a level playing field—for favorable outcomes. However, critics of these attempts to influence legislative outcomes argued that Lockheed's legislative success was in large part due to the campaign contributions it had made to the politicians who were key players. Central members of the House and the Senate involved in the Comsat legislation all received campaign contributions from Lockheed, both through its "PACs" and soft-money donations, and they were also the target of intense lobbying efforts.

PACs are groups of persons having common interests who seek to advance specific political plans by making contributions to candidates with similar or potentially similar views. Their common interests may be politically related or business-related; for example, all of a PAC's donors might be employed by the same company, labor union, or trade or professional association. Lockheed contributed $1,152,350 to the Republican and Democratic parties through its PAC in 2000 ($624,850 and $437,500 respectively). Democratic senatorial candidates received $81,500, and Republican senatorial candidates received $148,199. Democratic House candidates received $283,392, and Republican House candidates $504,628.

Lockheed's push to secure congressional endorsement also included the use of "hard money," or direct donations to specific politicians. Hard money contributions vary according to their source. PACs are able to donate $5,000 per election cycle (primary or general) to a candidate. The FEC also regulates how much individuals can donate to PACs ($5,000 as well) to limit an excessive funneling of funds from individuals through PACs to candidates. Individuals can donate only $1,000 per election (general or primary) to a candidate. Since Lockheed also sought approval from the Federal Communications Commission to declare it a "common carrier," it focused its efforts on those best able to help. Representative Bliley and Senator Burns were in a position to be helpful to Lockheed in both objectives, but at the time it was unclear whether or not they were willing to do so.

In the next election cycle, for the year 2000, Senator Burns received a $39,730 donation from a combination of Lockheed interests. This figure is not a direct donation from Lockheed; rather, it is the sum of donations from its PACs and interested individuals. These donations, whether by PAC or by employees, are governed by the FEC regulations previously described. Compared with contributions in the years before this election cycle, this figure represents a significant increase in contribution levels from Lockheed to Burns. Later in 2000, Burns introduced the satellite privatization measure that would have given Lockheed part of the package needed to buy Comsat. Bliley received a fairly standard contribution of $2,000. Lott and Hastert, who were jointly responsible for the legislation that allowed the acquisition to take place, received $8,000 and $10,250, respectively, in the 2000 election cycle. For Lott, this figure was consistent with previous donations from Lockheed. For Hastert, however, Lockheed's donation for the 2000 election made the company his ninth highest contributor (a list that Lockheed was not even on for the 1998 election).[3]

There are other indirect avenues by which businesses can show support for politicians. These include first-class flight tickets, free hotel stays, and even foundations and centers established in honor of politicians. For instance, while the Comsat legislation was pending before Congress, Lockheed gave a million-dollar donation to an academic center named after Senator Lott that was under construction at the University of Mississippi (the Trent Lott Leadership Institute). MCI Worldcom Inc., which *opposed* Lockheed on the Comsat legislation, also contributed a million dollars to this center. One advantage of this kind of gift is that it is tax deductible and does not have to be disclosed to the Federal Election Commission.

The nondisclosure rule has attracted critics. Fred Wertheimer, president of a public policy group called Democracy 21, said, regarding the proposed center, "It's very pleasant for the honoree, and very dangerous for citizens who are looking for a fair political process," implying that the rival donations were each made in order to influence the senator to adopt their perspective on the case.[4] In response to such criticisms, Senator Lott said that "The only thing benefactors will be 'buying' with their gifts are the desks, books, and other materials to help students in this new Ole Miss program."[5] The University of Mississippi stated that Mr. Lott had not been involved in fund-raising and that it was solely the university's idea to name the center after him.

Lockheed has also contributed to political campaigns using "soft money." These gifts are unlimited contributions that may be made by individuals, unions, corporations, or other groups, to a political party. These funds are generally claimed by political parties to be used for "party-building" endeavors, rather than for specific candidates. These funds, however, can be distributed to certain areas or political races at the discretion of the party. The unlimited nature of this type of contribution offers a way to give substantial amounts to a political team without running afoul of limits on contributions. In 2000, Lockheed contributed $1,152,350 in soft money—Democrats receiving $457,500 and Republicans receiving $694,850. It is impossible to trace how much of this money was diverted to specific federal election races, but this activity provides an additional means by which Lockheed (and other corporations) can support politicians.

Lockheed spent far more money in trying to persuade politicians to their point of view through bipartisan *lobbying*. In "Corporate PAC Campaign Contributions in Perspective," Professor Jeffrey Milyo and two associates found that, in general, lobbying expenses far exceed PAC contributions. These general findings apply to Lockheed, in particular. Lockheed spent $11,170,000 on lobbying in 2000, $1,152,350 in soft money donations, and $1,017,719 in PAC contributions. Milyo and associates suggest that one-time PAC donations are best understood as "entrance fees" that provide access to a legislator without engendering an "obligation" to support needed legislation. That is, monetary contributions serve as introductions to politicians but do not require reciprocal responses. Companies can then follow up through lobbying campaigns that inform those same politicians of the needs and interests of the groups the lobby represents.[6]

Lockheed spent money to lobby senators and members of Congress from both parties. Lott, then Senate majority leader, served as the day-to-day manger of business on the Senate floor and was responsible for working with each committee on all legislation and for scheduling the sequence and manner of its debate. Lott was thus in a key position to influence the progress of the Comsat legislation. Lockheed hired one former Lott staffer and listed his job description on a registration form as to "identify business relationships for [Lockheed Martin Global Telecommunications] in Mississippi that will benefit the state."[7] Such business relationships could include building a spaceport in Mississippi that would increase employment opportunities and bring in new capital, boosting the economy of the state. Speaker of the House Hastert was also in a pivotal position. The speaker chairs the House of Representatives and holds broad powers, including right of recognition on the floor and the ability to set the agenda by deciding the order and time that legislation comes before the House.

The many lobbyists hired by Lockheed included several who were closely connected to the Democratic party. Peter Knight was one of former Vice President Al Gore's political advisers; he sat on the board of the Comsat Corp. and is a long-standing lobbyist for Lockheed. Lockheed's lobbyist-list also boasted former Democratic representatives Beryl Anthony of Arkansas and veteran Democratic insider Tom Quinn (both well-known in Clinton circles). Former Democratic national Chairman Charles Manatt—among Washington's most able lobbyists—was, along with Knight, named a Comsat director.[8]

In pursuit of members of Congress and those influential with the administration, Lockheed put together a lobbying team that included members from eleven lobbying firms. Comsat had seven additional firms available. Lockheed openly acknowledges that it engages in such lobbying efforts but insists that there is nothing inappropriate about it and that such efforts are not geared towards politicians of a particular political persuasion. The company states that its focus "wasn't just Senator Lott" but the "overall Democrats and Republicans we wanted to improve our relationship with."[9] The larger goal of its ongoing efforts is to keep politicians in both parties aware of Lockheed's interests and concerns, and particularly to demonstrate how important it is that legislation be passed in Lockheed's favor. Teams coordinate with each other in targeting and contacting relevant officials in both parties and in holding informational seminars for them. Although some may question these practices, Lockheed's rivals also hire lobbying teams to represent their interests. Like Lockheed, they see lobbying not as the abuse of access by powerful aberrant groups or corporations, but rather as the modus operandi of corporations that seek to be efficient and profitable.

Lockheed and other defense contractors are dependent on government contracts for revenues. Lockheed received over $18 billion in U. S. government contracts in 1999, including $12.6 billion from the Pentagon and more than $2 billion from the Department of Energy.[10] From this perspective, political donations are essential to economic survival, with rival defense firms competing for key contracts and favorable legislation. Those who are unable to sustain economic and informational support services for politicians, the argument goes, will be unlikely to survive, or at least will not be financially competitive. Contributing money is viewed as an essential part of conducting business, since the contributions help determine the level of exposure of a company's interests. Companies perceive this to be a determining factor in how government contracts are awarded. Politicians also benefit from this relationship. They receive money for federal election campaigns and even for the promise of new industries and jobs to help bolster the economies of their home states.

CAMPAIGN FINANCE REFORM IN 2002

The McCain-Feingold campaign finance law took effect on November 6, 2002. The bill bans soft money and prevents so-called "issue" ads by special interest groups that mention a candidate and run just prior to an election. The bill's soft-money restrictions could greatly impact the way campaign funds are raised. In the case of Lockheed, this reform entails that the company could not repeat the $1,152,350 that it contributed to political parties in the 2000 election cycle. However, it is still allowed under this legislation to maintain PAC contributions ($1,017,719 in 2000) and lobbying expenditures ($11,170,000 in 2000).

Since passage of the McCain-Feingold campaign finance law, both the Republican and the Democratic parties have achieved record-high fundraising levels.

NOTES

1. Leslie Wayne, "Into the Telecommunications Maze: Lockheed Faces Many Obstacles in Bid for Satellite Company," *The New York Times*, February 2, 1999, p. C1.
2. News Release from the House Commerce Committee on February 17, 2000. Accessed at: http://www.presageinc.com, *Communications Satellite Reform Online Information* (as posted June 11, 2002).
3. www.opensecrets.org (as of January 2003). This website includes campaign contribution information for each candidate for each race by election and election cycles.
4. Frank Bruni, "Donors Flock to University Center Linked to Senate Majority Leader," *The New York Times*, May 8, 1999, p. A1.
5. *Ibid*. Lott received $993,593 in 1999–2000 PAC contributions, according to the Center for Responsive Politics.
6. Jeffrey Milyo, David Primo, and Timothy Groseclose, "PAC Campaign Contributions Have Little Influence," The Irving B. Harris School of Public Policy Studies, the University of Chicago, *Policy Brief*, vol. 1, no. 4 (June 13, 2002), p. 1 (analysis of a study based on statistical information).
7. Greg Schneider, "Lockheed Martin's Change of Course Pays Off," *The Washington Post*, February 21, 2000, p. F6.
8. Robert D. Novak, "Big-Money Washington," *The Washington Post*, December 10, 1998, p. F5.
9. Greg Schneider, "Lockheed Martin's Change of Course Pays Off," *The Washington Post*, February 21, 2000, p. F6.
10. www.indg.org/Lockhee2.htm

Italian Tax Mores

The Italian federal corporate tax system has an official, legal tax structure and tax rates just as the U.S. system does. However, all similarity between the two systems ends there.

The Italian tax authorities assume that no Italian corporation would ever submit a tax return that shows its true profits but rather that a corporation would submit a return that understates actual profits by anywhere between 30 percent and 70 percent; their assumption is essentially correct. Therefore, about six months after the annual deadline for filing corporate tax returns, the tax authorities issue to each corporation an "invitation to discuss" its tax return. The purpose of this notice is to arrange a personal meeting between them and representatives of the corporation. At this meeting, the Italian revenue service states the amount of corporate income tax that it believes is due. Its position is developed from both prior years' taxes actually paid and the current year's return; the amount that the tax authorities claim is due is generally several times that shown on the corporation's return for the current year. In short, the corporation's tax return and the revenue service's stated position are the operating offers for the several rounds of bargaining that will follow.

The Italian corporation is typically represented in such negotiations by its *commercialista,* a function that exists in Italian society for the primary purpose of negotiating corporate (and individual) tax payments with the Italian tax authorities. Thus, the management of an Italian corporation seldom, if ever, has to meet directly with the Italian revenue service and probably has a minimum awareness of the details of the negotiation other than the final settlement.

Both the final settlement and the negotiation are extremely important to the corporation, the tax authorities, and the *commercialista.* Since the tax authorities assume that a corporation *always* earned more money this year than last year and *never* has a loss, the amount of the final settlement—that is, corporate taxes that will actually be paid—becomes, for all practical purposes, the floor for the start of next year's negotiations. The final settlement also represents the amount of revenue that the Italian government will collect in taxes to help finance the cost of running the country. However, since large amounts of

---

money are involved and two individuals having vested personal interests are conducting the negotiations, the amount of *bustarella*—typically a substantial cash payment "requested" by the Italian revenue agent from the *commercialista*—usually determines whether the final settlement is closer to the corporation's original tax return or to the fiscal authority's original negotiating position.

Whatever *bustarella* is paid during the negotiation is usually included by the *commercialista* in his or her lump-sum fee "for services rendered" to the corporate client. If the final settlement is favorable to the corporation—and it is the *commercialista*'s job to see that it is—then the corporation is not likely to complain about the amount of its *commercialista*'s fee, nor will it ever know how much of that fee was represented by *bustarella* and how much remained for the *commercialista* as payment for his or her negotiating services. In any case, the tax authorities will recognize the full amount of the fee as a tax-deductible expense on the corporation's tax return for the following year.

About ten years ago, a leading American bank opened a banking subsidiary in a major Italian city. At the end of its first year of operation, the bank was advised by its local lawyers and tax accountants, both of whom were from branches of U.S. companies, to file its tax return "Italian-style," that is, to understate its actual profits by a significant amount. The American general manager of the bank, who was on his first overseas assignment, refused to do so both because he considered it dishonest and because it was inconsistent with the practices of his parent company in the United States.

About six months after filing its "American-style" tax return, the bank received an "invitation to discuss" notice from the Italian tax authorities. The bank's general manager consulted with his lawyers and tax accountants who suggested that he hire a *commercialista*. He rejected this advice and instead wrote a letter to the Italian revenue service not only stating that his firm's corporate return was correct as filed but also requesting that they inform him of any specific items about which they had questions. His letter was never answered.

About sixty days after receiving the initial "invitation to discuss" notice, the bank received a formal tax assessment notice calling for a tax of approximately three times that shown on the bank's corporate tax return. The tax authorities simply assumed that the bank's original return had been based on generally accepted Italian practices, and they reacted accordingly. The bank's general manager again consulted with his lawyers and tax accountants, who again suggested that he hire a *commercialista* who knew how to handle these matters. Upon learning that the *commercialista* would probably have to pay *bustarella* to his revenue service counterpart in order to reach a settlement, the general manager again chose to ignore his advisers. Instead, he responded by sending the Italian revenue service a check for the full amount of taxes due according to the bank's American-style tax return, even though the due date for the payment was almost six months hence; he made no reference to the amount of corporate taxes shown on the formal tax assessment notice.

Ninety days after paying its taxes, the bank received a third notice from the fiscal authorities. This one contained the statement "We have reviewed your corporate tax return for 19_____ and have determined the [the lira equivalent of] $6,000,000 of interest paid on deposits is not an allowable expense for federal purposes. Accordingly, the total tax due for 19_____ is lira _____." Since interest paid on deposits is any bank's largest single expense item, the new tax assessment was for an amount many times larger than that shown in the initial tax assessment notice and almost fifteen times larger than the taxes that the bank had actually paid.

The bank's general manager was understandably very upset. He immediately arranged an appointment to meet personally with the manager of the Italian revenue service's local office. Shortly after the start of their meeting, the conversation went something like this:

> **General Manager:** You can't really be serious about disallowing interest paid on deposits as a tax-deductible expense.
>
> **Italian Revenue Service:** Perhaps. However, we thought it would get your attention. Now that you're here, shall we begin our negotiations.[1]

NOTE

1. For readers interested in what happened subsequently, the bank was forced to pay the taxes shown on the initial tax assessment, and the American manager was recalled to the United States and replaced.

Pâté at Iroquois Brands

On April 6, 1985, proxy materials mailed by Iroquois Brands of Greenwich, Connecticut, to its shareholders contained a controversial proposal about its importation of goose liver pâté from French suppliers. The question put to shareholders was whether they wished the corporation to investigate charges of animal cruelty in the practice of force-feeding the geese used to make the pâté in France.

The officers of Iroquois Brands did not voluntarily place this proposal on the proxy agenda for shareholders. The issue had come to prominence through the persistent efforts of a single shareholder, Peter C. Lovenheim, who believed that the charges of inhumane treatment had substance and relevance for shareholders. Lovenheim, who held two-hundred shares of stock, was initially attracted to the company because of its health food orientation and its broad range of specialty products. When he received proxy materials detailing a new product, Edouard Artzner Pâté de Foie Gras, an expensive food created for French restaurants and the gourmet food market, he was distressed and felt betrayed. A proponent of animal welfare, he objected to what he believed to be cruelty to geese.

PREPARATION OF THE PRODUCT

Foie gras (literally, "fat liver") is an expensive food originally created for French restaurants and the gourmet food market. Foie gras comes from the livers of specific breeds of domesticated geese raised on a carbohydrate-rich diet. Various preparations of fresh foie gras and pâté de foie gras are the most popular and the most profitable items on the menus of many French restaurants.

Geese have been fattened in France and a few other countries to produce foie gras since the Roman period. The French cities of Strasbourg and Perigueux have become world famous for the quality of their foie gras. Roughly 20,000 French farmers make their livelihood from foie gras production. Most of their farms are so small and specialized that a ban on foie gras would produce significant economic costs to these farmers. Although France still produces about 60 percent of the world's foie gras, it is produced and marketed in several countries, including the United States. Some countries, includ-

This case was prepared by Tom L. Beauchamp and Kelley MacDougall. Not to be duplicated without permission of the holder of the copyright, © 1989, 1992, 1996, 2003 by Tom L. Beauchamp.

ing Germany,[1] prohibit the feeding practices required to produce marketable goose livers on grounds that the practice is immoral.

Commercial production of fresh foie gras and pâté using force-feeding methods—known as *gavage* ("cramming") in France—aims to enlarge an animal's liver through mechanical force-feeding of up to six-and-a-half pounds of salted, cooked maize per day, per animal, for up to one month. The prevailing practice is to restrain the animal's body in a metal or canvas brace and mechanically pump the maize through a funnel-and-tube device that is inserted several inches down the goose's throat, using techniques that prevent regurgitation. Each feeding takes approximately one minute in duration and is repeated two to six times a day until the liver enlarges to several times its original size. The average weight of the goose roughly doubles; the average liver roughly triples in size. The weight of the liver may increase tenfold in two weeks and may account for up to 10 percent of the animal's total weight.[2]

It has been reported by some who study force-feeding that geese strongly resist the feeding machines and find it difficult to breathe after their livers have expanded. There is physical discomfort in the bloated condition of the gastrointestinal tract. However, defenders of force-feeding contend that there is no reason to believe that the geese are caused pain and significant suffering or that any malformation or disease produced by the swelling of the liver causes the animal to suffer in the short period of time prior to slaughter. Defenders of force-feeding argue that if these geese were unconfined and in migration, they would, like wild geese, consume much larger amounts of food than they normally do. The argument is that geese are fitted by nature for some expansion of their livers.

Various arguments about the psychology of geese are difficult to assess. Konrad Lorenz notes in his well known work *The Year of the Greylag Goose*[3] that the emotions of the goose are particularly difficult for the novice student—including many experienced farmers—to discern. Little can be determined by the passive facial expressions on geese, and the meaning of bodily communications are even more difficult to decipher. Yet, Lorenz argues, a close student of geese can read the meanings of both facial expressions and bodily movements. For example, the position of the neck tells a great deal about whether the goose is disheartened, feeling submissive, and the like. Lorenz claims to be able to tell when geese are sad, feel threatened, feel uncertain, and feel tense; but he thinks that novices are unable to detect these emotions.

LOVENHEIM'S CONCERNS

Lovenheim obtained just over the 5 percent support from holders of stock necessary to introduce the issue to shareholders and management. Lovenheim wished to have mailed to the shareholders the proxy materials advocating the formation of a committee to investigate the methods used to fatten the geese. However, Lovenheim met with stern resistance from management. Officers refused to include his proxy materials in the shareholders' report because managers believed that the only relevant criteria for shareholder consideration were economic, and this was not an economic issue.

Lovenheim rejected this thesis. He maintained that ethical and social issues should not be excluded from proxy materials simply because these issues failed to be of economic interest and significance. He and other like-minded shareholders saw the proper treatment of animals as a perennial problem in Western morality that any sensitive person should consider. These shareholders wanted other members to be aware of the cruelty that was involved in the production of the "specialty food" now sold by Iroquois.

Lovenheim maintained that if undue stress, pain, and suffering are inflicted upon the geese, it is questionable whether further distribution of this product should continue unless a more humane production method is developed. Lovenheim was able to enlist the support of several animal welfare groups. For example, the American Society for the Prevention of Cruelty to Animals (ASPCA) said of force-feeding: "This is not just raising animals for food. This is an aberrant and unethical practice."[4] John F. Kullberg, the executive director of the organization, explained the ASPCA's position on the force-feeding of geese:

> We consider the force-feeding of geese an act of cruelty and remain committed to having this practice stopped.
>
> Hundreds of thousands of geese are subjected to force-feeding yearly. The pain and stress they endure is very real. The fact that all of this is justified solely on the basis of producing a luxury food item not only promotes the unethical stand that the end justifies the means, but makes the matter even more objectionable because of such a meaningless end.
>
> We are distressed that the results of this inhumane feeding practice are promoted for sale in the United States. It is further the opinion of our legal counsel that force-feeding violates several state anti-cruelty laws.[5]

The Humane Society of the United States also condemned this process as unnecessarily cruel to animals.

In his proposal, Lovenheim requested that a committee be formed to study the methods by which the French supplier produced pâté and then to report to shareholders its findings, together with an opinion about whether this process caused undue distress, pain, and suffering to animals. Management at Iroquois Brands denied that there was a need for such a committee. It cited figures that discounted the financial importance of the pâté, claiming that the company suffered a net loss on the product. Its figures may be summarized as follows:

Iroquois's annual revenue:	$141 million
Iroquois's annual profit:	$6 million
Iroquois's sales from pâté:	$79,000
Iroquois's net loss on pâté:	$3,121

Management acknowledged the importance of moral problems that arise when animals are treated in a cruel manner. However, the company contended that the real issue is whether a reseller of the end product should be responsible for the means of production. The board claimed to "deplore cruelty to animals in any form"[6] and commended the Humane Society for its work to alleviate the problem of cruelty to animals in the United States. However, it did not view itself as responsible for French practices over which it had no control. It maintained that, upon importing the pâté, the federal Food and Drug Administration tested and approved the product, thereby lifting any responsibility that Iroquois may have had.

Iroquois also argued that it was illogical to form a panel to study an issue that the company could not control, especially when the costs of obtaining expert consultation would exceed any reasonably anticipated profit from the product. Furthermore, management contended that even if a committee were formed, it would have little, if any, impact on Iroquois's actual business and even less impact on the world pâté market or the feeding practices in France.

Lovenheim rejected this line of argument. He claimed that, although Iroquois Brands might not itself force-feed the geese, it did import, advertise, and sell the end product. Iroquois was indirectly supporting animal mistreatment, was complicit in causing animal suffering, and therefore must be held responsible. The availability of a market for products obtained in this manner, he maintained, contributes to the continuation of such treatment.

ENTER THE COURTS

This struggle between management and shareholder was presented to a U.S. District Court, where the issues turned on legal technicalities rather than on substantive ethical questions. At issue in the courtroom was whether a 1983 rule of the Securities and Exchange Commission (SEC) would determine the outcome of this dispute. This rule allows a company to omit proxy materials proposed by shareholders if the relevant operation of the firm—in this case imported pâté—accounts for less than 5 percent of the firm's total assets and is not "otherwise significantly related to the issuer's business." Because importing and selling pâté did not account for the required 5 percent, Iroquois management did not feel compelled to issue the proxy materials.

Judge Oliver Gasch, admitting that the case involved a close call, sided with Lovenheim.[7] Judge Gasch held that the history of the rule in question showed no decision by the SEC that allowed a company to base its judgments solely on the economic considerations on which Iroquois relied. Upon learning of Judge Gasch's order that the proxy material must be sent to shareholders, Lovenheim said that he hoped his effort "reasserts the rights of shareholders in all companies to bring moral issues to the attention of management."[8]

The unit that imported the pâté was soon sold by Iroquois Brands, thereby leaving a moot and unresolved issue.[9]

NOTES

1. FRG, Protection of Animals Act [Tierschutzgesetz] 3, 7. This clause is a general prohibition of force-feeding animals except when necessary for the sake of their health.
2. Dominique Hermier, "Plasma Lipoproteins and Liver Lipids in Two Breeds of Geese with Different Susceptibility to Hepatic Steatosis: Changes Induced by Development and Force-Feeding," *Lipids* 26 (May 1991), pp. 331–39, esp. 331, 333–34; R. Rouvier et al., "Parmètres génétiques des caractères de croissance, de gavage et de foie gras. . .," *Génét. sél. Evol.* 24 (1992), pp. 53–69; M. A. I. Salem et al., "Studies on Fatty Liver Production from Aged Geese and Ducks. I. Serum Protein, Glucose and Cholesterol," *Egypt Journal of Animal Production* 23, no. 1–2 (1983), pp. 109–12; M. A. I. Salem et al., "Studies on Fatty Liver Production from Aged Geese and Ducks. II. Fatty Acid Composition of Liver and Some Chemical Aspects," *Egypt Journal of Animal Production* 23, no. 1–2 (1983), pp. 113–18.
3. *The Year of the Greylag Goose* (New York: Harcourt Brace, 1978).
4. American Society for the Prevention of Cruelty to Animals, Supporting Statement to Shareholders' Proposal. Included in Appendix 3 in the legal opinion cited in note 7 below.
5. From a letter written January 13, 1984, by ASPCA Executive Director John F. Kullberg. Included in Appendix 5 in the legal opinion cited in note 7 below.
6. Notice of 1983 Annual Meeting of Shareholders and Proxy Statement, Tuesday, May 10, 1983.
7. *Peter C. Lovenheim v. Iroquois Brands Ltd.* U.S. District Court, Washington, DC, Civil Case No. 85-0734 (May 24, 1985). The data and arguments presented before this court have been consulted in developing the facts in this case.
8. Philip Smith, "Shareholders to Be Given Pâté Question," *The Washington Post*, March 28, 1985, p. E3.
9. Personal correspondence with attorney Ralph L. Halpern of Jaeckle, Fleischmann & Mugel (Buffalo, New York), April 13, 1988.

How Reserve Mining Became Cleveland-Cliffs

The "Reserve Mining Case" has for decades been central in the struggle to protect both the environment and the financial health of industries that discharge waste materials. Though Reserve Mining no longer exists under this name, its successor has survived, though barely. The history of this company shows how difficult and important it is to fairly and knowledgeably regulate an industry in the cause of the environment.

Four steel firms created the Reserve Mining Company in 1939 for the purpose of mining and crushing taconite (low-grade iron ore). The name *Reserve* was used because in 1939, the iron ore was considered a long-term investment in need of new technology to make processing efficient. In an expensive and innovative move, Reserve Mining decided in 1944 to locate its prospective plant on Lake Superior and began to acquire the land in 1945. Establishing the plant on this great body of water was ideal because taconite processing requires large amounts of water. The taconite must be crushed into fine granules and collected into pellets before the residue is flushed back into the water. After nine hearings, the state of Minnesota issued the necessary environmental permits in 1947.

In 1948, the U.S. Army Corps of Engineers granted Reserve a permit to construct harbor facilities that called for the deposit of tailings (the residue waste product) in Lake Superior. The taconite was to be mined near Babbitt, Minnesota, and then shipped by rail approximately forty-five miles to the plant on Lake Superior's northwest shore. Work began on the Lake Superior facility in 1951, and full operations commenced at the plant in 1955. The town of Silver Bay was built for these mining operations. Reserve employed 80 percent of the 3,000 adult inhabitants of Silver Bay, and the state's total taconite workforce grew to 9,000. The operation proved so successful that between 1956 and 1960, Reserve sought and received permission for substantially increased production and correspondingly increased discharges of waste products into Lake Superior. Reserve achieved a final modest rise in production in 1965. This increase brought Reserve's annual production capacity to 10.7 million tons of pellets. To achieve this level, Reserve dumped 67,000 tons of waste

This case was prepared by Tom L. Beauchamp and revised by John Cuddihy, Joanne L. Jurmu, and Joseph Folio. Not to be duplicated without permission of the holder of the copyright, © 1982, 1992, 1996, 2003 by Tom L. Beauchamp.

material into Lake Superior each day. The state had approved these discharges under the assumption that this waste would sink and remain forever at the lake bottom.[1]

Presson S. Shane of the George Washington University School of Business has described the basic technology at the facility as follows:

> Taconite is a hard, gray rock in which are found particles of magnetite, a black oxide of iron which is magnetic and has the approximate oxygen content designated as Fe_3O_4. The deposits of taconite near Babbitt, Minnesota are sufficiently near the surface to permit their being taken from open pits. The taconite is crushed to a nominal 4 inch size and hauled along the Reserve railroad line to Silver Bay at a rate of about 90,000 tons per day.
>
> At Silver Bay the crushing operation is continued in order to free the particles of iron oxide for recovery and molding into pellets. A series of crushers, rod mills, ball mills, and magnetic separators are operated in processing the water slurry of ore. Two million tons of water are taken from Lake Superior each day (and returned) in the processing. The low-iron tailings are discharged back into the lake in the direction of a trough about 500 feet deep a few miles offshore. The discharge stream comprises the tailings, and the finest fraction, about 1½ percent solids, forms a dense current which flows toward the bottom of the lake. The magnetically recovered particles are the concentrate which is compressed to a cake with 10 percent moisture. It is then mixed with bentonite, which is a cohesive agent, and rolled into green pellets about ⅜ inch in diameter. The pellets are hardened by heating to 2350° F and are then ready for loading into ore boats at Silver Bay for the trip to the blast furnaces in Cleveland, Youngstown, Ashland, etc.[2]

ENVIRONMENTAL LITIGATION BEGINS

Serious environmental questions about Reserve's discharges first arose in 1963, when U.S. Senator Gaylord Nelson of Wisconsin investigated the possibility of water pollution violations in the United States. By 1968, Senator Nelson, a Taconite Study Group, and Secretary of the Interior Stewart Udall began to express concern about pollution in Lake Superior. In 1971 through 1972, the Environmental Protection Agency, the U.S. Justice Department, and the Minnesota Pollution Control Board (of the Minnesota Pollution Control Agency, or MPCA) all charged Reserve with violations of the Federal Pollution Control Act. They argued that the plant was discharging mineral fibers into the air, that the water discharges could be hazardous to health, and that drinking water supplies were endangered. Similar fibers were known to cause asbestosis, mesothelioma, and various cancers. Past concerns had primarily pertained to water pollution, including effects on fish life and the water supply, but as the courts began to tackle these issues, the focus shifted to threats to human health.

In 1973, a U.S. District Court in Minnesota entered an order closing Reserve's Silver Bay facility on grounds that it was discharging dustlike asbestiform (asbestoslike) particles into both the air and the water. Asbestos workers had been shown to be vulnerable to cancer when they inhaled the product. Some 200,000 persons drank the water from Lake Superior, and many more might potentially be affected by airborne fibers. Reserve appealed this decision to the Eighth Circuit Court of Appeals, where Judge Myron H. Bright summarized the situation in an extremely influential opinion in environmental law delivered on June 4, 1974:

> Although there is no dispute that significant amounts of waste tailings are discharged into the water and dust is discharged into the air by Reserve, the parties vigorously contest the precise nature of the discharge, its biological effects, and particularly with respect to the waters of Lake Superior, its ultimate destination. . . .
>
> The suggestion that particles of the cummingtonite-grunerite in Reserve's discharges are the equivalent of amosite asbestos raised an immediate health issue, since the inhalation of amosite asbestos at occupational levels of exposure is a demonstrated health hazard resulting in asbestosis and various forms of cancer. However, the proof of a health hazard requires more than the mere fact of discharge; the discharge of an agent hazardous in one circumstance must be linked to some present or future likelihood of disease under the prevailing circumstances. An extraordinary amount of testimony was received on these issues. . . .
>
> The theory by which plaintiffs argue that the discharges present a substantial danger is founded largely upon epidemiological studies of asbestos workers occupationally exposed to and inhaling high levels of asbestos dust. A study by Dr. Selikoff of workers at a New Jersey asbestos manufacturing plant demonstrated that occupational exposure to amosite asbestos poses a hazard of increased incidence of asbestosis and various forms of cancer. Similar studies in other occupational contexts leave no doubt that asbestos, at sufficiently high dosages, is injurious to health. However, in order to draw the conclusion that environmental exposure to Reserve's discharges presents a health threat in the instant case, it must be shown either that the circumstances of exposure are at least comparable to those in occupational settings, or, alternatively, that the occupational studies establish certain principles of asbestos-disease pathology which may be applied to predicting the occurrence of such disease in altered circumstances.
>
> Initially, it must be observed that environmental exposure from Reserve's discharges into air and water is simply not comparable to that typical of occupational settings. The occupational studies

involve direct exposure to and inhalation of asbestos dust in high concentrations and in confined spaces. This pattern of exposure cannot be equated with the discharge into the outside air of relatively low levels of asbestos fibers. . . . In order to make a prediction, based on the occupational studies, as to the likelihood of disease at lower levels of exposure, at least two key findings must be made. First, an attempt must be made to determine, with some precision, what the lower level of exposure is. Second, that lower level of exposure must be applied to the known pathology of asbestos-induced disease, i.e., it must be determined whether the level of exposure is safe or unsafe.

Unfortunately, the testimony of Dr. Arnold Brown indicates that neither of these key determinations can be made. Dr. Brown testified that, with respect to both air and water, the level of fibers is not readily susceptible of measurement. This results from the relatively imprecise state of counting techniques and the wide margins of error which necessarily result, and is reflected in the widely divergent sample counts received by the court. . . . In commenting on the statement, "This suggests that there are levels of asbestos exposure that will not be associated with any detectable risk," Dr. Brown stated:

"As a generalization, yes, I agree to that. But I must reiterate my view that I do not know what that level is. . . ."

A fair review of this impartial testimony by the court's own witnesses—to which we necessarily must give great weight at this interim stage of review—clearly suggests that the discharges by Reserve can be characterized only as presenting an unquantifiable risk, i.e., a health risk which either may be negligible or may be significant, but with any significance as yet based on unknowns. . . .[3]

The court's reluctance to pronounce or even attempt to quantify an actual health hazard was a victory for Reserve, although the court went on to suggest that better air control and the "termination of Reserve's discharges into Lake Superior" should take place as quickly as possible. Judge Bright, speaking for the court, then granted Reserve a seventy-day stay of Judge Lord's order on the condition that Reserve submit an adequate pollution-control plan. Reserve was also required to continue the work under way on the development of alternate disposal sites.

DISPOSAL PLANS

Reserve soon announced plans for an on-land disposal facility to be called Mile Post 7. Reserve applied to the state of Minnesota to construct this new facility. However, the state rejected these plans and entered into negotiations with Reserve. On April 8, 1975, the Eighth Circuit Court of Appeals handed down a much-anticipated decision on Reserve's responsibilities:

We adhere to our preliminary assessment that the evidence is insufficient to support the kind of demonstrable danger to the public health that would justify the immediate closing of Reserve's operations. We now address the basic question of whether the discharges pose any risk to public health. . . .

Plaintiffs' hypothesis that Reserve's air emissions represent a significant threat to the public health touches numerous scientific disciplines, and an overall evaluation demands broad scientific understanding. We think it significant that Dr. Brown, an impartial witness, whose court-appointed task was to address the health issue in its entirety, joined with plaintiff's witnesses in viewing as reasonable the hypothesis that Reserve's discharges present a threat to public health. Although, as we noted in our stay opinion, Dr. Brown found the evidence insufficient to make a scientific probability statement as to whether adverse health consequences would in fact ensue, he expressed a public health concern over the continued long-term emission of fiber into the air. . . .

The . . . discussion of the evidence demonstrates that the medical and scientific conclusions here in dispute clearly lie "on the frontiers of scientific knowledge." . . .

As we have demonstrated, Reserve's air and water discharges pose a danger to the public health and justify judicial action of a preventive nature.

In fashioning relief in a case such as this involving a possibility of future harm, a court should strike a proper balance between the benefits conferred and the hazards created by Reserve's facility.

Reserve must be given a reasonable opportunity and a reasonable time to construct facilities to accomplish an abatement of its pollution of air and water and the health risk created thereby. In this way, hardship to employees and great economic loss incident to an immediate plant closing may be avoided. . . .

We cannot ignore, however, the potential for harm in Reserve's discharges. This potential imparts a degree of urgency to this case that would otherwise be absent from an environmental suit in which ecological pollution alone were proved. Thus, any authorization of Reserve to continue operations during conversion of its facilities to abate the pollution must be circumscribed by realistic time limitations. . . .[4]

In all essentials, Judge Bright and his colleagues on the court of appeals had reversed their earlier views, now holding that Reserve's water and air discharges did create a major public health threat and that the courts need not shy away from decisions in the face of scientific uncertainties. (The judges shrouded their apparent reversal in legal technicalities.)[5]

For several years following this decision, various courts argued that, as the court of appeals put it, "the probability of harm is more likely than not."

However, neither side succeeded in providing definitive scientific evidence, and the controversy's focus shifted to the problem of finding a satisfactory on-land disposal site.

ON-LAND DISPOSAL FACILITY BUILT

Reserve and the state continued to dispute every health issue mentioned earlier, and each won major victories in the courts. Reserve repeatedly threatened to close its Silver Bay facility permanently in the face of costs imposed by courts and the state. Finally, the two sides struck a bargain. On July 7, 1978, Reserve agreed both to build the new facility at Mile Post 7 and to satisfy the stringent conditions on which the state insisted for approval of the permits. The total investment in the new facility was set at $380 million. The renovated facility contained one of the world's largest and most expensive pollution control programs. In addition, the company agreed to stop all discharges into Lake Superior by April 15, 1980. It carried out this promise, and the new facility began operations in August 1980.

Several scientific studies of health hazards had been completed by July 1978, and other studies followed. These studies, several sponsored by Reserve, did not show any significant increase in disease related to asbestos in the region or in plant workers. Studies showed no buildup of asbestiform bodies in the lung tissue or in the bloodstream of persons drinking water from Lake Superior. Reserve's workforce did not show a significant outbreak of asbestosis or any similar disease; none of its employees had ever developed a dust-related disease.[6] Nevertheless, Reserve could not prove that there would not be latent and serious long-term effects in twenty years, as is commonly the case with asbestos-caused diseases.

RESERVE CEASES OPERATIONS

With the decline of the steel industry in the early 1980s, Reserve's economic situation declined. High-grade Brazilian ore became available to steelmakers for a price well under that of taconite.[7] The decline in the auto industry also contributed to the steel industry's problems. After 1982, Reserve experienced a number of temporary shutdowns and employee layoffs. While operating at 40 percent of capacity, Reserve was forced to lay off 1,200 of its 2,600 employees between 1982 and 1986.[8]

After using the on-land settling pond for four years, Reserve requested permission to build a filtration plant to allow the company to resume the dumping of waste water into Lake Superior. According to Reserve, the operation needed the filtration plant because its settling ponds were filling up sooner than expected. This condition was the result of the fact that Reserve's facilities were operating well under capacity. Water was collecting quicker because less of it was being recirculated through the plant.[9]

Reserve claimed that the filtration plant was the only viable alternative to a complete shutdown. Management also claimed that the filtration process would remove more than 99 percent of the pollutants and would make the water "safe to drink."[10] Plant discharge would be between 2,500 and 3,500 gallons per minute. The estimated cost of plant construction was approximately $2 million. Reserve hoped to have it operational within six months. The Minnesota Pollution Control Board received the request, and after three board meetings filled with controversy, approved the permit under the condition that the proposed filtration plant represent the best available technology.[11]

This permit allowed Reserve to dump water into Lake Superior as long as the fiber content was at or below one million fibers per liter. On those days when the fiber content exceeded that limit, the water was to be dumped on land and recycled until it met standards. The filtration plant was built and became operational late in 1984. Reserve monitored the fiber content by sending samples to the Minnesota Health Department Laboratory for analysis.

Reserve was dealt a severe blow on July 17, 1986, when LTV Steel, which owned 50 percent of Reserve, declared Chapter 11 bankruptcy. Problems included smaller than expected steel shipments in the second quarter and lower pricing levels. Reserve's facilities temporarily closed while Armco Inc., LTV's partner, surveyed the situation. Armco considered operating Reserve on its own or finding another partner for the operations, but neither option was deemed financially feasible. On August 7, Armco placed Reserve too into Chapter 11 bankruptcy. The move was linked to the weakening financial circumstance and the general economic outlook; no direct connection was made between the costly installment of the on-land disposal site and the bankruptcy.

In August 1986, unemployment for the state of Minnesota was between 5 and 6 percent, whereas Lake County (including Silver Bay) experienced rates of approximately 40 percent. Some families of the laid-off workers remained in the area, but many others elected to leave. All of the 2,200 laid-off or retired Reserve employees lacked health care and pension benefits until mid-1987.[12] Although the plant did not operate again until 1990, Reserve continued to recycle water into Lake Superior that collected in the on-land facility. After the shutdown, the water quality was well below the 1 million fibers-per-liter limit.

"RESERVE" REOPENS

On June 12, 1989, the Colorado-based Cyprus Minerals Company acquired Reserve's assets with a $52 million purchase in New York's Federal Bankruptcy Court. The purchase followed a year of negotiations between Cyprus, state representatives, and Reserve's court-appointed trustee. Cyprus, the second-largest copper producer in the United States, purchased Reserve to "enter the iron ore industry, and to provide stability for the company."[13] Immediately after the acquisition, Cyprus renamed Reserve the *Cyprus Northshore Mining Corporation* and implemented a $29.9 million "program to refurbish the former Reserve mining and processing operations for production of high quality [taconite] pellets."[14] Cyprus Northshore called for regional employment applications from former Reserve employees and quickly received over 3,000 such applications. By 1992, Cyprus Northshore employed 420 people, 94 percent of whom were former Reserve employees.[15]

Responsibility for the upkeep and oversight of Mile Post 7, the facility's on-land tailings-disposal basin, was assumed by the State of Minnesota, until Cyprus increased production. Though Cyprus was fined for a few environmental infractions, the plant steadily improved its environmental protection devices throughout the early 1990s.[16]

INDUSTRY STRUGGLES
AND NORTHSHORE'S REACTION

In 1994, Cleveland Cliffs, Inc. ("Cliffs"), the nation's largest iron ore supplier, purchased the taconite plant from Cyprus but retained the name "Northshore Mining Corporation" for this facility. Cliffs had aspirations for expansion of the plant, which was stagnating because of Cyprus's financial difficulties.[17] Early in 2000, company officials announced that they intended to build a plant at Northshore that would produce bricks that were 95 percent iron, as opposed to the standard pellets that contained 65 percent iron. Many in the industry believed that this strategy was the step needed to sustain the taconite industry for the long term.

Cliffs argued that its projected expansion would have minimal environmental impact but also acknowledged that there would be a slight increase in the emission of mercury, sulfur dioxide, and other pollutants. Environmental opponents argued that any increase of pollutants emitted stood to further damage lakes and rivers that were already under an advisory as a result of past pollution problems.[18] In response, Cliffs provided an Environmental Awareness Worksheet to the MPCA, offered to complete an Environmental Impact Statement, and reminded the public that the proposed plant would create thousands of jobs in the region.[19]

However, in June 2000, Cliffs became more cautious about its financial commitments and asked the MPCA to delay a pending decision on the permit to build the new plant. The company was concerned with the stumbling LTV Steel Mining Company, which had announced its imminent and permanent closure.[20] The entire industry then faced economic problems, and all talk of expansion had ceased.

In September 2001, Cliffs temporarily shut down its Northshore plant until December.[21] During this period, Cliffs announced a bold venture to purchase the mining properties of the defunct LTV Corporation. Its plans included the assumption of all environmental liability in an effort to restructure the steelmaking process.[22] After a report from the U.S. International Trade Commission, it appeared to many in business and government that Minnesota and other states were the economic victims of subsidized foreign imports in steel. Twenty-six domestic U.S. steelmakers had recently gone bankrupt, and the industry had lost 25,000 jobs as a result.[23] The steel industry pointed to these figures and the new report as evidence that it needed immediate assistance from the government. Though President Bush had authorized the Trade Commission's investigation, the bureaucratic nature of the process did not lead to a timely government response.[24]

Cliffs announced in mid-November 2001 that it was collaborating with Kobe Steel to produce iron nuggets, which are 97 percent iron, by building a pilot plant at its Northshore facilities. These nuggets, by contrast to pellets that are 65 percent iron, have a much higher market value. Cliffs hoped that the nugget process "could represent a major break-through in iron-making technology as it requires only a rotary hearth furnace, which means both lower capital and operation costs."[25] Some believe that this change is the only way that the industry can survive. Cliffs hopes, as of this writing, that the pilot plant will be functional within a year.[26]

Environmentalists have recently been restrained in their comments as Cliffs attempts to revitalize its Northshore plant. Cliffs has modified its permit for the research and development of its pilot plant and still must examine the environmental aspects of its proposed expansion. Cliffs maintains that the reduced energy requirements for its new process will produce a smaller impact on the environment.[27] On a related note, Minnesota's Blue Ribbon Committee is presently studying the feasibility and safety of using taconite waste in road construction and in sand. This proposal faces the same environmental issues that taconite has always struggled with. However, this proposal, if approved, would create a new income for the region and a very different process for disposing of the waste.[28]

Just as Cliffs was in the midst of restructuring, President George W. Bush announced on March 5, 2002, that, as a result of the Trade Commission's report, he was imposing a tariff of up to 30 percent on imported steel products. The tariff, a combination of flat and graduated rates depending upon the specific steel import, is a three-year plan whose goal is to provide the domestic steel industry with the opportunity to restructure to compete against the influx of foreign, often subsidized, imports. International reaction to the tariff has been hostile, threatening a retaliation.[29] The European Union announced that it would pursue retaliatory quotas and tariffs.[30] Other countries filed formal complaints with the World Trade Organization (WTO), which ruled against the U.S.[31]

Cliffs has reported that the 30 percent tariff on flat-rolled products will greatly assist in recovery "from the surge of imports that has crippled the domestic steel market."[32] The steel industry had lost 31 companies to bankruptcy in the four years prior to Bush's new policy.[33]

The impact of the tariffs for companies like Cliffs remains uncertain. The tariffs may not be enough to preserve many U.S. steel companies for the long term.[34] As the taconite industry searches for new answers, the old environmental concerns persist. Though these concerns appear to have abated in the face of the massive problems facing the industry, politicians continue to struggle with the dual goals of promoting jobs and setting thresholds of acceptable risk. After more than a half-century of struggle with the problems generated by the Reserve Mining case, few are confident that they can predict where the balance will finally be struck.

NOTES

1. The early history in this case relies on E. W. Davis, *Pioneering with Taconite* (St. Paul: Minnesota Historical Society, 1964). Points of history in the 1970s sometimes depend on Robert V. Bartlett, *The Reserve Mining Controversy* (Bloomington: Indiana University Press, 1980); and on a telephone conversation with Professor Bartlett in April 1982 about details not covered in the book.
2. Presson S. Shane, "Silver Bay: Reserve Mining Company" (1973). Reprinted by permission of Professor Shane.
3. 498 F.2d 1073 (1974).
4. 514 F.2d Series, 492 (1975).
5. A useful analysis of this second decision is found in William A. Thomas, "Judicial Treatment of Scientific Uncertainty in the *Reserve Mining* Case," *Proceedings of the Fourth Symposium on Statistics and the Environment* (Washington, DC: American Statistical Association, 1977), pp. 1–13.
6. Bartlett, *Reserve Mining Controversy*, p. 209.
7. Bill Richards, "Minnesota Iron Range Is Hurt and Despairing as More Plants Close," *The Wall Street Journal*, November 26, 1984, p. 1.
8. "Reserve Mining Schedules Another Operations Suspension," *Skillings' Mining Review* (March 26, 1983), p. 5.
9. Bill Sternberg, "Reserve Mining Waste Plan Draws Fire from Activist Mize," *Marquette Mining Journal* (May 26, 1984).
10. *Ibid.*
11. The following information on the filtration plant is the result of a telephone conversation with Robert Criswell of the Minnesota Pollution Control Agency on April 1, 1987.
12. Telephone interview, Gene Skraba, staff representative, United Steelworkers of America, Hibbing, Minnesota, April 6, 1987.
13. "Cyprus Minerals Co. Enters Iron Ore Industry with Start of Pellet Production at Cyprus Northshore Mining Corp.," *Skillings' Mining Review* (January 13, 1990), pp. 2–8.
14. *Ibid.*
15. John Myers, "Babbitt Mine Reopens with a Bang," *Duluth News-Tribune*, December 30, 1990, p. 5.
16. Larry Oakes, "Silver Bay Wrestles over Taconite," *Star Tribune*, January 29, 2000, p. 1D.
17. Lee Bloomquist, "Mining Company Addresses Environmental Concerns about Minnesota Project," *Duluth News-Tribune*, February 24, 2000.
18. *Ibid.*
19. *Ibid.*
20. Lee Bloomquist, "Minnesota Mining Firm to Decide on Future of Pellets Production or Pig Iron," *Duluth News-Tribune*, June 6, 2000.
21. Lee Bloomquist, "Mining Firm Closes Taconite Production Plants in Duluth," *Duluth News-Tribune*, September 15, 2001.
22. Thomas Gerdel, "LTV OK's Deal to Sell Mining, Power Facilities," *The Plain Dealer*, October 11, 2001, p. C1.
23. Lee Bloomquist, "Trade Commission Reports U.S. Steel Industry Hurt by Cheap Imports," *Duluth News-Tribune*, October 23, 2001.
24. *Ibid.*

25. E-mail correspondence with Ralph S. Berge, Public Relations official at Cleveland Cliffs, February 6, 2002. www.cleveland-cliffs.com

26. Lee Bloomquist, "Construction of Silver Bay, Minn., Iron Nugget Pilot Plant Advances," *Duluth News-Tribune*, November 14, 2001.

27. E-mail correspondence with Ralph S. Berge, Public Relations official at Cleveland Cliffs. E-mailed on November 30, 2001 and responded on February 6, 2002. www.cleveland-cliffs.com.

28. Lee Bloomquist, "Minnesota Mining Group Studies Use of Taconite as a Construction Material," *Duluth News-Tribune*, October 30, 2001.

29. Warren Vieth, "Bush to Impose Tariffs on Steel in Rescue Move," *The Los Angeles Times*, March 6, 2002, p. A1.

30. Michael Harrison, "EU to Escalate Steel Dispute by Imposing Strict Import Quotas," *The Independent* (London), March 19, 2002, p. 19.

31. Elizabeth Olson, "Europe Presses U. S. on Steel Tariffs," *The New York Times*, March 20, 2002, p. W1; David Nicklaus, "Tariffs, Bankruptcy Breathe New Life into Steel Industry," *St. Louis Post-Dispatch*, April 2, 2003, p. C1. The tariffs did reinvigorate U. S. steel markets, but European countries can now impose penalties.

32. E-mail correspondence with Ralph S. Berge, Public Relations official at Cleveland Cliffs, March 18, 2002. www.cleveland-cliffs.com

33. Robert Zoellick, "The Reigning Champions of Free Trade," *Financial Times* (London), March 13, 2002, p. 19.

34. Warren Vieth, "Bush to Impose Tariffs on Steel in Rescue Move," *The Los Angeles Times*, March 6, 2002, p. A1

Regulating Emissions: From Acid Rain to Global Warming

"Acid rain" is the term used to refer to pollution caused by higher than normal acidity in rain, fog, snow, and the like. Created by burning coal and other fossil fuels, it has been cited in numerous scientific studies as the leading cause of lake acidification and fish kills in the northeastern United States and southeastern Canada. Acid rain has adversely affected human health, forest ecosystems, farmlands, groundwater, the exposed surfaces of buildings, and many manufactured items. Environmental activists and many politicians have targeted the coal industry and its power-generating and industrial consumers as primary causes of acid rain.

Experts have pointed to the gaseous sulfur dioxide that is released into the air when coal with a high sulfur content is burned—primarily in utility power plants and some industrial plants. The sulfur dioxide and nitrogen oxides from vehicles and oil burner emissions combine with water vapor to produce sulfuric and nitric acids. Carried by prevailing winds, perhaps far from the emission source, these acids infiltrate precipitation and lower its pH levels. Pure rain is naturally somewhat acidic, with a pH level of 5.6 (6.0 is neutral). The degree of acidity increases exponentially as the pH level decreases. Rainfall with pH levels of 3 or 4 is common in the eastern United States and Canada and thus is anywhere from 10 to over 100 times more acidic than a normal 5.6. Levels as low as 1.5, roughly the acidity of battery acid, have been reported.[1]

Ecological systems have natural alkaline properties that can neutralize moderately acidic rain, but continued precipitation with low pH levels endangers the environment. Large fish kills often occur in the early spring because, as environmentalist Anne LaBastille has graphically depicted,

> all winter, the pollutant load from storms accumulates in the snowpack as if in a great white sponge. When mild weather gives the sponge a "squeeze," acids concentrated on the surface of the snow are released with the first melt. This acid shock . . . produces drastic changes in water chemistry that destroy fish life.[2]

This case was prepared by Nancy Blanpied, Tom L. Beauchamp, and Joseph Folio, and revised by Sarah Westrick, Cathleen Kaveny, Joanne L. Jurmu, John Cuddihy, and Jeff Greene. Not to be duplicated without permission of the holder of the copyright, © 1992, 1996, 2003, by Tom L. Beauchamp.

Areas that have struggled with acid rain in the northeastern United States and southeastern Canada are naturally low in alkaline buffers, which neutralize the acids. As an acidification byproduct, toxic metals such as aluminum are leached from the earth's surface. The aluminum proves lethal to fish and other life-forms, and fish that survive may become poisonous to predators who eat them, including, in some cases, humans.[3] Forty-one states have issued strict warnings regarding the consumption of freshwater fish. Concerned about high mercury levels, officials in some states have urged women of childbearing capacity or those nursing young children to severely limit their consumption of all local, freshwater fish.[4]

REACTIONS TO ACID RAIN

Environmental groups, several states in the United States, and the Canadian government all voiced increasing concern in the 1970s about the deleterious effects of acid rain. In 1977, the U.S. Congress responded by amending the Clean Air Act to address problems of state compliance. The solution received mixed reviews from environmentalists and the coal industry alike. The amendment permitted established coal plants to continue to operate while merely reducing their emissions levels. Conversely, new plants, most of which were prone to burn low-sulfur coal already, had to meet stricter standards. They had to install "scrubbers," that is, equipment for flue-gas desulfurization. In the end, the older, high-sulfur-burning coal plants were enabled to maintain a competitive advantage over newer, more environmentally sound plants. This step extended the lives of these old plants.[5]

Because the devastating consequences of acid rain were attributed to coal, attention was also focused on coal mines and the mining of high-sulfur coal. Coal mining is a major industry in Ohio and West Virginia. "Coal jobs" in West Virginia provided employment for 125,000 people in 1979, but that number has decreased steadily to 45,000 in 2001.[6] Ohio's mining industry employs roughly 3,000 people, down from 14,000 in the 1970s.[7] Ohio coal, which has a particularly high sulfur content, is used throughout the region and has been thought by environmentalists to be one of the primary sources of the acid rain in the northeastern United States and southeastern Canada. However, existing environmental regulations controlling the use of high-sulfur coal have generally had a negative impact on the region's economy. Miners fear for their jobs, and unemployment in coal-mining regions has increased.

Historically, those concerned about this economic decline have cautioned against an additional regulatory intervention. The National Coal Association reported that because of the greater use of low-sulfur coal and scrubbers in power plants, there was little more sulfur dioxide in the air than there was in the late 1940s. Additionally, because of the many unknowns about acid rain, *The Wall Street Journal* cautioned as follows in mid-1980: "Precipitous regulatory action by EPA could cost utilities and other industries billions of dollars. Until more is genuinely known about acid rain, these expenditures may end up only going down the drain."[8] Despite such warnings, the EPA proceeded with regulatory efforts (by targeting coal- and oil-fired power plants) until the Reagan administration ordered that *The Wall Street Journal's* advice become official government policy. However, scientific evidence-gathering continued, as did controversies over how to read the evidence, and an investigatory panel placed the burden of responsibility for environmental deterioration on coal-burning industries. The "circumstantial evidence" of a causal connection between coal burning and environmental damage, it argued, was overwhelming. The panel recommended stringent control measures.[9]

The uncertainty of the scientific community provided critics of regulation the room to maneuver in two respects. First, in the spirit of the editorial in *The Wall Street Journal,* the critics could point to the unreliable association between sulfur emissions and acid rain. Second, even if sulfur was conceded to be the cause of acid rain, it remained difficult to target particular utility plants as the source. Tracking the atmospheric routes of acid rain from sources to destinations has always been a daunting and complex problem. It has been difficult to determine with precision who has been responsible for the deteriorating situation. The issue of acid precipitation across the U.S.-Canadian border received extensive attention. In March 1985, the United States and Canada appointed special envoys to study the issue and make recommendations for its resolution. One major recommendation in their January 1986 report was a five-year, $5 billion program to develop innovative technology for new and existing discharge sources. In addition, many other "solutions" to acid rain were proposed.[10]

As the scientific evidence of increased sulfur pollution mounted, the problem of acid rain was felt still more acutely. In November 1990, President George Bush signed into law new amendments to the Clean Air Act. Among the amendments' major provisions was a nationwide utility emissions cap on sulfur dioxide emissions of 8.9 million tons a year by the year 2000, and they were to be kept at this level beyond 2000. The Bush administration argued that this cap represents a 10-million-ton reduction from the levels of a decade earlier. The largest sulfur dioxide cuts for the first five years, through Phase I of the initiative, were from roughly 250 plants, as it required them to reduce emissions by 3.5 million tons per year. Phase II, effective in 2000, required all remaining plants (ones that were cleaner to begin with) to come under the national cap on emissions.[11]

These Amendments were the first to make use of tradeable permits, or allowances, for SO_2 emissions. Each year, the EPA issued a proportional amount of allowances to the respective plants, each allowance permitting 1 ton of emissions for that year. In turn, these plants were able to sell their allowances to other plants that were not able to meet the necessary reductions, or they could "bank" them for future use. However, allowances could not be borrowed from the future to compensate for the present. Failure to have adequate allowances for actual emissions would result in severe economic penalties for the plant. This market-based approach fell in line with President Bush's ideals, since it did not mandate *methods of reduction,* but rather *results.* Some environmentalists purchased allowances themselves, thereby ensuring that the overall emissions cap would be lowered by the amount purchased. In this plan, though, the costs would still have to be borne by someone.[12]

Title IV of these 1990 amendments details acid rain controls. A major part of the projected reduction in sulfur dioxide was to come by substituting low-sulfur coal for the popular high-sulfur coal. Industry watchers call the acid rain provisions "a boon for low-sulfur coal producers, since a large part of this reduction will be obtained through substituting low-sulfur coals for the higher-sulfur fuels now used" and also a boon for rail carriers, which now must truck the coal farther and in larger quantities.[13]

Midwestern coal producers have experienced economic problems as a result of this section of the bill. In Illinois, for example, the production level and employee population have dropped from 60 million tons and 18,000 miners in 1980 to only 40 million tons and 4,500 workers in 2001.[14] The drop in employment in Ohio cited earlier is yet another example of how the shift to low-sulfur coal has impacted midwestern companies. Consequently, the coal companies in these areas have been searching for viable alternatives. A pilot plant in Ohio is exploring coal gasification technology, which involves extracting and burning only certain gases from coal, thereby preventing harmful emissions prior to combustion.[15] Additionaly, support for this "clean-coal" technology was found in the Bush adminstration of 2001, which pledged $2 billion to research for this technology over the ensuing ten years.[16] Many midwestern coal producers are hoping that these new technologies will catch on and allow their industry to survive.

Total industry emissions between 1995 and 1997 turned out to be one-third *less* than the total designated "allowances"; 37 percent of the reduction came from the installation of scrubbers and 44 percent came by switching to low-sulfur coal. An economic analysis indicated that even regions of the midwest and Appalachia actually shifted more low-sulfur coal, or at least lower-sulfer coal. The "targeted" states of Ohio, West Virginia, and Pennsylvania accounted for 37 percent of the total reductions. The midwest demonstrated the greatest reductions in emissions. Additionally, the means of each plant varied with the economics of its particular situation. Those plants in the west and southeast, closer to low-sulfur coal, began to switch fuel types. Plants not close to these areas more often invested in scrubbers.[17]

Though the economics is complex, the general cost of compliance with legal requirements was lower than estimates had predicted. The cost of scrubbers, though more expensive than fuel-switching, was roughly half of what was predicted, and their cost (per unit) is expected to continue to decrease through Phase II. Switching to low-sulfur coal was cheaper for plants, yet the cost to convert their furnaces and the variable price of low-sulfur coal as a commodity mitigated the difference between this method and scrubbing. In other words, once scrubbers are installed, their use can be increased accordingly to comply with new allowance restrictions, whereas switching to low-sulfur coal leaves power companies dependent upon the price, especially as they require more of it to meet the changing allowances.[18]

Though plants have generally complied and emissions have been reduced, the phenomenon of acid rain has not disappeared. SO_2 emissions have been reduced by 29 percent since 1990, and acid rain levels decreased by 25 percent between 1995 and 1999.[19] However, scientists have noted, specifically in the northeast, that forests and lakes are not recovering at the desired rate. Some observers of the situation note that stringent regulations were not implemented until 1995, as the Amendments specified, and things have at least improved since then. They add that Phase II required plants to cut emissions 50 percent below 1980 levels. Nonetheless, scientists and environmentalists still point to utility companies, which are responsible for 60 percent of the SO_2 emitted. These critics are again asking for increased regulations. They believe that though the sulfur content of the rain has decreased by 38 percent, environmental factors, such as the depletion of natural buffers to the acid by the previous years of unregulated pollution, demand a more drastic cut. Otherwise, these areas will not recover.[20]

Many critics are quick to point to loopholes in current legislation, such as the New Source Review Clause that permits older plants to continue operating under old emissions standards. The clause requires these plants to adhere to the new regulations only when they are modified to increase capacity or emissions. The thought is that older plants must either conform or close. The Bush administration announced in 2002 that it would pursue lawsuits against companies that have not complied with this stipulation. Since these suits were initiated by the Clinton administration, they were expected to be ignored by the Republicans, but Bush vowed to uphold the provisions of the Amendments.[21]

The Bush administration has, nonetheless, been less regulation-minded than the Clinton administration. On January 1, 2003, Bush loosened the EPA interpretation of the New Source Review rules. This alteration permits hundreds of older power plants to operate without being legally obligated to upgrade their pollution controls, thereby decreasing the potential grounds for lawsuits. The administration contends that this approach will ease standards that are too rigid, allowing these plants to become more efficient, and consequently to reduce pollution. Detractors argue that this plan cripples the efforts to control acid rain and other emission pollution.[22] However, the administration has scheduled a Clear Skies initiative with a goal of slashing emissions of sulfur dioxide, nitrogen oxide, and mercury by 70 percent. Environmentalists still hope for a more comprehensive program that goes beyond the attack on these specific emissions. Much of the debate between these parties appears to rest, as it long has, on different assessments of the economic sacrifice that should be demanded of the relevant industries.

GLOBAL WARMING: SAME PROBLEM, SAME SOLUTION?

Global warming came to the forefront of environmental politics in the 1990s as international concern spurred conferences to discuss this phenomenon. From its earliest exploration, though, global warming has been and remains a contentious issue. Experts have long debated the impact of carbon dioxide emissions, and more specifically its tendency to trap sunlight in our atmosphere. Some who support regulation warn of drastic shifts in weather patterns that affect all types of life, accompanied by exponentially rising sea levels that could engulf coastal cities. Critics on the opposite extreme have dismissed these claims, because they either deny the scientific hypotheses or contend that humans will have to dread only warmer weather and more plentiful crop yields. As it has emerged over the years as perhaps the greatest environmental threat of our time, global warming has been addressed in a manner strikingly reminiscent to that of the acid rain problem. It is not clear whether these issues will be treated as fundamentally similar, but one salient fact is that only regulation can decrease the amount of carbon dioxide produced, and those regulations will affect the same utility plants, and consequently citizens, that acid rain has affected.

Global warming, much like acid rain, is a complex problem that has undergone scientific scrutiny over the years. The process at first glance seems uncomplicated: Carbon dioxide is released by human factors, such as coal or automobile use, and as the carbon dioxide rises into the atmosphere, it traps sunlight within the atmosphere. It thereby "warms" the earth through what has been styled "the greenhouse effect." The process, however, involves some other key factors. Scientists point out that many other substances contribute to this greenhouse effect, like water vapor and clouds. Models have demonstrated that these two substances magnify the effects of carbon dioxide alone by three to four times.[23]

Over the years, scientists have come to support overwhelmingly the thesis that carbon dioxide is a contributing factor to the global warming phenomenon. The nation's investor-owned electric utilities have generally argued that there is no conclusive evidence linking carbon dioxide to the greenhouse effect and have contended that even if there were, there is still no concrete proof that this occurrence is necessarily a bad thing. These arguments would question why companies should be forced to spend so much money to solve a problem that may not even be happening.

In recent years the scientific debate has shifted to the rate at which temperatures are changing and the effects that this rate change will have on the world. Parallel to this discussion is one regarding the extent and effects of proposed regulation. Few solid facts exist concerning the rate of warming. First, changes in climate are inevitable for at least fifty years as a result of the "unrealized" heat from emissions that are stored in the world's oceans. Second, "to merely maintain the current level of carbon dioxide in the atmosphere, emissions would have to cut by more than 50 percent."[24]

International concern has been expressed through conferences, most notably the Kyoto Protocol of 1997. Signed in Japan by 160 nations, including the United States, signatories agreed in theory to reduce carbon dioxide emission levels to 5 percent below 1990 levels by 2010. When the treaty was brought back to the U.S. Senate for advice and consent, however, it did not receive the necessary votes. When President Bush took office in 2001, he made clear that he had no intention of attempting to ratify the Protocol. The main objections throughout from politicians and business persons have been twofold. One is that such a drastic change is too costly for apparently insignificant results, and the other is that the treaty fails to include large industrialized nations whose emissions rates are great and steadily increasing. It offers them only "voluntary" goals. Since the United States is directly responsible for 23 percent of the entire world's greenhouse gas emissions, many in the international community argue that the U.S. lack of participation would be a detrimental step in the attempt to halt global warming.[25]

The economic forecasts based on accepting the Kyoto formula do not paint a favorable outcome. The U.S. Department of Energy notes that the direct impact will be high prices for energy, thereby decreasing demand and further injuring the mining and coal regions discussed previously. They predict that gas and energy prices will rise, workers' wages will fall, and unemployment will increase. Energy-intensive industries, such as those that produce automobiles, steel, paper, and chemicals, would all suffer. Increased costs for transportation would harm U.S. agriculture as domestic goods and exports are challenged by cheaper imports.[26]

The alternatives offered by Bush are similar to those utilized to address the problem of acid rain. Bush advocates a cap-and-trade style approach that will permit the market to regulate emission reductions. There is one striking difference, though, between acid rain and global warming. The problem of acid rain was targeted, affecting specific areas, and the cause of these effects could be addressed with legislation. With global warming, the issue is truly global, and governments cannot point to particular harms for which the emitters are responsible. In this sense, any solution must be global, and the lack of this consensus is the main argument currently offered against Kyoto. If only developed countries were regulated, 80 percent of the world would go unregulated. Studies indicate that developing nations, led by China, India, and Brazil, will surpass the major industrialized nations for total carbon dioxide emissions within the next twenty years. This point has led the current U.S. administration to deem the domestic costs of such a treaty as too significant, especially when there is a prospect of uncertain returns.[27]

Nevertheless, some companies have been encouraged by state governments to act voluntarily despite the absence of strict federal mandates. Whether for economic or environmental reasons, companies like Xcel Energy of Minneapolis have proposed to reduce their greenhouse gas emissions preemptively. In May 2002, the company announced its plans to convert one coal-burning plant to burn natural gas instead, and it said that it would add powerful pollution control methods to its other coal plant. The pollution controls, which include scrubbers and filters, and conversion to burn natural gas are an investment of $600 million. This action was spurred by favorable state legislation that permits utility companies to recover the cost of their efforts by increasing the price that it bills its customers.[28]

In January 2003, a group of major corporations created the first voluntary program to reduce greenhouse gas emissions by cap and trading. The program, called the Chicago Climate Exchange, obligates members to reduce emission levels or face sanction. With DuPont, Ford, International Paper, Motorola, American Electric Power, and the city of Chicago already on board, the Exchange is courting new members (although critics point out that there are no mandatory limits).[29] California has also attacked the problem of greenhouse gases by passing legislation that tightly regulates carbon dioxide emissions from vehicles. Since in the majority of the states carbon dioxide emissions are from vehicles, these standards will have a dramatic effect. Additionally, when the emission standards are changed in 2009, analysts believe that the effects will affect the entire country because vehicle manufacturers are not likely to produce different automobiles for one state. The most vulnerable target of this legislation are sport utility vehicles (SUVs), which are often criticized for their inefficient gas/emission ratios.[30] Though these solutions are far from comprehensive, they do represent a growing demand for action to reduce greenhouse gas emissions.

NOTES

1. Lois R. Ember, "Acid Pollutants: Hitchhikers Ride the Wind," *Chemical and Engineering News* (September 14, 1981), p. 29.
2. Anne LaBastille, "Acid Rain: How Great a Menace?" *National Geographic* 160 (November 1981), p. 672.
3. Robert H. Boyle, "An American Tragedy," *Sports Illustrated* (September 21, 1981), p. 75.
4. Robert Braile, "Warning Sound on Safety of Seafood," *The Boston Globe*, March 11, 2001, p. 1.
5. A. Ellerman et al., "A Political History of Federal Acid Rain Legislation," in *Markets for Clean Air: The U.S. Acid Rain Program* (New York: Cambridge University Press, 2000), pp. 13–21.
6. Timothy Gardner, "Appalachia Is Hoping to Cash in on Coal Boom," *Pittsburgh Post-Gazette*, June 21, 2001, p. E8.
7. Tom Diemer, "Bush Fans Embers of Coal Research," *The Plain Dealer*, June 24, 2001, p. 1A.
8. "Review and Outlook: Acid Rain," *The Wall Street Journal*, June 20, 1980.
9. Committee on the Atmosphere and the Biosphere, *Atmosphere-Biosphere Interactions* (Washington, DC: National Academy Press, 1981).
10. Alan Skrainka and Daniel Burkhardt, "Acid Rain: What's an Investor to Do?" *Public Utilities Fortnightly* (August 31, 1989), p. 33.
11. A. Ellerman et al., "A Market-Based Experiment," in *Markets for Clean Air: The U.S. Acid Rain Program* (New York: Cambridge University Press, 2000), pp. 3–12.
12. *Ibid.*
13. Richard G. Sharp, "The Clean Air Act Amendments: Impacts on Rail Coal Transportation," *Public Utilities Fortnightly* (March 1, 1991), p. 26.
14. Kevin McDermott, "Aid for Illinois' Coal Industry Is a Hot Topic Among State Legislators," *St. Louis Post-Dispatch*, May 6, 2001, p. A15.
15. Brad Floss, "Coming Clean with Coal," *The Ottawa Citizen*, June 22, 2001, p. B3.
16. Gary Polakovic, "Smog Feared in Power Buildup," *Los Angeles Times*, July 16, 2001, p. A1.
17. A. Ellerman et al., "Title IV Compliance and Emission Reductions, 1995–97," in *Markets for Clean Air: The U.S. Acid Rain Program* (New York: Cambridge University Press, 2000), pp. 109–140.
18. A. Ellerman et al., "Cost of Compliance with Title IV in Phase I," in *Markets for Clean Air: The U.S. Acid Rain Program* (New York: Cambridge University Press, 2000), pp. 221–250.

19. Ricardo Bayon, "Trading Futures in Dirty Air," *The Washington Post*, August 5, 2001, p. B2.
20. Beth Daley, "Acid Rain Resists 90s Fix," *The Boston Globe*, March 26, 2001, p. A1.
21. Elizabeth Shogren, "Administration Sticking with Clinton Pollution Suit," *Los Angeles Times*, January 16, 2002, p. A14.
22. Katharine Seelye, "9 States in East Sue U.S. Over New Pollution Rules," *The New York Times*, January 1, 2003, p. A1.
23. Richard Lindzen, professor of meteorology at MIT, "Dialogue: How Dangerous Is Global Warming?" *Los Angeles Times*, June 17, 2001, p. M3.
24. Seema Mehta, "Earth's Forecast: More Heat," *Los Angeles Times*, June 19, 2001, p. Cal.1.
25. Elizabeth Shogren and Gary Polakovic, "Bush Seeks to Curb Power Plant Emissions, Set Climate Goals," *Los Angeles Times*, February 15, 2002, p. A18.
26. Charli E. Coon, "Why President Bush Is Right to Abandon the Kyoto Protocol," *The Heritage Foundation Backgrounder*, no. 1437, May 11, 2001. www.heritage.org/library/backgrounder/bg1437.html
27. *Ibid.*
28. As Senia, "Tackling Global Warming," *Utility Business*, June 2002, p. 6.
29. Peter Behr and Eric Pianin, "Firms Start Trading Program for Greenhouse-Gas Emisions," *The Washington Post*, January 17, 2003, p. A14.
30. Cat Lazaroff, "California Law Will Limit CO_2 Emissions from Cars," *Environment News Service*, July 22, 2002.

CHAPTER FOUR

Competitive Markets

Seizure of the S.W. Parcel

The European Petroleum Consortium (EPC) is a major European oil company with several affiliates and subsidiaries in the United States. In November 1983, EPC leased three contiguous parcels of land near Chico, California—exactly 300 acres, subdivided into three distinct units of 100 acres—from a wealthy farmer, Mr. Buck Wheat. The parties signed three oil and gas leases, one for each of the three contiguous parcels, which were labeled N.W., S.W., and N.E. because of their geographical locations.

Within a year a significant gas-producing well had been drilled on the S.W. property, and Mr. Wheat was earning royalties from the gas production. In the fourteen years following the lease, Mr. Wheat earned in excess of $2,500,000 in royalties from this well. By 1997, he was also making millions of dollars per year on other wells that oil and gas companies were operating on his 1,500 acres of property.

Under the terms of the EPC lease, EPC had the option to extend the lease under the original terms of royalty payments for as long as oil or gas was being produced on any parcel of the land that had been leased. If production ever ceased for a period of one year, the agreement would be invalid. If there were no producing wells on a parcel and EPC wished not to extend the lease on that parcel, EPC was required to file a quitclaim deed (a deed of conveyance that is a form of release of rights) to this effect.

In November 1998, the lease was scheduled to expire. EPC notified Mr. Wheat by a phone call ninety days prior to the expiration date of the lease of its intention to extend the lease on *one* parcel of land, the S.W. parcel, but *not* on the other two. Mr. Wheat responded that he naturally was pleased that royalty payments would continue. Under the terms of the lease, EPC had thirty days beyond the date of expiration to record the quitclaim deed with the county and to record the continuation of the lease arrangement. Twenty-two days beyond the expiration date, EPC did file both the quitclaim and the extension; and twenty-nine days beyond the expiration date, an EPC official had a copy delivered to Mr. Wheat by a messenger service. EPC was not required by the terms

This case was prepared by Tom L. Beauchamp. It is based on factual circumstances of a conflict between one large and one small oil firm; all names have been changed. Not to be duplicated without permission of the holder of the copyright, © 2003 by Tom L. Beauchamp.

of the lease to deliver this copy, because Mr. Wheat had already been notified by phone of its intentions and the requisite legal documents had been filed.

Thirty-one days beyond the expiration date, Mr. Wheat signed an oil-and-gas lease on all 100 acres of the *producing S.W. parcel* with Oklasas Oil Company, a small independent headquartered in Anadarko, Oklahoma. That is, Mr. Wheat leased to Oklasas the very same S.W. parcel on which EPC believed it had an exclusive lease. Obviously two exclusive leases to competitors on the same property cannot both be valid.

Mr. Wheat's new lease of the S.W. parcel and his rapid change in relations with EPC were the result of an inadvertent clerical error and the enterprising activities of Mr. B. Sly, president of the Oklasas Oil Company. He devised a method of acquiring leased land that is highly unconventional but that has thus far paid off handsomely. He hired a low-salaried clerk to go into several California counties known to have a large number of producing gas wells. The clerk checks all the leases that have been filed, looking for technical violations of the law or for lease loopholes. Whenever a technical violation or potential problem is found on the lease of a producing property, Mr. Sly contacts the owner of the property and makes a lease offer that exceeds the terms found in the original lease. Mr. Sly can afford to give the property owner a much larger percentage of the royalties than is conventional, because he has no significant drilling costs and encounters no real speculative risk in an industry filled with drilling risk.

Only about 15 percent of the landowners are willing to meet and discuss the possibility of a lease with Mr. Sly because most believe they have a prior commitment to the company with which they have signed an agreement. About 10 percent renegotiate with the company with which they originally signed the lease; they often use Mr. Sly's offer as a way of obtaining better terms in a new lease, although they do not negotiate terms as favorable as Mr. Sly's. Instead of providing the landowner with the standard one-sixth royalty share, Mr. Sly offers one-third, doubling the owners' royalties overnight.

Mr. Sly has been able to sign agreements with approximately one-third of the 15 percent who are willing to meet with him. Thus, he eventually comes to terms with about 5 percent of his contacts. His clerk finds one promising legal problem or technical violation that suggests an invalid lease for every nine days of full-time research. Mr. Sly is already bringing in over $3.9 million annually for Oklasas from the wells he has acquired on these properties, and his operating costs are extremely low because he obtains only properties with producing wells.

Very fortunately, from Mr. Sly's perspective, his clerk was working in the county offices on the day EPC filed its quitclaim deeds and extension. The clerk's trained eye detected a serious error almost immediately: EPC had inadvertently quitclaimed the S.W. parcel and extended the lease on the nonproducing N.W. parcel. This error resulted from a slip of the pen; the clerk at EPC had written "N.W." on the form rather than "S.W." Although EPC had a system set up precisely to avoid such "erroneous legal descriptions," the error passed through six checkpoints in six offices at EPC without detection.

Within two hours of the clerk's discovery of the misfiling in the county office, the relevant papers had been copied and sent by overnight mail to Mr. Sly. Two days later he was in California to pay a visit to Mr. Wheat. After a two-hour meeting, they were joined by their lawyers for a lunch and an afternoon meeting, and by 5 o'clock an agreement had been signed. Neither party had contacted EPC to ascertain whether a mistake had been made, but it was only too obvious to them that a mistake had indeed been made.

Mr. Wheat asked not only that he be given a one-third royalty share but also that Mr. Sly lease, for a sum of $7,500 per year, the N.E. property that had been quitclaimed and then drill on that property. (EPC had said several times that it was not interested in drilling on this property after it had discovered gas on the S.W. property.) Mr. Wheat also asked for a full indemnification in the event of a lawsuit by EPC. That is, he asked to be fully secured against loss or damage in the event of a lawsuit over the leases, including any loss from the shutdown of operations at the well. Mr. Sly agreed that he would pay all legal costs and reimburse for any loss that Mr. Wheat might incur.

This was not a difficult decision for Mr. Sly. In oil and gas leases, the written record is everything, so far as the law is concerned. One simply cannot tell the legal status of the property unless there is a written legal record. Unrecorded statements of intention and verbal promises count for nothing. Mr. Sly's lawyer was certain that no suit by EPC would stand a chance of success.

The next day Sly's lawyer notified EPC of the new arrangement and told it to abandon the property immediately. Within twenty-four hours EPC replied that it considered the negotiations over this property to have been in bad faith. EPC said it considered any entry upon the land and any drilling to constitute a trespass and also to be in bad faith. EPC added, however, that it was willing to negotiate and settle out of court, because it was responsible for the clerical error. Oklasas replied immediately that it was not interested in negotiation.

EPC felt that it had been targeted by a fraudster but did not want to admit in public that it had been abused as a result of its own mistake. Although EPC wanted to sue, it was not clear that anything illegal had been done—only that something avoidable and embarrassing had occurred.

Edward Reece's Search for Contractors

INTRODUCTION

Edward Reece paced up and down as the slides came off the printer. His presentation was more or less ready, and he was feeling pretty confident about the meeting that afternoon. He clicked forward, putting his final "Recommendations" slide on the screen of his laptop. He had deliberately left this slide unfinished just in case of any last-minute change of heart. However, after six weeks of interviews, meetings, and analysis, he was ready to fill in the name of the researcher that he would recommend for carrying out the protocol on the Lipidolve project. All that remained was for him to summarize his justification of the decision in three or four bullet points.

EDWARD REECE

Eddie Reece considered himself a retired research scientist. He had thirty years experience developing and testing therapeutic treatments. He was proud of his accomplishments and for years had decorated his office with examples of over 150 patents that had been made in his name. He had carried out some of his most successful research in the medical school of South Eastern University. However, ten years previously he had made the leap to the for-profit world and had spent the last five years of his career supervising the research program of Unified Pharmaceuticals.

Four years ago, Eddie had retired to Austin, Texas, because of deteriorating health. However, the southern climate had been good for him, and gradually a life that revolved around his daily game of golf had lost some of its appeal. Recently, he began to try and find some part-time consulting work that would rekindle his interest in science and research. Through a golfing friend he was introduced to Michael Stokes, the CEO of Aqua Scientific Solutions.

This case was prepared by John McVea for the purpose of discussion and education on the role of ethics in the field of biotechnology. The materials were developed as part of "Bioethics and Biotechnology: A Collaborative Project of the University of Virginia Institute for Practical Ethics, Georgetown University's Kennedy Institute of Ethics and Law Center, and the Johns Hopkins University Berman Bioethics Institute." The work was sponsored by a grant from the Greenwall Foundation. The case is printed by permission of the principal investigators.

Stokes was impressed with Reece's background and told Reece that he had a perfect consulting job for him that would give Reece the chance to see whether he was ready for part-time work.

AQUA SCIENTIFIC SOLUTIONS

Aqua was a small, successful pharmaceutical business. Most of Aqua's existing products were specifically targeted to rare diseases and disorders.

Its latest development was particularly critical to the firm's strategy over the next few years. Several years ago, as part of some basic research, Aqua had come across a chemical compound that seemed to slow the absorption of fatty compounds in otherwise healthy rats. This product, initially named *Lipidolve*, seemed to have potential in the lucrative market for the control of obesity. The size of this market, together with the projected low costs of manufacture for Lipidolve, had the potential to transform Aqua from a niche researcher in the drugs business into a major competitor.

Lipidolve had successfully completed phase 1 and phase 2 trials and now was entering the final and most critical trial on voluntary human subjects. Stokes had approved the preparation of an Investigating New Drug (IND) application with Aqua as the sponsor; however, the firm was required to appoint a principal investigator to carry out the work.

Principal investigators were normally academic clinicians who carried out human-subjects research within colleges of medicine or universities. In this case, however, Stokes had yet to make a decision about the principal investigator. Stokes realized that he now faced one of the most critical decisions of his career—to whom should he assign the human subjects protocol for Lipidolve? What criteria should he use? What relationship should this clinician have with the Aqua organization when the stakes were so high?

These were the questions that Stokes had asked Reece to consider. He thought that Reece's research and business experience were ideal for offering advice to the executive team that would make the decision by August 30. He had offered Reece a six-week consulting contract ending with a presentation on August 14. He specifically asked Reece to consider the following issues:

- To whom should Aqua give the contract, and how should Aqua structure the agreement between that person and the firm?
- What were the risks and justifications for each of the options available to the Aqua organization?

THE OPTIONS

In order to consider all of the options, Reece spent the next month reviewing the set of external candidates that had been pulled together by the vice president of research, Louise Laporte. Laporte had been assisting him in carrying out an initial screening of the candidates. They used their personal experience and the initial application materials that the candidates had supplied to eliminate researchers who did not appear to have sufficient experience or else had no track record in this type of trial. This effort left them with six qualified and experienced candidates.

Reece visited each of these candidates and carried out an in-depth interview including a detailed tour of the facilities in which the work would be carried out. At this point, two more candidates were eliminated.

The final four candidates were all considered equally capable of carrying out high-quality research within the time-scale required. Therefore, Reece began an initial round of negotiations to determine how each candidate expected to be compensated for the work. At a minimum, all of the proposed contracts would cover the trial expenses and appropriate allocated overhead costs including the researchers' compensation. Moreover, if the trials went well, they had the potential to leave a small excess or profit for the researchers. However, some of the contracts offered significantly more scope for profit than others. The result of these negotiations were as follows:

1. Dr. Joshua Rosenfelt was a professor of medicine at University College in Pittsburgh. He had successfully carried out dozens of successful protocols and had an excellent reputation for the quality of his work. However, Rosenfelt was extremely busy. He currently was involved in at least four other trials, three for charitable medical research institutions and one for a drug firm in a completely unrelated field. Reece had some concerns over how the priorities would be set between the competing projects. Rosenfelt requested compensation as follows: His research department would receive $500,000 in advance to cover the cost of the trials. In addition, Aqua would supply $200,000 worth of laboratory equipment to the university, which would remain the university's property after the trial.

2. Dr. Alex Century was a specialist in dietary research at the De La Ferla Medical School in Denver, Colorado. Century was particularly interested in the Lipidolve compound and had done research on similar compounds in the past. Century's department was extremely well funded and had received a number of public and private grants over the last ten years. Indeed, some of the private gifts had enabled Century to build up an endowment that allowed him to carry out some internally funded original research. Century requested compensation as follows: Aqua would donate $300,000 to his research endowment and another $300,000 on completion of the work. In addition, Century would receive a milestone bonus of $10,000 worth of Aqua Scientific Solutions stock if the work was completed within twelve months.

3. Dr. Elaine Boyle was a specialist in intestinal biology at the Marjorie B. and Mitchell K. Carlock Center for Dietary Research at the Westminster Hospital in Cambridge, Massachusetts. She had one of the largest practices in the country dealing with adult obesity. The Carlock Center was involved in dozens of trials on obesity involving both drug treatments

and a range of dietary treatments. Reece noted that Dr. Boyle had the advantage of a large pool of patients with obesity problems that she was willing to use for the research. Because of the special contribution that she felt her practice could give the research, Dr. Boyle had proposed an incentive-based compensation structure. She would receive $2,500 for every patient who completed the trial, up to a maximum enrollment of 300 patients.

4. Dr. Douglas Kuczynski was a leading medical researcher at Bay University in California and was widely regarded as one of the most innovative researchers in the field. On top of an impressive history of medical research, he had a number of entrepreneurial interests. He was also CEO and president of a biotechnology firm that had been formed with the right to exploit a number of his research patents, as per an agreement he had made with the university. In line with his entrepreneurial spirit, Kuczynski had proposed that the deal be structured as follows. In compensation he would receive stock options in Aqua. The options would give Kuczynski the right to buy up to 100,000 ordinary shares in Aqua Scientific Solutions at a price of $10 per share. The current price was $12 per share. The block of options could be exercised only between twelve and eighteen months, after the commencement of the trials.

THE MEETING

Reece stared blankly back at his computer screen. He had analyzed all the options endlessly. Depending on the assumptions made about the success of the product, it could be argued that, financially, there was little to differentiate the offers. On the other hand, the structure of the deals certainly might have different motivational effects on the researchers and might be perceived differently by the general public. Several other issues had made him wonder what was the right thing to do.

The first alternative of paying a flat fee to Dr. Rosenfelt's department seemed to simplify some of the issues. But would the lack of incentives give the project a low level of priority and lead to delays in completing the results?

The second alternative held back some of the payment until completion of the project and gave Dr. Century a strong incentive to finish the project on time. But was it legitimate to reward a scientist for the delivery of results?

The third alternative had the advantage of a guaranteed pool of patients. The incentive system would encourage Dr. Boyle to recruit as many patients as possible and to deliver results on time. However, might this sort of contract encourage Dr. Boyle to take shortcuts, and was this possibility something that Aqua should worry about?

The fourth alternative of a contract based on stock options had a number of advantages. Issuing options would not appear as a cost on the income statement of Aqua. If the trial failed, the options would have little value, and the cost of the trial for Aqua would be much reduced. And options, like some of the other incentives, would encourage Kuczynski to place a high priority on the work.

On the other hand, if the trial was successful and Aqua succeeded with its new strategy, Kuczynski could earn huge rewards. Aqua's investment banker's best estimate for the future value of Aqua shares was $17. At this price Kuczynski would earn $700,000 for the work. However, Reece knew that share-price forecasting is an inexact science, and other advisers had produced estimates between $18 to $42 per share. Therefore, depending on the success of Lipidolve, Kuczynski could personally reap windfall profits of up to $3 million. Could this level of compensation be justified? How would it play to shareholders, participants in the trial, or the general public? Aqua already rewarded all its employees with stock options. Was it right to reward contracted scientists in the same way?

Reece knew that time was of the essence for Aqua, but so was the accuracy and reliability of the trial. On the other hand, he did not want to support an alternative that might encourage wrongdoing by any of the scientists. Furthermore, some of the alternatives made him think about the issue of informed consent. Should the researchers have to reveal the nature of their contracts to the patients? Did patients have the right to know the extent to which the researcher who was supervising their trial was being paid by the drug manufacturer? If so, was Aqua responsible for making sure that the researchers followed appropriate informed-consent procedures?

Reece got up and started to wander around his office, doing imaginary golf swings with his rolled-up presentation. Despite all the analysis, he had a gut feeling about this situation. He knew that he was going to be grilled pretty hard by the management team about the criteria he was using to propose or reject each option. He put down the slides, sat down at his computer, and started filling out some bullet-points that summarized a set of principles to support his decision.

Lilly's Consultation with Hostile Corporations

Lilly Advisers is a consulting firm based in the Maryland suburbs of Washington, D.C. The firm consults about contract administration and construction management with architectural firms and construction companies and their respective clients. The firm employs attorneys, engineers, architects, and accountants. They work in teams assembled for individual, discrete projects. The company secures properly written contracts for clients, protects against failures to execute contracts, and prepares contract releases.

Merv Rodgers is the president of Lilly Advisers. He is a lawyer specializing in conflict resolution, breach of contract, and contract amendment. He previously worked for the American Arbitration Association and two smaller consulting firms. He is a member of several professional organizations in both law and engineering. He has twice been retained by the governor of Maryland as an expert consultant to assist in the renovation of state-owned buildings in Maryland. His dossier contains a strong letter of praise and recommendation from the governor for his contribution to the state.

Several years ago Lilly entered into a *consulting agreement* with the Green Acres School System in Northern Virginia to address some problems that had arisen during the construction of two new high schools. Merv personally directed the team of consultants. The circumstances were these: A small construction company—Meyerhoff Builders—had been awarded the contract to build the two schools, but the entire project had been under the direct supervision of Stewart & Sons, a large, experienced, and prestigious architectural firm heavily involved in construction management. Because of unseasonable rains, add-ons to the contract, subcontractor delays, an extremely cold winter, and disagreements between the architects and the school board, the project was running behind the major dates in the contract. More troublesome was the fact that the school board had disagreed more than once with both the architects and the construction company on critical matters, causing still further delays.

At one point it was unclear whether any party to the contract was willing to work with the other on the construction of the *second* high school.

The school board hired Merv and his team to advise its members about how to proceed under these tense circumstances. After several weeks of investigation, the Lilly team submitted a confidential written report to the Green Acres School Board on February 15, 1999. It was called the *First High School Report.* This report analyzed the contract and critically evaluated the work performed to date by the contractor (Meyerhoff Builders) and the architectural firm (Stewart & Sons). Lilly was already familiar with Stewart & Sons, with whom it had worked as an adviser on three previous projects, all of which had been successfully completed. The consulting work associated with these projects, none of which involved the Green Acres School, had been smooth, efficient, and free of problems. Each project involved consulting on an out-of-state construction contract. Lilly had thereby come to know how Stewart & Sons operates and the methods it endorses. It knew, for example, that Stewart & Sons thinks of itself as a construction manager no less than a group of advisory architects.

In the *First High School Report,* the Lilly consulting group, which Merv headed, criticized Stewart & Sons's on-site management. Lilly argued that Stewart & Sons had (1) taken too much control over scheduling, (2) abused its position by improperly supervising the construction developments, (3) let several construction company failures go unreported, and (4) assumed scheduling duties not granted in the contract. Lilly maintained that Stewart & Sons's failures to control the scheduling properly was the single biggest factor in the construction delays and that Stewart and Sons was making an unusually large profit for the part of the project involving its administrative control.

After Lilly filed the report with the school board, the existence and contents of the report remained confidential, although Stewart & Sons knew that Lilly had been retained by Green Acres as a consultant. On the basis of this report, the Green Acres School Board demanded that both the Meyerhoff Construction firm and Stewart & Sons renegotiate with the school board. However, the *reason* given by the school board for renegotiation was the construction delays; the contents of the report were not mentioned and remained entirely confidential. After two months of difficult negotiation, all parties somehow found their way to an amendment to the contract, called the "amended agreement." They settled all outstanding issues and ended the first phase (the first school) of the two-phase project. They also agreed to move next to the second phase (the second school) under the altered format presented in the amended agreement.

However, the haggling over the amended agreement caused tension, and each party felt abused by the other. The school board believed that, as a result of Lilly's evaluation of undue profit, Stewart & Sons had assumed a very uncompromising and aggressive negotiating stance. Each party felt that it had compromised too much, but all signed the legally binding amended agreement on June 30, 1999. Construction resumed under the new terms.

During the next eight months, additional problems arose over the construction of the second high school. The school board and the architects again found themselves in disagreement about the architects' performance. The two parties were quarreling over several problems about specifications, quality of materials, and management responsibility. At this point, Stewart & Sons—still unaware of the contents of the written *First High School Report*—contacted Lilly to see whether Lilly would be interested in becoming a consultant for *Stewart & Sons* in this new round of disputes with Green Acres. Neither company considered this contact surprising, because Stewart & Sons had worked successfully with Lilly on the three previous projects. They agreed over the phone to meet informally to discuss the possibility.

On September 24, 2000, Lilly made a formal sales presentation to Stewart & Sons. At this meeting Merv represented Lilly. He felt that he had to disclose his firm's relationship with the school board. He reported to representatives of Stewart & Sons that Lilly had performed prior consulting work for Green Acres on some of its projects, including the first high school. Merv disclosed that Lilly had "evaluated the construction management documents and contracts" for the school board. He said that they had made some confidential suggestions to school officials about the various issues of which owners and contractors need to be aware, especially when disputes exist among the parties. However, Merv disclosed neither the existence of the criticisms in the *First High School Report* nor the full scope of the consulting.

On November 7, 2000, the architects' lawyer, Sam Shapiro, contacted Merv about what were the precise representations made in the past to the Green Acres School Board and whether there might be any problem of conflict of interest. They talked for a few minutes by phone, and Merv assured Sam that "there was nothing in any work for the school board that would stand in the way of Lilly's now advising Stewart & Sons." Merv noted that Lilly has a mechanical, well-designed system that is applied to each potential consulting job that explores whether conflicts of interest exist. He said that he personally had reviewed the work for Green Acres and found no problem of conflict of interest. Merv reported that he had to be especially diligent in screening for conflicts because Lilly had worked for *both* clients on several previous contracts. Merv concluded by saying, "If there had been any sort of conflict that would now put Stewart & Sons at risk, I would not even consider accepting the job." Foremost in Merv's mind in making this statement was that the work done for Green Acres was done for a *former* client on a *former* project—namely, the *first* high school. In his view, that consulting project was concluded.

Neither of these two lawyers asked the other for anything in writing; nor did either take notes about the telephone conversation. Sam assumed that Merv meant that no negative judgments had been reached in the report to Green Acres about the architects' performance. Stewart & Sons had always believed that any problems about the construction contract had been between the construction firm and the school board. The company had no reason to suppose that Lilly might have negatively evaluated Stewart & Sons's performance.

On the basis of this assurance, on November 8, 2000, Sam Shapiro and other representatives of Stewart & Sons authorized a contract for Lilly's services. Merv himself signed the agreement.

During the next four weeks, the disputes over the construction worsened between Stewart & Sons and the Green Acres School Board. The latter sued both the construction firm and the architects. Lawyers representing Stewart & Sons soon discovered the *First High School Report*, which Lilly was required by law (at the demand of the Green Acres School Board) to deposit with the court. As soon as representatives of Stewart & Sons read this report, they were astonished and bitterly angry over what they saw as misrepresentation and conflict of interest by Lilly officials, principally Merv.

As Stewart & Sons viewed the situation, a conflict of interest existed for Lilly *and* an inadequate disclosure had been made of prior consulting work for Green Acres; these failures placed the firm in legal jeopardy because its own chosen consultant was on record as challenging the firm's competence (in the *Report*). Stewart & Sons had known all along that Lilly had the *potential* for some sort of conflict because there *might* have been something in the confidential relationship with Green Acres that would have presented a conflict. But Lilly had explicitly assured Stewart & Sons that there was no reason to be concerned about that past relationship. Lilly could not disclose the precise contents of a confidential report, of course, but Stewart & Sons saw no reason why the fact that negative evaluations had been tendered to the school board could not have been mentioned.

Merv evaluated the situation very differently. He knew that he had a *potential* conflict of interest in coming to an agreement with Stewart & Sons. But he had worked very hard within his firm to overcome the potential conflict by assigning an entirely different consulting team for Stewart & Sons than the team that had been assigned to consult with Green Acres. He had carefully instructed every employee associated with the first project not to disclose anything about that project to those assigned to work with Stewart & Sons on the second project. He also isolated himself from any knowledge of the facts during the Stewart & Sons consultation, because he had himself been on the first consulting team. He did not permit second-team members to have access to the *First High School Report* or any documents involved in the first consultation. He did not allow any knowledge or discussion of the vital services that Lilly had performed for Green Acres to reach the second consultation team. He restricted access to documents that criticized Stewart & Sons's performance, which were in a corporate file.

But as Stewart & Sons sees it, in the absence of an adequate disclosure about the nature and existence of the *First High School Report*, the conflict of interest was actual, not merely potential, and was not eliminated by Merv's various maneuvers; Lilly therefore should have declined to enter the arrangement. Stewart & Sons regards it as virtually certain that in a circumstance of adequate disclosure, neither it nor Green Acres would have consented to Lilly's new business arrangement with Stewart & Sons. Stewart & Sons believes that it was owed a disclosure of the existence of those opinions by Lilly officials that impugned the integrity and honesty of Stewart & Sons, thereby exposing it to legal jeopardy. The confidential nature of the report to Green Acres provided no excuse for the failure to disclose that *some* statements in the report might prove to be detrimental to Stewart & Sons's interests.

Merv is puzzled by this reaction. He had designed what he saw as a flawless strategy of eliminating all possible revelation of the original consulting arrangement. He did so precisely to prevent all problems of conflict of interest, and he does not see even a single person with a conflict of interest. The accusation that he should have disclosed both the existence and the nature of the report to Stewart & Sons particularly irritates him. Because the report was *confidential,* he believes that he had an ethical obligation *not* to disclose its content. He therefore could not have disclosed either the services that Lilly had performed for Green Acres or the fact that Lilly criticized Stewart & Sons's performance. He had chosen his words very carefully in all conversations with Stewart & Sons so that they were aware that Green Acres had consulted in confidence with Lilly about the high school contract and that the confidential character of the consulting precluded any form of disclosure about it. He now says to himself, "Didn't I make this clear to Stewart & Sons? What did the company expect me to say about a confidential relationship other than that it existed? Is not that disclosure as much of a disclosure as is ethically permissible?"

The more he thinks about the situation, the more Merv believes that the charges against him have been fabricated to extricate Stewart & Sons from a difficult situation. The architects initiated the contact with Lilly knowing that there had been a consulting relationship and that the contracts had been evaluated. With that knowledge, it was up to Stewart & Sons to decide whether to write a contract with Lilly, and it had decided to do so. Merv thinks that he disclosed all that a client could reasonably ask and that the client had in fact been in a good position to make a reasonable judgment about whether to come to an agreement with Lilly. Why would anyone suppose that he should have been the person to decide not to proceed, rather than the *client's* being responsible for that decision?

Moreover, when he signed the contract with Stewart & Sons, Merv knew effectively nothing about the nature of the *later* disputes over the second high school. As he saw it, he had a new and singular relationship with Stewart & Sons unaffected by his past connection to the Green Acres School Board. The most important element of Merv's thinking is his sincere conviction that no conflict truly existed, because the job that Lilly performed for Green Acres was not the same as the new Stewart & Sons project. At other companies, he had known many consultants to work for two different parties who were both contractually involved in the same construction project. This practice was, so far as he could see, acceptable and prevalent in the world of construction consultants. The decisive industry standard for conflict of interest was not "both parties are on the same project," rather it was "one party is placed at risk by virtue of consulting with both parties." As long as there is no significant risk of harm, Merv had never worried about working for more than one of the different parties to the same contract; nor did he know anyone in the industry who worried about it.

As he slumps into his office chair, Merv's eyes fall on the latest letter from Stewart & Sons. The letter informs him that Stewart & Sons would not pay a penny of the $102,500 owed on the consulting contract. Stewart & Sons has good lawyers, and Merv knows that if he becomes involved in a lawsuit, he could spend more than $100,000 in legal fees, with no guarantee as to outcome. "But," he thinks, "I should spend the hundred grand." Merv's considerable anger has settled into determination.

Venture Capital
for Rubbernex Paints

On a Saturday morning in April 2002, five good friends met in the basement of John Kleinig's house near Palo Alto, California. They saw each other frequently because they carpooled to work at the Globe Coating Company, one of the world's largest manufacturers of fine paints, varnishes, and protective coatings. Globe had consistently surpassed other manufacturers in the development of several new products and had put together the industry's finest research staff. The five commuters and friends were all members of this exceptionally capable research staff. Two were research scientists. The other three handled administration, research protocol development, and computer records.

Kleinig was Globe's research division manager, a position he had obtained five years ago after fifteen years of working with the company. He also was the acknowledged leader of this group. Each of the other four had more than ten years of experience with the company. They all believed that Kleinig was the person most responsible for making their research division the best in the world. These five men jointly knew virtually everything of importance about research, administration, secret formulas, the competition, suppliers, and the general industry. Along with thirteen other key people in the division, these five men had helped develop several products vital for Globe's leading position.

During their commutes, the five had ample opportunity to criticize their peers and to discuss the cumbersome, bureaucratic, and slow operation of research at Globe. Over a period of several months, they gradually became convinced that they could conduct far more advanced research on new coatings in upcoming years than could their proud but somewhat content and even complacent colleagues. Therefore, they met on this Saturday morning to put the final touches on a business plan for which they hoped to find funding.

Kleinig and another group member, Jimmy Liang, had already drafted and discussed a tentative business plan. Their idea for a new venture centered on the strategy of constructing a plant to manufacture "thin film" coatings. These protective coatings are new products pioneered and marketed by Globe, which had devoted ten years of research to the development of three forms of the coating. The film coating is so thin that it is invisible to the eye and allows various forms of electrical and adhesive contact as though no coating existed,

This case was prepared by Tom L. Beauchamp. Not to be duplicated without permission of the holder of the copyright, © 2003 by Tom L. Beauchamp.

yet it provides all the protection of traditional clear coatings. The technology has a marvelous potential for application, from wood floors to fine furniture and metals manufacturing. It is the most innovative new product in the coating industry and has not, as yet, been applied in as many industries as some observers believe it can be.

This product was originally conceived by Kleinig himself in a series of meetings with two of his associates in management at Globe, one a chemist and one an engineer. Globe already had vaguely similar, somewhat unsuccessful coating applications on the market. Kleinig and his associates had been able to overcome problems with these coatings by adding several ingredients and innovative manufacturing processes. They recognized, as the research proceeded, that these ingredients and processes were trade secrets proprietary to Globe. Kleinig had personally masterminded the research protocol, though almost all of the research had been conducted by teams under the two chemists, both of whom had subsequently retired. Without the efforts of these three managers, Globe would never have had the will or the expertise to produce these products. Of course, Globe did underwrite all of the costs of the ten years of research, which by the beginning of 2002 had been returned in earnings many times over.

Globe has always been primarily interested in thin films to produce superior paints and clear coatings on *wood* products. About two years ago Kleinig thought that he saw a very different application. He thought that he could put an even thinner film on computer heads and similar moving parts to protect those parts from wear. This idea, which is what he and his carpooling friends have been discussing on the way to work, has come to form the nucleus of their proposals for funding. Between July and the end of August 2002, a friend of Kleinig's, Jay Ewing, critiqued the evolving business plan numerous times and helped Kleinig develop contacts with several venture capitalists. He also arranged for a meeting with the Los Angeles specialty law firm of Lion and Lion to provide legal counsel.

In early September, Kleinig met with various venture capitalists. A September 9, 2002, meeting proved to be the decisive one. Kleinig hit it off beautifully with a representative of a large East Coast venture capitalist, HH Ventures of Philadelphia. This representative was already convinced that thin coating promised major technological innovations in the paint and varnish industry and that the five men represented the epitome of coating knowledge. Their discussion of personnel and business plans lasted approximately two-and-a-half hours, and both men admired each other's integrity and capability by the end of the meeting. Between September 10 and 18, Kleinig and HH representatives placed fifteen evening phone calls to cement the basis for an agreement between HH and what was to be Rubbernex Industries.

On September 19, 2002, Kleinig resigned from Globe. Because he had at the time almost completed an agreement with HH Ventures, he reached the conclusion that he could no longer in good conscience remain a loyal Globe employee. The other four group members did not resign at this point, because they were not holding direct discussions with HH and therefore were not parties to any agreement, even though they knew about the pending arrangements.

At his "exit interview" with his supervisor and a Globe lawyer, Kleinig encountered a hostile and an intimidating environment. Globe told him in straightforward terms that if he were to put his knowledge and skills to work with another company by utilizing Globe trade secrets, he would face a vigorous lawsuit. His supervisor told him that Globe was seriously concerned that its trade secrets and confidential business information would be misappropriated. Kleinig was asked to sign a letter that enumerated 168 broadly worded trade secrets that he could not transmit or use. Since he had himself been an inventor of or designer of many of these trade secrets, he refused to sign. At the same time, he assured Globe that there would be no misappropriation of proprietary information. His supervisors nonetheless continued to focus heavily on moral and legal problems of the appropriation of trade secrets.

By the conclusion of the exit interview, those present had negotiated their way to the following tentative arrangement: In advance of taking a new job or developing any product, Kleinig would consult with his ex-supervisor at Globe to ensure that there would be no trade secret violations. He also would submit a plan to show that any market he wished to explore would not conflict with already established Globe markets. Beyond the list of 168 broadly worded trade secrets, the interview participants did not discuss the nature of trade secrets or trade secrets specific to thin film technology. Nothing was mentioned about computer-head applications.

In a September 21, 2002, meeting, Kleinig, three HH representatives, and lawyers representing both parties signed a tentative agreement to fund Rubbernex Industries. The contract gave Rubbernex funding for one month to allow for further development of the business plan. HH also had the month to evaluate its position with the choice of dropping its interest at the month's end or trying to reach a final agreement for major funding. The agreement included an offer of further financing after one month, conditional on a *due diligence* review. In this context, "due diligence" means, in large part, that HH has obligations of due care when money is given to assist in a business start-up. This is a standard of proper care requiring that the venture capital firm competently and thoroughly investigate a proposal's business viability and take all reasonable steps to protect against violations of the rights of all affected parties.

The September 21 meeting involved lengthy discussions about Kleinig's exit interview, about Globe's concerns for its trade secrets, and about HH's need for assurances that no trade-secrets problem existed. Kleinig reassured them that he could "build thin film coatings using many different alternative chemicals and processes" and that Globe should have no basis for concern by the time Rubbernex developed the new processes. The next day, Jimmy Liang and the group's chief scientist, Jack Kemp, resigned from Globe. One week later the final two group members resigned.

Globe officials told all four during their exit interviews that the company was considering a suit against Kleinig to protect its trade secrets and warned all that if they joined him, they faced the same suit. Globe officials told all four that company officials could prove that Kleinig had conspired with other individuals to steal Globe's secrets as early as nine months before leaving the company.

These officials would not, however, specify the trade secrets when requested by Kemp to do so; nor would they state the identities of the "other individuals."

Henry Hardy was the man at HH who had the responsibility, in the end, for deciding whether the package called a *tentative agreement* (to fund and implement a business plan for a new manufacturing company) between venture capitalist HH and the five entrepreneurs would stand as written, be rewritten, or be cancelled. It was Hardy's massive personal fortune that constituted the venture capital that fuels HH. He had at first decided not to fund Rubbernex because of his lawyer's explicit concern that Globe's threat of a lawsuit was not idle. But Hardy had left open the possibility that Globe could be mollified or that the trade-secrets problem could be handled in an honest and a forthright manner. Besides, Hardy had never liked the idea of lawyers' calling the shots in the world of business.

Hardy had personally taken charge of HH's due diligence review, which he usually left to subordinate officers. He first hired the best firm in New York to do reference checks on the entrepreneurs. These consultants were asked to examine their professional credentials, their professional integrity, and all former or existing employment contracts that they had signed. Hardy next commissioned a thorough review of the legal questions surrounding trade secrets by a specialist law firm. He also hired twelve outside consultants at American universities to review the feasibility of the entrepreneurs' scientific claims and asked in each case for an evaluation of whether the venture could be successfully launched without using Globe's trade secrets. He then requested a thorough review of HH's financial and legal position by his in-house lawyer and three of his program directors.

Hardy examined the enterprise's business viability by having two of his most trusted consultants examine every feature of the Rubbernex proposal. He commissioned a review by a Wall Street security analyst of the coating industry and held discussions with two other venture capitalists who had in the past been involved with trade-secrets issues. He also asked for an appraisal by Kleinig of whether he would need further direct hires from Globe to fulfill his plan's staffing requirements.

Hardy then attempted to contact Globe executives to ask them to review the Rubbernex business plan for possible trade-secrets problems. Following the course sketched out during Kleinig's exit interview, Hardy's proposal to Globe invited company engineers and chemists to spend time in any future Rubbernex manufacturing facility for observational purposes to ensure that there were no trade-secrets violations. He was prepared to divulge any formulas used for thin film coatings and to allow a neutral inspector to examine Rubbernex's formulas by comparison with Globe's to see whether there were any violations. In their reply, Globe's lawyers issued a warning that the technology of thin film coatings was proprietary to Globe and that if any venture capital was forthcoming from HH, Hardy would personally be named in a lawsuit.

This response angered Hardy, as he thought he was fully satisfying the conditions that Globe had itself laid down in the exit interview and verbal agreement with Kleinig. He felt that, whereas he had offered numerous concessions to Globe to ensure that there were no moral or legal violations, Globe had taken a hostile position of nonnegotiation solely to prevent potential competition. At about this time, Hardy's internal and external legal advisers submitted reports stating that with enough chemical and engineering ingenuity and sufficient venture capital to buy expensive new West German machinery, the potential existed to introduce sufficient modifications to claim a new product that was a true industry advance, not at all a mere clone of the Globe product. However, his advisers judged it necessary to qualify their reports with the following statement: "I cannot ensure that there will be no violation of trade secrets unless I am able to examine the trade secrets, and law and ethics prohibit me from doing so." That is, since they did not know exactly what constituted a trade secret at Globe, they were not in a position to ensure that there would be no violation.

HH Ventures's due diligence standards had consistently equaled or surpassed those in the industry, and Hardy could not imagine a more thorough review than he had done. But this was his first foray into the territory of a trade-secrets problem, and he was perplexed by the fact that there is no way to examine whether a trade-secrets violation is likely to occur. He remained uncertain of both how much ingenuity the entrepreneurs had (although he knew that in the past they had not lacked for a wealth of new ideas) and of what the trade secrets are that could not be utilized. He came to appreciate that his consultants could not recognize the exploitation of a Globe trade secret by the entrepreneurs even if it were to occur. Each of his consultants had simply said that the potential existed for the entrepreneurs to make thin film coatings through, as a court opinion once put it, "skillful variations of general processes known to the particular trade,"[1] but no one could say for sure whether the potential would be actualized.

Hardy's legal consultants had supplied him with the standard legal definition and analysis of trade secrets, which his consultant report-sheet summarized as follows:

> A trade secret consists of any formula, device, pattern, or compilation of information used in business that gives one an opportunity to obtain advantage over competitors who do not know or use it. It is not a secret of any sort, but a process or device for continuous use in the operation of the business. An exact definition of trade secrets is not possible, but there are factors that can be considered in determining whether something is a trade secret: general knowledge, employee knowledge, the adequacy of protective guarding, the value of the information, the amount of money expended in development of the secret, and ease of acquisition or duplication. An employee in possession of confidential information that could damage the economic interests of an employer if disclosed is under an obligation of confidentiality that remains in force when the employee leaves the firm and takes employment elsewhere. However, under common law it is not a breach of any obligation owed to an employer to plan for a new competitive venture while still employed, even though the employee has an opportunity to observe (what will

later be) a competitor's secrets, and even though the employee may leave with a wealth of experience in and knowledge about the competitor's processes, products, research, and financial matters.

Hardy saw that this legal definition makes a sharp distinction between a company that *owns* a formula, device, or process that has been *disclosed* in confidence to one or more employees, and a company whose formula has been *developed by those employees while employed* at the company. He had learned that in some of the more innovative industries, employees are typically instrumental in creating or advancing a formula, device, or process through their own ingenuity and skills. The greater the extent of an employee's role in creating or otherwise improving the confidential information or property, the greater the employee's apparent claim to a right to use it elsewhere, and the less an employer's right to claim sole possession. Hardy had come to believe that the entrepreneurs who came to him for funding were in this latter circumstance.

It therefore seemed unfair to the entrepreneurs to keep them from starting Rubbernex simply because their former employer was intimidating them. As Hardy saw it, these employees had two main types of obligation to Globe: contractual obligations based on their employment contracts and obligations to ensure that the new venture would use only independently developed competitive technologies (thus avoiding violations of trade secrets, patents, and proprietary designs). Although there is some disagreement and ambiguity, Hardy's reference checks and technical consultants all said that these obligations likely could be satisfied in this case.

His consultants had also pointed out that the law of trade secrets is amorphous, conceptually muddy, and formed from a number of different areas of law in a patchwork manner. The law attempts to foster innovation and progress without either leaving firms the victims of faithless employees or placing employees in a situation of servitude. An employer has a right to his or her intellectual property, but the employee also has a right to seek gainful employment that requires the application of his or her knowledge and abilities. If employees could be prevented by intimidation from moving from one firm to another, technological growth and diffusion could be stifled.

Hardy agreed with this perspective. He therefore favored funding the entrepreneurs even though his lawyers had stated their belief that two lawsuits were a virtual certainty, one against the former Globe employees for misappropriation of trade secrets and the second against HH Ventures for a failure of due care. Hardy denied the latter charge because it implied that he had performed an inadequate due diligence review prior to an investment. He considered this charge groundless. He had always been both cautious in his due diligence reviews and bold in his business planning. He has been cautious this time, he thinks, and he will fund this venture.

NOTE

1. *Aetna Building Co. v. West,* 39 Cal. 2d 198, at 206.

Banning Cigarette Advertising

Beginning in the late 1950s, pressure grew from the health care community for a government study on the health hazards of smoking. The hazards had been discussed for years, but no definite conclusions had been clearly demonstrated. In 1962, in response to pressure from the medical community, President Kennedy asked the surgeon general to study the risks of smoking. As circumstances evolved over many years, the emphasis slowly shifted from the risk of the product to the ethics of its advertising, in part because the risks became clear. During the Clinton administration, the Food and Drug Administration (FDA) and various antismoking coalitions proceeded to vigorously attack cigarette manufacturers for the way they market their products. In light of unfavorable legal decisions and mounting popular and political pressures, the tobacco industry began to address the concerns about smoking, especially those surrounding its advertisements. This conflict has persisted, unabated, into the twenty-first century.

THE EARLY SURGEON GENERAL'S REPORT

In the early 1960s, Surgeon General Luther Terry assumed the task of evaluating over 8,000 previous studies on the effects of smoking. The goal of the committee he assembled was to decide the question "Is smoking bad?" The committee consisted of persons selected to provide as much impartiality as possible. This committee concluded and reported that smoking was a substantial cause of certain diseases.

Government officials responded by considering the regulation of cigarette advertising. Critics of the tobacco industry claimed that advertisements that showed healthy, happy, and sexually appealing men and women smoking were encouraging increased consumption, especially by American youth. Congressional examination resulted in the passage of the Federal Cigarette Labeling and Advertising Act (1965). The purposes of the act were to provide for the uniform labeling of all cigarette packages and to inform the public of the health risks associated with smoking.[1] The act required that the warning label

This case was prepared by Tom L. Beauchamp and Joanne L. Jurmu, and revised by Anna Pinedo, Katy Cancro, Blaire Osgood, and Joseph Folio. Not to be duplicated without permission of the holder of the copyright, © 1992, 1996, 2003 by Tom L. Beauchamp.

"Caution: Cigarette smoking may be hazardous to your health" be included on every package in a conspicuous location.

The act preempted actions by other authorities to regulate cigarette advertising. No state or federal agency could require additional package labeling or warnings in advertisements for the life of the act. Originally, the Federal Trade Commission (FTC) had pushed to extend the act to require the warning label in advertisements.[2] Thus, the FTC was critical of Congress for not taking this step and other, more sweeping courses of action.

For their part, members of the tobacco industry were reserved. They agreed that the findings of the committee were significant, but they urged further medical research into the risks of smoking. Many studies that the congressional committee had evaluated were statistical. The industry believed that other forms of evidence based on biomedical research of the risks of smoking should be undertaken before definite conclusions could be drawn. Tobacco producers also adopted a voluntary advertising code. They vowed that in their ads, smoking would not be associated with manliness, sex appeal, or social charm.[3]

Advertising for cigarettes involves large expenditures. In 1967, the industry spent $312 million on ads. Of this figure, 73 percent, or $226.9 million, was spent on television advertising.[4] Eleven percent of 1967 advertising revenues were generated by cigarette ads.[5] The FTC conducted a new study based on industry figures and found that the average American was exposed to sixty seven cigarette commercials per month.[6] The agency concluded that such a high exposure rate was encouraging youth to begin the habit. In 1967, the FTC invoked the Fairness Doctrine with regard to cigarette commercials. The Fairness Doctrine, implemented in the 1950s, requires that broadcasters present both sides of a controversial issue. The FTC declared smoking to be a controversial issue and required that broadcasters make significant time available for antismoking messages. Antismoking interest groups were unable to afford advertising time in proportion to cigarette advertising, so broadcasters had to give them free air time. By 1970, the broadcast media had given antismoking messages roughly one-third of cigarette-related advertising time, at a cost of $75 million.[7]

BAN PROPOSED

In 1968, the Federal Communications Commission (FCC) announced a proposed rule to ban all broadcast ads.[8] Some groups called only for a stronger warning label that cited specific health risks or for warnings plus information on tar and nicotine content to be included on all packaging. The debate soon narrowed to those in favor of warnings only and those in favor of a ban on all ads.

ARGUMENTS IN SUPPORT OF THE AD BAN

Advocates of the ban acknowledged that adult smokers would not stop smoking even if all ads disappeared, but their hope was to prevent youths from starting. Teenagers presumably saw smoking glamorized in ads and tried to duplicate the glorified conduct. Ban supporters predicted that each successive generation would foster a smaller percentage of smokers and that eventually smoking would be eliminated. Any risk to jobs and the tobacco industry as a whole would be minimized because those people involved would have a chance to find other work and to invest in other endeavors. Ban supporters maintained that tobacco was a dangerous substance, unworthy of promotion through federally regulated broadcast media.

ARGUMENTS IN OPPOSITION TO THE BAN

Opposition to the ban rested primarily, from the industry perspective, on questions of First Amendment rights. They argued that tobacco is a legal product in the United States and that the federal government helps to subsidize tobacco farmers. State governments and the federal government depend on revenues generated by cigarette taxes. In 1968, the industry paid $4.1 billion in state and federal taxes.[9] With obvious state and federal backing for the manufacture of cigarettes, tobacco product manufacturers seemed to have the right to advertise their products under the freedom of speech provision of the Constitution. Banning tobacco industry ads was viewed by tobacco industry representatives as arbitrary discrimination against a targeted industry.[10]

A BAN ON BROADCAST ADVERTISING

Congress amended the Cigarette Labeling and Advertising Act in 1970 in the Public Health Smoking Act. The 1970 act provided for the banning of all cigarette ads "on any medium of electronic communication subject to the jurisdiction of the Federal Communication Commission."[11] To the dismay of cigarette producers, the antismoking ads continued in the absence of cigarette ads. The industry petitioned the FCC to be permitted significant time under the Fairness Doctrine to present industry views on smoking. The FCC denied the request, stating that the dangers of smoking were now well-known and that the issue was no longer controversial.[12]

By 1985, it became apparent that per capita cigarette consumption was decreasing while the national population was increasing. These data reflected a significant decline in smoking. The trend was expected to continue, according to projections made by the Centers for Disease Control, Office of Health and Smoking. By 1994, the per capita consumption of cigarettes was approximately 2,493, down from 3,370 cigarettes per capita in 1985.[13] The California Department of Health Services and the University of San Diego kept careful figures on California. In 1988, 26.7 percent of California's population smoked.[14] In 2000, that number was down to 17.2 percent.[15]

However, the medical community, notably the American Medical Association (AMA), has not been satisfied with these results. It was disappointed that the tobacco industry was still advertising heavily, generally by switching media—from electronic to print—and undertaking sponsorship of sporting events, such as the Marlboro race car tours.

CIGARETTE ADS IN PRINT MEDIA

After the 1971 ban, newspaper advertising and sponsorship of sporting events became major means of marketing cigarettes, as is still the case today. Newspapers are probably the major source of information transmitted to the public about the dangers of smoking cigarettes. Newspapers thus have an interest both in earning revenue from cigarette advertising and in informing the public about the dangers of what they advertise. Most newspapers are businesses with two goals—making a profit and satisfying the consumer—which in the case of cigarette advertising can conflict.

The *New Republic* once commissioned reporter David Owen to write an article on cancer and the cigarette lobby. He wrote a piece sufficiently blunt in stating the issues and laying blame that the *New Republic*'s editors killed the story. According to *USA Today*, "In the candid (and no doubt regretted) words of Leon Wieseltier, the editor who assigned it, the threat of 'massive losses of advertising revenue' did it in."[16] The editors of the *New Republic* had been willing to report on the dangers of smoking and on the pressures brought by lobbyists, but they were not willing to print the forcefulness with which Owen stated his case. Owen later published his piece in the *Washington Monthly,* where he depicted the industry as using newspapers and magazines to enhance the appeal of smoking by portraying the young smoker as healthy and sexy— precisely what the industry had agreed not to do.

According to research conducted by Kenneth E. Warner, this example of burying Owen's article is but one of many cases in which American news media have refused to report the dangers of smoking for fear of decreased advertising revenue.[17] *The Washington Post*'s ombudsperson, using statistics taken from the *New York State Journal of Medicine,* found that only 6 out of 1,700 daily American newspapers attempt wholeheartedly to report on the dangers of smoking.[18] However, the American Newspaper Publishers Association and the Magazine Publishers Association continue to appeal to First Amendment protections of the right to advertise and to present the facts as newspapers see fit in order to justify their view that this matter should be left up to each individual newspaper.

Most, if not all, advertising associations remain opposed to a ban on print cigarette ads. Ad agencies maintain that the government cannot ban an industry's ads merely because it does not like that industry's product. They remind Congress that if cigarettes are legal to sell, they should be legal to advertise. Furthermore, agencies believe that banning cigarette ads will not accomplish the goal of reducing consumption by youth. Several studies have found that young smokers are most often influenced to start smoking by friends and parents, rather than by media ads.[19]

In 1985, the AMA set a goal of having a smokeless society by the year 2000. In the attempt to achieve this goal, the association again proposed a total ban on all cigarette advertising. Although it turned out to be unsuccessful, this proposal served as a stimulus to restrict tobacco advertisement and also spurred further debate. Most major cigarette companies did reduce their share of print advertisements. The FTC reports that the amount spent on media advertising was significantly down by 1994. However, newspaper ads constituted only a fraction of the $6 billion budget spent on other advertising techniques such as giveaways, coupons, and event sponsorship.[20] Tobacco marketers decided to focus on the use of discount ads, point-of-sale displays, and sponsorship of sports events to replace print advertisements. After television ads were banned and print advertising seemed targeted for strict regulation, the cigarette industry put more than 90 percent of its marketing dollars into nonprint advertising.[21] These techniques are mostly directed to those who already smoke rather than potential smokers. For example, Philip Morris, marketer of the nation's largest-selling Marlboro brand, developed the Philip Morris magazine in 1985. The magazine, a voice of the industry, was distributed, as of 1997, to 13 million readers.[22]

CIGARETTE ADS IN THE 1990s

During the 1990s, former Health and Human Services Secretary Louis W. Sullivan mounted a vigorous criticism of cigarette marketing by accusing the industry of incorrect, dishonest, and harmful advertising techniques. Sullivan was particularly distressed by the sponsorship of sporting events. The tobacco industry is firmly entrenched in the sports world with such sponsorships as the Winston Cup race car circuit. By sponsoring sporting events and splashing their names across billboards, sailboats, or race cars, tobacco companies are purchasing the advertising exposure on television that money cannot legally buy. A leader in the campaign against televised tobacco ads and the founder of the group *Doctors Ought to Care*, Dr. Alan Blum, stated, "I can find you tobacco brand logos on television every hour of every day."[23]

Sullivan judged the industry to be "trading on the prestige and image of the athletes to barter its products," while suggesting in its ads that "tobacco use is compatible with good health." Sullivan criticized social inaction over the last thirty years as vigorously as he criticized the industry: "It is immoral for civilized societies to condone the promotion and advertising of products which, when used as intended, cause disability and death."[24] Sullivan and other critics used two major arguments to challenge tobacco sponsorships. First, by using athletic men and women in its ads, the tobacco industry is attempting to create an image that the products are positively related to health and fitness. This association runs counter to all collected data on both exercise and disease. Second, many children watch the sporting events live or on television. Thus, they are exposed to cigarette advertising in a way that seems to defeat the purpose of the cigarette advertising ban.

The tobacco industry has reacted sharply to these criticisms, insisting that it has a right to market its product. The industry claims that Sullivan's comments are insulting in that they suggest that people have no choice about whether they should smoke and need the government to make the decision for them. Industry officials also cite the sports world's dependence on tobacco companies' financial support. The industry, which in 1993 spent approximately $80 million in sponsoring sporting events, received some support from the athletes involved. For example, Pam Shriver, a leading tennis player on the once-popular "Virginia Slims" tour, said that critics do not understand "how our tour evolved and how it's progressing and the opportunities that Philip Morris gave to women over the last 20 years. . . . If they asked us to endorse the product, that would be different. But personal endorsements versus [corporate] marketing vehicles that are perfectly legal are two very different things."[25]

Several proposals to combat these ads have been introduced by federal, state, and local governments. The city of Cincinnati set out in 1994 to remove any ad for tobacco products that appeared in bus shelters, buses, or outdoors. Baltimore imposed similar regulations.[26] After being accused by the Justice Department of strategically placing billboards in locations at professional sports stadiums that would frequently be shown on TV,[27] the Philip Morris Co. agreed to reposition all of its ads in sports stadiums.[28] In addition to that agreement, in 1994, Philip Morris ended its twenty-five-year connection with the Women's Tennis Association as the sponsor of the Virginia Slims tour.[29]

New regulations were proposed by the Clinton administration in 1995 regarding magazine advertisements and sponsorship of sporting events. The prospect of such restrictions provoked strong opposition from the tobacco and advertising industries, although public sentiment was generally supportive of the proposed legislation. A 1994 Gallup Poll indicated that "two-thirds of Americans—including almost half of all smokers—want the U.S. government to impose greater restrictions on cigarette advertising. For 53 percent that means a total ban. And 15 percent, while they don't support a total ban, said there should be greater restrictions."[30]

TARGET MARKETING

According to the Centers for Disease Control and Prevention in Atlanta, the cigarette industry is currently losing approximately 430,000 customers a year to lung-cancer and smoking-related deaths.[31] The percentage of adults who smoke dropped from 42.4 percent in 1965 to 25.7 percent in 1991,[32] and as of 2001, the rate further decreased to 22.7 percent.[33] As a result of this declining market, cigarette manufacturers need customers in alternative population segments. They favor advertisements that depict an optimum lifestyle, suggesting that one could enjoy that lifestyle when smoking certain cigarettes.

In the fall of 1991, Brown and Williamson Tobacco company launched its KOOL PENGUIN campaign. Arguably, this animated penguin with a spiked haircut and Bart Simpson attitude encouraged young people to take up cigarettes. The advertisements presented the penguin as a rebellious type, with lines such as "So I'm a penguin, deal with it." This tone appears to reinforce teenage rebellion and beliefs that smoking promotes friendship and social acceptability. However, Brown and Williamson denied that this campaign was designed to encourage young people to start smoking: "We're interested in reaching anyone over 21," said the spokesperson. "The reaction we got in focus groups was that this is a funny, appealing and eye catching way to sell our product."[34]

Then, in 1994, Camel introduced its animated character "Joe Camel" and his female counterpart "Josephine Camel" into their advertising strategy, though they insisted that such advertising themes did nothing more than promote the product to users. "Joe Camel" encountered scrutiny because of growing concern about advertising directed at youth. The California Supreme Court in San Francisco decided in 1994 to hear a case brought by a California woman against "Joe Camel." The court upheld the lawsuit because "the allegations against R. J. Reynolds were based not on smoking and health, but on a 'more general' duty imposed under state law 'not to engage in unfair competition by advertising illegal conduct,' namely, smoking by minors."[35] Alan Mansfield, the attorney representing the California woman, said that the legal challenge would "attempt to show RJR intentionally targeted minors with its ads, or that, upon learning the campaign affected youths, it failed to amend the now six-year-old campaign." As evidence, Mansfield cited a study that suggests that teen "smokers accounted for $476 million of Camel sales in 1991, compared with just $6 million garnered before the Camel campaign."[36]

The FTC decided in June 1994 not to take action against "Joe Camel." The FTC said that there was no evidence to support the hypothesis that "Joe Camel" entices children to begin smoking.[37] This decision, together with the Freedom of Speech Act and First Amendment rights, strengthened RJR's defense arguments in its various lawsuits.

Opposition to cigarette advertising is not confined to the American market. As of October 1, 1991, all cigarette advertising on television was banned throughout Europe. In May 2001, the European Parliament passed stringent legislation regarding the production and marketing of tobacco products. The crux of the legislation was a limit placed on the amounts of various chemicals per cigarette, made mandatory as of 2004: The maximum limits are set at 10 milligrams of tar, 1 milligram of nicotine, and 10 milligrams of carbon monoxide. The new laws make it illegal to use "misleading" terms, such as "light" or "mild," even if they are part of a product's registered trademark. It further stipulates that packaging must include large warnings, and it encourages individual countries to add graphic pictures that demonstrate the potential harms of smoking. These laws not only regulate tobacco in the EU countries but also affect its exports.

Tobacco companies believe that this unique attempt to limit the chemicals in cigarettes, not to mention the changes in packaging, will drastically reduce their profits as they compete against more potent products from countries outside of the EU. Though continuing litigation seems certain, these laws represent changing international sentiments toward the tobacco industry.

NEGOTIATED SETTLEMENT

In August 1996, President Clinton announced an executive order that declared nicotine to be an addictive drug, thereby relegating authority over its sale and advertisement to the FDA. This political move was an attempt to implement some of the same restrictions that the administration had previously considered. Coupled with public support, as manifested by the rise in individual and class-action law suits against the various tobacco companies, there was a powerful impetus to restrict the tobacco industry further.[38] Many states, led by their respective attorneys general, began to take up the case against tobacco companies. Their case focused on the harms of youth smoking, and specifically on the way that advertising promoted smoking.

Faced with these mounting pressures, the four largest tobacco companies (Philip Morris, R. J. Reynolds, Brown & Williamson, and Lorillard) entered into negotiations with the states. In November 1998, the states and the tobacco companies signed a detailed document, referred to as the Master Settlement Agreement (MSA). The MSA stipulated a number of restrictions for both the advertisement and business practices of the tobacco companies. Philip Morris now highlights the main points of the settlement on its website:

1. prohibition on "targeting" youth in cigarette marketing;
2. a ban on the use of cartoon characters in cigarette advertising;
3. a ban on most forms of outdoor tobacco brand advertising, such as billboards and transit ads;
4. prohibition on the distribution of tobacco branded merchandise, such as caps and t-shirts;
5. strict limitation on tobacco brand-name sponsorships;
6. prohibition on making material misrepresentations of fact regarding the health consequences of cigarettes;
7. prohibition on opposing specified legislative or regulatory youth-related tobacco control initiatives;
8. a requirement that the companies publicly disclose a wide range of previously non-public legal documents.[39]

The tobacco companies also agreed to provide the states with more than $200 billion over twenty-five years in compensation for the alleged harms of smoking, whereas $1.45 billion was designated to found the American Legacy Foundation, which will "conduct a national public education campaign," including advertising and education about the risks and harms of smoking.[40]

Although the MSA was heralded as a monumental shift in tobacco industry regulation, its scope remains unclear. Philip Morris was quick to announce that as of September 2000, it would cease to advertise in fifty magazines with young readers, thereby making good on its intent not to "target" youth, and demonstrating an effort to further separate itself from the other manufacturers.

The other three tobacco companies did not follow suit. According to the agreement, the companies must restrict their advertisements if more than 15 percent of a magazine's readers are under eighteen years of age or if that same age group represented more than 2 million readers. In August 2001, the *New England Journal of Medicine* published a study that concluded that the MSA had had almost no effect on advertisements directed at youth, because the "overall level of exposure of young people to this advertising remained high."[41]

The article further evaluated each of the companies. Brown & Williamson has reduced its level of advertising in magazines with many youth readers, but R. J. Reynolds and Lorillard have not. Both R. J. Reynolds and Lorillard have increased their advertising in magazines directed at youths since the MSA was signed. Despite the death of its animated Joe Camel (via the MSA), R. J. Reynolds has slightly increased its advertising in youth-oriented magazines, as has Lorillard.[42] The study also noted that the percentage of youths reached by ads for youth-brand cigarettes—defined as any brand smoked by more than 5 percent of high school smokers—has consistently remained around 85 percent.[43] The three tobacco companies chiefly in question have contended that the MSA established only guidelines, not laws.[44] These interpretations of the MSA by the tobacco industries have motivated its critics to push for tighter regulation.

After 2000, the movement against the tobacco industries clearly was focused in the courtroom. In September 1999, the federal government filed suit against the tobacco industries "to recover $25 billion per year the government spends on smoking related health costs."[45] Also suing in part under the civil racketeering statute (RICO), the government may collect triple damages if the case is successfully argued. Legal experts also noted that because of the potential for such a large reward and because of the vast legal resources of the government, the tobacco industries would likely focus on settling the case out of court.[46]

In July 2001, U.S. District Judge Gladys Kessler dismissed the portion of the government's case based on the Medical Care Recoveries Act and the Medicare Secondary Payer, leaving only the racketeering claims.[47] The remaining racketeering claims, according to Judge Kessler, pertain to the alleged "false and deceptive statements" about the addictive nature and health-related harms of their products.[48] As the case moved to trial, the government had to process over 1,700 document requests from the tobacco industry.[49]

In 2000, the U.S. Supreme Court decided that the FDA did not have the proper authority to regulate tobacco as a drug and therefore could not regulate its advertisements. In June 2001, it ruled five to four that states are not able to restrict the tobacco industries' advertising methods beyond the federally established limits. This ruling struck down a Massachusetts law banning tobacco ads near playgrounds and schools.[50] The struggle over proper limits for tobacco advertisements continues, with tobacco companies continuing to maintain wide discretion in the ways in which they advertise.

COUNTER ADS, CHANGING ATTITUDES, AND CORPORATE NAMES

The American Legacy Foundation (funded, pardoxically, by the four major tobacco companies under the conditions of the MSA), has produced several commercials and advertisements that graphically portray the harmful nature of cigarettes and that question the intentions of the tobacco industry. One ad shows young people piling 1,200 body bags in front of the headquaters of Philip Morris to symbolize the national average of 1,200 smokers that die in the United States every day from related illnesses. Another ad shows a woman attempting to enter the offices of Philip Morris with a machine clearly identified as a lie detector; she is quickly turned away. Though praised by antismoking advocates, the ads have drawn stern criticism from the very industry required to fund them. Philip Morris executives stated that these ads relied on "vilification" and "hatred," instead of education, as agreed to in the MSA. The industry even went as far as threatening lawsuits, though none has yet materialized.[51] This tit for tat between the tobacco industries and the government continues, even under the auspices of a settlement.

NOTES

1. "Controversy Over Cigarette Advertising," *Congressional Digest* 48 (June–July, 1969), p. 168.
2. *Ibid.*
3. "Smoking: One Year Later," *Time* 87 (January 22, 1965), p. 58.
4. "Controversy Over Cigarette Advertising," p. 169.
5. "Rising Battle," *Time* 93 (February 14, 1969), p. 85.
6. "Controversy Over Cigarette Advertising," p. 168
7. James L. Hamilton, "The Demand for Cigarettes: Advertising, the Health Scare, and the Cigarette Advertising Ban," *Review of Economics and Statistics* 54 (November 1972), p. 408.
8. "Rising Battle," *Time*, p. 85.
9. *Ibid.*
10. "The Moral Minefield of Cigarette Advertising," *Business and Society Review* 51 (Fall 1984), p. 14.
11. 15 U.S.C., #1335.
12. "A Bright Spark for Cigarette Makers," *Business Week* (December 26, 1970), p. 64.
13. "Surveillance for Selected Tobacco-Use Behaviors–United States, 1900–1994," *Morbidity and Mortality Weekly Report* 43 (November 18, 1994), p. 7.
14. Dan Morain, "Legislature Aims Fusillade of Bills at Tobacco Industry," *The Los Angeles Times*, March 10, 1993, p. A1.
15. Susan Duerksen, "S.D. County Smoking Rate 3rd-Lowest in U.S. in 2000," *The San Diego Union-Tribune*, December 23, 2001, p. B1.
16. Charles Trueheart, "The Tobacco Industry's Advertising Smoke Screen," *USA Today*, March 15, 1985, p. 3D.
17. Kenneth E. Warner, "Cigarette Advertising and Media Coverage of Smoking and Health," *New England Journal of Medicine* 312 (February 7, 1985), pp. 384–88.
18. Sam Zagoria, "Smoking and the Media's Responsibility," *The Washington Post*, December 18, 1985, p. A26.

19. Eugene E. Levitt and Judith A. Edwards, "A Multivariate Study of Correlative Factors in Youthful Cigarette Smoking," *Developmental Psychology* 2, no. 2 (1970), pp. 5–11; and E. E. Levitt, "Reasons for Smoking and Not Smoking Given by School Children," *Journal of Public Health* (February 1971), pp. 101–4.

20. Paul Farhi, "Clinton Mover May Doom Colorful Cigarette Ads," *The Washington Post*, August 11, 1995, p. D1.

21. Anthony Ramirez, "Advertising: Proposed Regulations," *The New York Times*, August 14, 1995, p. D6.

22. Melanie Wells, "Magazines Blur Lines," *USA Today*, November 3, 1997, p. 12B.

23. Mitchell Zuckoff, "Kicking the Connection," *The Boston Sunday Globe*, July 2, 1995, p. 65.

24. Alison Muscatine and Spencer Rich, "Sullivan: Cut Tobacco, Sports Links," *The Washington Post*, April 11, 1991, pp. A1, A4.

25. *Ibid.*

26. "Cincinnati Will Prohibit Outdoor Ads for Tobacco," *The New York Times*, June 4, 1994, p. A9.

27. For example, in Fenway Park in Boston, a Marlboro billboard had been placed above the right field bleachers and could be seen on TV every time the camera captured a home run or a play in the outfield. See Mitchell Zuckoff, "Is it safe or out? U. S., Philip Morris dispute Marlboro sign at Fenway Park," *The Boston Sunday Globe*, July 2, 1995, p. 66.

28. Mitchell Zuckoff, "Kicking the Connection," *The Boston Sunday Globe*, July 2, 1995, p. 65.

29. Suein Hwang, "Philip Morris Agrees to Stop Placing Ads in View of TV," *The Wall Street Journal*, June 7, 1995, p. B5.

30. Steven Colford and Ira Teinowitz, "Teen Smoking and Ads Linked," *Advertising Age* 65 (February 21, 1994), pp. 1+.

31. Centers for Disease Control, "Targeting Tobacco Use: The Nation's Leading Cause of Death," last updated September 6, 2001. www.cdc.gov/tobacco/overview/oshaag.html, viewed on January 25, 2002.

32. "Surveillance for Selected Tobacco-Use-Behaviors–United States, 1900–1994."

33. Susan Duerksen, "S.D. County Smoking Rate 3rd-Lowest in U.S. in 2000," *The San Diego Union-Tribune*, December 23, 2001, p. B1.

34. Paul Farhi, "Kool's Penguin Draws Health Officials' Heat," *The Washington Post*, October 23, 1991, pp. C1, C7.

35. Paul Barrett, "Supreme Court Gives Green Light to Suit Against Tobacco Concern's Cartoon Ads," *The Wall Street Journal*, November 29, 1994, p. A24.

36. Steven W. Colford, "Joe Camel Heads for Showdown in California Court," *Advertising Age* (December 5, 1994), p. 16.

37. Stuart Elliot, "The F.T.C. Explains Its Joe Camel Decision," *The New York Times*, June 8, 1994, p. D2.

38. Warren Richey, "Clinton Proposal an Attempt to Snuff out Teen Smoking," *The Christian Science Monitor*, August 23, 1996, p. 3.

39. "FDA and Tobacco," Philip Morris Companies, Inc., Press Room, as viewed on January 30, 2002. http://www.philipmorris.com/pressroom/lit_reg/microsites/fda_regulation/white_paper.asp

40. *Ibid.*

41. Charles King and Michael Siegel, "The Master Settlement Agreement with the Tobacco Industry and Cigarette Advertising in Magazines," *The New England Journal of Medicine* 345 (August 16, 2001), p. 509.

42. *Ibid.*, pp. 507–508.

43. *Ibid.*, pp. 508–510.

44. Alex Kuczynski, "Tobacco Companies Accused of Still Aiming Ads at Youths," *The New York Times*, August 15, 2001, p. A1.

45. Ron Scherer, "Federal Lawsuit Is Next Test for Big Tobacco," *The Christian Science Monitor*, September 23, 1999, p. 2.

46. *Ibid.*

47. "Judge Kessler Reaffirms Dismissal of Two Counts in DOJ-Tobacco Suit," Philip Morris Companies, Inc., Pressroom, as viewed on February 1, 2002. www.philipmorris.com/pressroom/press_releases/dojrelease.asp

48. Marc Kaufman, "Ashcroft Signals Support of Tobacco Suit," *The Washington Post*, October 7, 2001, p. A11.

49. *Ibid.*

50. Charles Lane, "Tobacco Industry Wins Ad Victory," *The Washington Post*, June 29, 2001, p. A1.

51. Peter Carlson, "Big Tobacco Burned by Cigarette Spots," *The Washington Post*, August 10, 2001, p. C1

Marketing Alcoholic Beverages and Its Impact on Underage Drinkers

The question of whether and in what forms alcoholic drinks are deliberately marketed to underage drinkers by the beer, wine, and spirits industries has been a perennial concern. Several marketing strategies have sustained the debate in recent years.

CISCO WINE

One influential case involved the drink Cisco, a wine strengthened with grape brandy and manufactured by the Canandaigua Wine Company of New York State. This product was brought into public view on the night of May 27, 1990, when intoxicated Maryland teenager Donnell Petite hurled rocks at motorists passing by on the Capital Beltway, causing permanent brain damage to a teenage passenger. Before the incident, Petite and his friends had purchased and consumed two 24-ounce bottles of Cisco.

Cisco's clear glass container and wraparound neck label made its appearance almost identical to that of standard wine coolers. However, the alcohol content was not equal in the two. The wine industry divides its products into three categories, each roughly defined by average alcohol content. Most wine coolers contain 4 to 5 percent alcohol. In comparison, the industry defines "table wines" as products containing up to a 14-percent alcohol level. Finally, the "dessert wine" category includes all wines with alcohol content above 14 percent, usually an 18- to 20-percent level. Classified by Canandaigua as a "fortified dessert wine," Cisco had a 20 percent alcohol content level, even though its packaging gave Cisco a "cooler style" appearance.

Consumer advocates such as the National Council on Alcoholism and Drug Dependence (NCADD) alleged that purchasers, particularly underage drinkers, did not realize the wine's potency because of its stylish packaging. These interest groups feared that the wine's cooler-style packaging could cause people to mistake Cisco for a regular wine cooler with a low-alcohol content.

This case was prepared, at different times, by John Cuddihy, Jeff Greene, Michael Hammer, and Dianna Spring, under the supervision of Tom L. Beauchamp. Not to be duplicated without permission of the holder of the copyright, © 1992, 1996, 2003 by Tom L. Beauchamp.

Cisco's potency also prompted U.S. Surgeon General Antonia Novello to declare Cisco "a dangerous fortified wine, and the ultimate 'wine fooler.' "[1]

Consumer complaints alerted various public interest organizations, including NCADD and the Center for Science in the Public Interest (CSPI), about the public's concern over Cisco's unadvertised potency. These organizations researched Cisco and its effects, and alerted the public to what they saw as the dangers of Cisco.[2] During this time Canandaigua used the slogan "Cisco takes you by surprise" as a marketing technique.

Disturbed by the results of its research, NCADD—in cooperation with CSPI, Mothers Against Drunk Driving (MADD), and Representative John Conyers (D-Mich.)—asked Canandaigua to voluntarily withdraw Cisco from sale and to alter its marketing techniques to better inform the public of Cisco's alcohol content. Southland Corporation, the owner of 7-Eleven stores, decided to remove Cisco from all of the company-owned stores[3] and sent letters to the remaining stores, all of which are run by franchises, strongly urging them to discontinue selling the product.[4] In similar actions, the state of Maine banned all sales of Cisco, and a midwestern food chain (Food-4-Less) removed the fortified dessert wine from its shelves.

Canandaigua's management never acknowledged any validity regarding these concerns. Though the company agreed that Cisco's twelve-ounce bottle bore "some resemblance" to the wine coolers produced by the Seagram's and Gallo companies, it contended that the superficial likenesses did not warrant a packaging adjustment.[5] Canandaigua pointed to Cisco's distinctive packaging features: "Whereas wine coolers are almost universally sold in 4-packs of bottles, Cisco is sold in single bottles."[6] The company also maintained that "Cisco's 'hot,' high-alcohol taste immediately tells the consumer it is not a low-alcohol cooler."[7] However, faced with growing pressure to repackage Cisco and properly identify the drink's potency to distinguish it from a wine cooler, Canandaigua announced new marketing and labeling plans in October 1990. It opted to label Cisco bottles with the warning "This is not a wine cooler" in the largest print allowed under federal regulations, and it agreed to remove the controversial point-of-purchase slogan "Cisco takes you by surprise."

However, NCADD and CSPI continued their grass-roots campaigns to get Canandaigua to redesign Cisco's packaging to look like a fortified wine instead of a wine cooler. As consumer advocates feared, teenage intoxication cases involving Cisco continued to increase, despite Canandaigua's warning labels.[8] The mushrooming public uproar over Cisco soon attracted the attention of Congress, the Treasury Department's Bureau of Alcohol, Tobacco, and Firearms (BATF), and the Federal Trade Commission, which gave consumer advocates the opportunity to effect national regulatory action against Cisco. Though some state governments supported the Cisco recall movement, they wielded no authority outside of their borders. Despite the government's concerns and occasional requests or demands, Canandaigua did not repackage Cisco.

Canandaigua Chairman Marvin Sands contended in early 1991 that Cisco had been made the scapegoat for the problem of underage drinking. The company insisted that consumer groups had targeted Cisco for action, even though other, stronger dessert (strengthened) wines enjoyed national marketing without negative publicity. Canandaigua's management argued that popular sherries, ports, and marsala wines rivaled Cisco's alcohol content levels, whereas other alcoholic beverages, such as brandy, contained 40 percent alcohol. Cisco's producers insisted that the advocacy groups unfairly "made what is true of a class of beverages appear to be true of Cisco only."[9] Canandaigua considered the groups' actions discriminatory because they ignored the alcoholic content and effects of other strengthened brands.

According to Sands, "Cisco doesn't play any more of a role [in alcohol abuse] than any other brand. We've never had a single complaint about it from a consumer, retailer or wholesaler. All we've seen are allegations and accusations."[10] In later correspondence with Representative George Miller, Sands stated that "When [Cisco] is consumed responsibly by persons over 21, there is no 'serious health hazard' associated with Cisco."[11]

Nonetheless, NCADD and federal officials independently pressed their cases. Faced with the serious potential of a ban on all Cisco shipments outside New York State—unless it altered Cisco's bottle and label design—Canandaigua's management finally reached an agreement with federal authorities. On February 4, 1991, Canandaigua officials presented proposed modifications to Cisco's packaging to Surgeon General Novello. The plans changed Cisco's bottle color from clear to dark green and replaced the bottle's short neck with a longer, more slender neck. Canandaigua altered the twelve-ounce bottle label so that it read "THIS CONTAINER SERVES 4 PEOPLE AND IS BEST SERVED OVER ICE." The company also retained its warning label "This is not a wine cooler" on all Cisco bottles. According to Sands, "The new Cisco package looks like no other product on the market today."[12] Company officials made the new bottles available to distributors during the spring of 1991.

The Surgeon General, the Federal Trade Commission, and the BATF announced that these changes satisfactorily addressed their objections about the former package, and the government abandoned its plans for regulatory action against Canandaigua.

ALCOPOPS

In 1996, a drink called Hooper's Hooch gained sufficient popularity in Britain that companies such as Bass (a British brewer) and Anheuser-Busch began testing Hooch and similar drinks in the United States.[13] Hooch was the first wave of a group of alcoholic lemonades, colas, and orange drinks now known as "alcopops." Today, these drinks are found in a number of labels and flavors. They are often more alcoholic than beers and cater to tastes already familiar to youthful customers. Some firms see this new market niche as an opportunity to target the "aging children of baby boomers." This group, who are "reaching drink age" and who were "raised on cartons of fruit drinks," is "attracted to a beverage that combines the sweet taste of juice with alcohol," said M. Shanken Communications, which produced *Impact's Wine Study 2001.*[14]

Concerns about the marketing of these drinks are not unlike those in the marketing of Cisco: "These drinks are there to help people who don't have a taste for alcohol to develop one," said Mark Bennett of the British advocacy group Alcohol Concern.[15] More recently, in the United States, the Center for Science in the Public Interest—the same group that led the criticism of Canandaigua's Cisco—attacked Hooper's Hooch and other "alternative beverage brands"—such as Smirnoff Ice and Mike's Hard Lemonade—claiming that the "sweet and fruity alcoholic beverages are trying to woo kids."[16] Subsequent to this claim, CSPI conducted a study of name-brand recognition and consumption of alcopops in the fourteen to eighteen age group. The study found that 86 percent of those who first tried alcopops did so because of the taste. Thirty percent of teens reported that alcopops provided the drinks they would most like to try, in comparison with 16 percent for beer and 16 percent for mixed drinks.

In May 2001, CSPI filed a complaint—similar to complaints against Cisco—with the Bureau of Alcohol, Tobacco, and Firearms and the Federal Trade Commission calling for "label and marketing changes" to make the marketing strategies less targeted to youth.[17] (As of February 2003, no action had been taken in response to the CSPI complaint.)[18] CSPI claims that youths fourteen to eighteen years of age are lured by "malternatives" because of the colorful packaging and the flavors, which are marketed for a younger taste.[19] In September 2002, CSPI again wrote to the Director of the Bureau of Alcohol, Tobacco, and Firearms. CSPI stated that the consumer is not adequately protected by current regulations.[20] A study conducted by CSPI in June 2002 concluded that underage drinkers believe that alcopops contain hard liquor and that when they see television advertisements for these products, they falsely associate them with hard-liquor brands such as Jack Daniels.[21] CSPI considers the marketing misleading because of the explicit use of brand names such as Smirnoff and Skyy (suggesting vodka), when in reality these drinks do not contain hard-liquor. Alcopops is merely a carbonated malt beverage that contains sweet flavoring to mask the taste of the alcohol so that it tastes like juice or soda.

According to BATF this marketing is "not in itself misleading." When packaged as a malt beverage, alcopops became more available to underage drinkers. In contrast to distilled products like vodka, which cannot be sold in convenience stores such as 7-Eleven, malt beverages are allowed to be sold in convenience stores. Thus, alcopops uses awareness of the hard-liquor association while being more easily accessible to underage drinkers (approximately eight times as many outlets could carry the product).

Beverage corporations deny accusations that they are targeting youth. "We've never had a serious complaint from anyone that we're marketing these products to underage kids," said Phil Lynch, vice president of communications for Brown-Forman, which marketed Jack Daniel's Country Cocktails, another "alternative beverage brand." Marketers of various brands also maintain that they are careful to monitor the placement of ads to avoid those under twenty-one.[22] They question whether a high rate of teenage recognition of name brands is indicative of a strategy of targeting youth. Regarding the alleged link between advertising and underage drinking, Charles Atkins, who conducted the last FTC study on the subject in 1985, had this to say: "It depends on who is interpreting the data. I think the impact of alcohol advertising on underage drinking is probably small, but still significant."[23] The same questions that surrounded Cisco's labeling and marketing here reappear.

Also similar is the confusion over what these beverages are and how much alcohol concentration they contain. In February 2001, Glacier Bay Vodka, another "alternative beverage," launched into the alcopop niche by creating a fruity drink using orange, berry, cran-grapefruit and lemonade flavors, spiked with vodka, in the end creating a drink with a 5.9 percent alcohol "kick."[24] This niche is quickly growing in popularity and is making up for the void after wine coolers peaked in popularity in the late 1980s and early 1990s.[25] Although the alcohol content of alcopops and alternative beverages ranges between 5 percent and 7 percent, considerably under Cisco's 20 percent, critics wonder whether consumers, because of the light, fruity tastes of these drinks, realize that they are about as potent as most beers. This question is largely unanswered in empirical studies.

Conflicts have occurred between manufacturers over the marketing of these drinks. In February 2002, the National Advertising Division of the Council of Better Business Bureaus in New York forwarded a complaint to the FTC and ATF after Mark Anthony International—producer of Mike's Hard Lemonade—complained that Smirnoff Ice was using deceptive marketing techniques. Mark Anthony claimed that marketing the product using Smirnoff Vodka's "red color and eagle logo" was "confusing consumers into expecting Smirnoff vodka to be an ingredient in Smirnoff Ice when it contains no vodka."[26]

ABSOLUT AND OTHER VODKAS

The marketing of hard liquor has recently resurfaced as part of the controversy about alcohol advertising and its effects on underage drinkers. Controversy started with Absolut vodka, which has drawn a great deal of attention over the last twenty years. It has run what is widely considered to have been one of the most successful marketing campaigns ever. As Ben Wightman in *Public Relations Quarterly* notes, "The dream of any advertiser is to create an ad campaign so recognizable and so popular that the ads become news themselves. . . . Absolut Vodka's 'Absolut campaign' has gone down in the collective consciousness of American culture."[27] The Absolut campaign has come to be considered both art and news. Still, as Charles Madigan notes, "Vodka is vodka, by definition—potatoes, grain, molasses. No matter what it is distilled from, it comes out strong and clear and tastes pretty much the same. In the case of Absolut, it was the packaging and marketing that made the difference."[28]

For nearly twenty years—peaking in popularity in the late 1990s—Absolut has used ads that intentionally placed the Absolut bottle in "various shapes and settings." For example, an ad titled "Absolut San Francisco" displayed the bottle shrouded in fog; "Absolut Hitchcock" had a bottle reminiscent of Alfred Hitchcock's profile. In 1996, Absolut published the "Absolut Book: The Absolut Vodka Advertising Story," which had sold 150,000 copies by 1997.[29] These ads have taken on great popularity with teens and even preteens. Critics see a clear association between this marketing strategy and teen-friendly icons such as Joe Camel. They express concern about ads that create "spillover" by their appeal to underage drinkers. Kirk Davidson, professor of business ethics at St. Mary's College, stated, "I think Absolut is one of those curiosities that you really can't explain or plan for. . . . But there are plenty of examples, mostly beer and malt beverages, where the manufacturers can well be criticized, just like Joe Camel, for aiming at the margin."[30]

Reports about Absolut are often based on anecdotal evidence. For example, the *Christian Science* Monitor asks, "How do you measure the impact of Absolut vodka ads on Beth Gadomski? Beth, 17, has covered an entire wall of her bedroom with 150 Absolut vodka ads."[31] The *Washington Post* describes two other girls, Allie Kligman, thirteen at the time, and her then sixteen-year-old sister Jillian, who both also collected Absolut ads.[32] The Absolut website, too, is an artistic journey. In praise of the website, Edwin Mitchell-Finch writes, "Non-vodka drinkers would still enjoy the browse for a colorful journey. You can even use the site to send an e-card to a friend."[33] Another marketing tool, the website has extended the debate over Absolut's influence on underage drinkers. The site requires that a person be of legal drinking age in order to use the site, but an underage user is still able to go back, even without closing the browser, and present himself or herself as legally of age even after denying it.[34]

Many critics are more subdued in their assessment of Absolut ads than they have been of other hard liquors, particularly in expressing concerns about advertising on television. Absolut has generally stayed away from television and radio, primarily advertising in venues like the *New Yorker,* the *New York Times Magazine,* and *Art in America*—as well as *Sports Illustrated* and *Rolling Stone,* whose audiences are younger. Laurie Lieber, director of the Center on Alcohol Advertising, said, "We're most interested in reducing children's exposure on TV, radio and at point of sale. Magazine ads are a different issue. . . . An argument could be made that if kids are getting hold of these, there are ways to intervene without curbing the advertiser."[35]

An unofficial voluntary ban existed on advertising alcohol on television for fifty years. NBC television attempted to end this agreement in 2002 when it decided to air Smirnoff Vodka advertisements created by Diageo PLC—the United Kingdom–based company that owns Guinness, Smirnoff, and Johnny Walker.[36] This decision met with resistance from the medical community and the political arena. The American Medical Association (AMA) and the House of Representatives voiced opposition, claiming that research has proven that children are overexposed to advertisements for alcohol on television. However, it is worth nothing that NBC itself imposed nineteen self-regulations on its proposed Smirnoff Vodka advertisements, including allowing them to appear only after 9 P.M. and requiring the minimum age of all actors in the ad to be thirty years old. After 9 P.M. at least 85 percent of the viewers are estimated to be of legal drinking age. An additional self-imposed requirement for advertising on television was for the company to pay for social advertising against drunk driving.[37]

The House of Representatives threatened to hold a hearing on NBC's advertising policy unless it canceled the deal with Diageo PLC. Additional criticism of NBC came from beer advertisers, who hope to maintain their monopoly on airwave advertisements. NBC's advertising campaign never aired because of the opposition from Washington politicians and the beer and wine industries.[38]

NOTES

1. Public Statement of Antonia C. Novello, U.S. Surgeon General, press conference, January 9, 1991.
2. *FYI—Cisco Campaign Chronology.* Published by the National Council on Alcoholism and Drug Dependence, Inc., n.d., pp. 1–2.
3. "7-Eleven Stores to Remove Their Cisco Wine Supplies," *The Wall Street Journal,* January 9, 1991, p. B3.
4. Telephone conversation between Southland spokeswoman Mrs. Rosemary Fischer and John Cuddihy, January 28, 1991.
5. April 24, 1991, telephone conversation between John Cuddihy and Canandaigua Wine Company legal counsel Robert Sands.
6. *Cisco: The Controversy, the Facts, Actions,* p. 12. Privately published by the Canandaigua Wine Company, 1990.
7. *Ibid.*
8. Dr. Joseph Wright, pediatrician at the Children's National Medical Center in Washington, DC, *FORTIFIED WINES: A Wolf in Sheep's Clothing,* press release, November 1990. Dr. Wright's patients averaged 15.3 years of age, leading him to say, "Kids think it's a more benign product than it actually is. Kids are deceived by the color, taste, and packaging resemblances to wine coolers. Cisco represents an extreme health hazard to underage drinkers." Personal interview with Dr. Joseph Wright, February 6, 1991.
9. *Ibid.,* p. 7.
10. Laura Bird, "Novello Brands Cisco a 'Wine Fooler,'" *Adweek's Marketing Week,* January 14, 1991, p. 6.
11. Letter from Mr. Richard Sands, president, Canandaigua Wine Company, to Representative George Miller, chairman, Select Committee on Children, Youth, and Families, January 29, 1991.
12. *Canandaigua Unveils New Package for Cisco-Brand Fortified Wine,* Canandaigua Wine Company press release, February 5, 1991.
13. Tara Parker-Pope, "Spiked Sodas, Illicit Hit with British Kids, Head for U.S.," *The Wall Street Journal,* February 12, 1996.
14. Ellen Lee, "Danville, Calif.-Based Drink Maker Offers Low-Alcohol Vodka Beverages," *Knight Ridder/Tribune Business News,* February 10, 2001.
15. Tara Parker-Pope, "Spiked Sodas, Illicit Hit with British Kids, Head for U.S.," *The Denver Post,* February 18, 1996.

16. Theresa Howard, "Health Group Targets 'Alternative' Alcohol Beverage Marketing," *USA Today,* May 9, 2001.
17. *Ibid.*
18. Correspondence with CSPI Alcohol Policies Project. April 17, 2002.
19. *Ibid.*
20. Letter to BATF Director Bradley Buckles: http://www.cspinet.org/booze/BATFLetter 20917.htm
21. *Ibid.*
22. Correspondence with CSPI Alcohol Policies Project, April 17, 2002.
23. Ron Scherer and Nicole Gaouette, "Critics Take Aim at the Effect of Hip Commercials on Kids," *The Christian Science Monitor,* December 26, 1996.
24. Ellen Lee, "Danville, Calif.-Based Drink Maker Offers Low-Alcohol Vodka Beverages," February 10, 2001.
25. *Ibid.*
26. Stuart Elliott, "Two Agencies Receive Complaints on Promotion of Smirnoff Drink," *The New York Times,* February 22, 2002.
27. Ben Wightman, "Absolut: Biography of a Bottle," *Public Relations Quarterly,* Summer 2001, p. 6.
28. Charles M. Madigan, "How the Swedes Pulled It Off," *Across the Board,* May/June 2001, p. 84.
29. Kathleen Day, "Collecting, or Being Collected?; Teens' Absolut Ad Fad Raises Fear of Backlash on Alcohol Marketing," *The Washington Post,* August 2, 1997.
30. *Ibid.,* p. F1.
31. Ron Scherer and Nicole Gaouette, "Critics Take Aim at the Effect of Hip Commercials on Kids," *The Christian Science Monitor,* December 26, 1996.
32. Kathleen Day, "Collecting, or Being Collected? Teens' Absolut Ad Fad Raises Fear of Backlash on Alcohol Marketing," *The Washington Post,* August 2, 1997, p. F01.
33. Edwin Mitchell-Finch, "New Media Choice: Absolut.com," *Marketing,* February 22, 2001, p. 15.
34. See http://www.absolut.com
35. *Ibid.*
36. http://www.bizforward.com/wdc/issues/2002-03/firstforward/page03.shtml
37. http://www.hlclaw.com/Publications/Newsletters.asp?ID=245&Article=1403
38. Theresa Howard, "After Criticism, NBC Calls Off Liquor Ads," *USA Today,* March 21, 2002.

Nike's Defense of Its Vietnamese Factories

Like many other American apparel makers, Nike uses various subcontractors in Asia to manufacture its products. Some 150 Nike subcontracted factories employ more than 450,000 workers. In Nike's early days, before orders shifted to lower-cost suppliers in Taiwan and South Korea, the company imported its shoes from Japan. Soon, even Taiwan and South Korea became too expensive for this highly competitive market, and suppliers moved their factories to China and Indonesia. Then Nike found Vietnam. Soon Nike became Vietnam's largest single employer. Its factories in Vietnam are run by the company's South Korean and Taiwanese contractors, who employ tens of thousands of Vietnamese. By 1998, one out of every ten pairs of Nike shoes came from Vietnam. Shipments of Nike shoes alone accounted for 5 percent of Vietnam's total exports.[1]

One of Southeast Asia's poorest economies, Vietnam has an official rural unemployment of about 27 percent in some regions. It seeks foreign investment to create jobs and bring in manufacturing expertise. However, unlike many governments that do not investigate worker abuses, Vietnam pays close attention to the practices of its foreign investors and has some of the region's toughest laws aimed at protecting workers. It ensures a minimum wage, sets overtime limits, and permits strikes. Vietnamese government officials, however, have divided priorities. While union leaders say that they are duty-bound to defend workers, investment planners want trade unions to not scare away foreign investors. If Nike were to pull out of Vietnam, 35,000 Vietnamese would be out of work.[2]

ALLEGATIONS OF ABUSE

In the mid-1990s, allegations of worker abuses in factories that contracted with Nike began to mount. An investigation of Nike labor practices in Vietnam was launched in 1998. The report found that by not directly running the factories where its products were made, Nike had little control over internal labor conditions. The report, focusing on factories in and around Ho Chi Minh City,

This case was prepared by Sasha Lyutse, under the supervision of Tom L. Beauchamp. Not to be duplicated without permission of the holder of the copyright, © 2003 by Tom L. Beauchamp.

found local supervisors using abusive and humiliating practices to punish Vietnamese workers. Nike denied that workers were being abused in these factories, insisting that the company did not tolerate abuse and required its manufacturers to take "immediate and effective measures to deal with it."[3] There may have been isolated cases of poor management, the company said, but such cases have never been "typical of Nike factories."[4]

Nike also noted that it has contracts with factories that employ at least 500,000 workers in more than fifty countries, so that there are bound to be local problems, including cultural differences, that sometimes make it difficult to impose American-style business and management practices.[5] In order to mitigate these differences, the company said, a Nike training manager works with subcontractors on problems of sexual harassment, physical and verbal abuse, and listening skills. The 1998 report found that Nike had "a fine code of conduct" but that its local contractors consistently violated it.[6]

COMPARATIVE SALARY LEVELS

In 1998, Nike employees at the Sam Yang factory, just outside Ho Chi Minh City, were paid $1.84 a day. Their average monthly salary was $48.00, slightly better than Vietnam's $45.00 minimum wage for this region. With this salary, Nike workers could meet their basic needs, including food and shelter, but little else. Nike and its suppliers were paying competitive wages—no worse and no better than those paid by other foreign shoe and clothing manufacturers.[7]

Nike is one of the world's most profitable sportswear companies. Phillip Knight, founder of Nike's $9 billion sports-apparel empire, signs sports superstars to multimillion-dollar contracts to advertise Nike sneakers that sometimes sell for $100 or more on the American market. A pair of Nike sneakers is unattainable for a worker at the Sam Yang factory, who works six days a week and makes roughly $600 a year, half the average income in Ho Chi Minh City, but about four times the annual earnings in more remote rural regions of Vietnam.[8]

THE NIKE RESPONSE

Pressure on Nike to enforce its vision of good labor practices has continued for years. Criticism has come from American college students demanding that their sports teams drop Nike products, a series of petitions signed by politicians, and anti-Nike web-sites. Nike has responded by creating a labor monitoring department and has translated its code of conduct into eleven languages so that more workers could read it. At the Sam Yang factory, the local owners issued a ten-point "action plan" based on many of the 1998 report's recommendations. They held a union election, signed a labor contract with workers, and improved working conditions. The factory also got a new manager, increased trainees' wages, and cut down on overtime. Most workers got a 5 percent raise, which came to about 8 cents more per day.[9]

In addition, Phillip Knight made six promises regarding Nike shoe factories during a May 12, 1998, speech at the National Press Club in Washington, D.C.:

- All Nike shoe factories would meet U.S. Occupational Health and Safety Administration indoor air quality standards.
- The minimum age would be raised to 18 for Nike shoe factories, 16 for clothing factories.
- Nike would include non-governmental organizations, or NGOs, in factory monitoring, and the company would make inspection results public.
- Nike would expand its worker education program, making free high-school equivalency courses available.
- A micro-enterprise loan program would be expanded to benefit 4,000 families in Vietnam, Indonesia, Pakistan and Thailand.
- Research and forums on responsible business practices would be funded at four universities.[10]

However, a subsequent report issued by the Global Exchange concluded that "the projects Knight announced have been of little benefit to Nike workers" or "have helped only a tiny minority, or else have no relevance to Nike factories at all." "Nike workers," it said, "are still forced to work excessive hours in high pressure work environments, are not paid enough to meet the most basic needs of their children, and are subject to harassment, dismissal and violent intimidation if they try to form unions or tell journalists about labor abuses in their factories."[11]

A 2001 report by the Global Alliance—this time an initiative sponsored by Nike itself in response to persisting criticism—again presented evidence of abusive labor practices in Southeast Asian Nike subcontracted factories, including physical, verbal and sexual abuse. According to the report, 96 percent of workers claimed that they did not make enough money to meet their basic needs.[12]

ALLEGATIONS OF FALSE ADVERTISING

Between 1998 and 2003, Nike's human-rights problems resurfaced in the public eye in a new form. In the mid-1990s, Nike began to counter allegations of worker abuses. The company attempted to justify its workers' wages and to explain working conditions at its overseas plants. It commissioned a study, which it publicized in the media, concluding that its workers were well-treated, paid twice the local minimum wage, provided with health care, and protected from physical abuse.[13] This response was to critics who alleged that Nike was treating the sweatshop-issue more as a public relations problem than a serious human rights matter.

In 1998, Nike was sued by San Francisco activist Marc Kasky for *false advertisement*. Kasky alleged that Nike violated California's false-advertising and unfair-competition statutes when it made false statements in interviews, letters to newspapers, and other nonadvertising forums, extolling the benefits of globalization and defending its overseas labor practices.[14] Kasky claimed that Nike was inaccurate and focused solely on protecting its image and selling more sneakers, not bringing about real change in labor practices. He also asserted that Nike deliberately made false statements aimed at misleading the public when it denied that its subcontractors mistreated workers in Southeast Asian shoe factories.

In May 2002, the California Supreme Court allowed Kasky to pursue his suit under a California state consumer-protection law, ruling that Nike's public statements could be construed as a form of advertising. The Court applied its ruling to statements that appear in op-eds and editorials, as well as to comments made to reporters (thus, not limited to paid commercial advertisements).[15] In Nike's case, the speech at issue included communications such as letters to the editor, in which the company responded to public criticism about alleged workplace conditions in Asian-contracted footwear factories.[16] According to Kasky's attorney, "The lawsuit specifically describes numerous factual misrepresentations Nike made to the public about the labor practices in the factories that manufacture its shoes. These misrepresentations were not part of any political debate, but were made by Nike to encourage customers to buy a pair of its shoes."[17]

Nike, joined by a diverse group of public interest organizations, businesses, media outlets, and associations—including The New York Times Co., Pfizer, CNN, and the U.S. Chamber of Commerce—urged the United States Supreme Court to review the California ruling. The U.S. Supreme Court has agreed to hear the case. At stake is whether corporations should be given free speech rights to defend themselves and their practices without fear of being sued. In support of Nike, some two-dozen news organizations have said in court filings that a fear of lawsuits would keep company executives from talking freely to the public and the press and could lead to a flood of lawsuits against companies merely for defending themselves. Nike and its supporters say that the ruling could apply to almost any public statement a company might issue regarding its corporate practices, including a remark to the media, thus deterring corporations from communicating even on matters of genuine public interest.[18]

On its website, Nike points out that the U.S. Supreme Court has defined commercial speech as "speech that does no more than propose a commercial transaction" and that the Nike statements cited in the suit did not "propose a commercial transaction" in any respect. "Nike editorials, comments to reporters, and even direct communications to consumers," the company maintains, "neither discussed particular products nor addressed the price or quality of the Nike line of goods."[19] As a result of the California court decision, Nike also announced that it would break precedent and would not in 2003 publicly release its 2002 annual corporate responsibility report. This report reviews the initiatives and progress the company has made in its labor compliance, community affairs, sustainable development, and workplace programs. The company also recently declined to participate in several media interviews and declined invitations to speak at various business and academic forums about such issues as globalization. The company asserts that there is now a danger that even true statements, made publicly, could be deemed misleading.[20]

NOTES

1. "Nike Battles Labour Charges; U.S. Firm Makes Changes After Alleged Worker Abuses in Vietnam," *The Toronto Star*, April 2, 1998, p. D8.
2. *Ibid.*
3. *Ibid.*
4. "Labor-rights Group: Nike, Knight Not Living Up to 1998 Promises," *The Associated Press State & Local Wire* (May 16, 2001), from web.lexis-nexis.com
5. *Ibid.*
6. "Nike Battles Labour Charges; U.S. Firm Makes Changes After Alleged Worker Abuses in Vietnam," *The Toronto Star*, April 2, 1998, p. D8.
7. *Ibid.*
8. *Ibid.*
9. *Ibid.*
10. "Labor-rights Group: Nike, Knight Not Living Up to 1998 Promises," *The Associated Press State & Local Wire* (May 16, 2001), from web.lexis-nexis.com
11. *Ibid.*
12. "The Living Wage Project to Brief Members of Congress on Nike Labor Abuses," *PR Newswire Association, Inc.* (April 3, 2001), from web.lexis-nexis.com
13. "Supreme Court to Take up Nike and Free Speech," *The San Francisco Chronicle*, January 11, 2003, p. A3.
14. "Nike Ruling: Just How Chilling Is It? An Answer May Have to Come From Washington," *National Law Journal* 25 (January 20, 2003), p. A9.
15. "U.S. Supreme Court Agrees to Hear Landmark First Amendment Case," *PR Newswire Association, Inc.* (January 10, 2003), from web.lexis-nexis.com
16. *Ibid.*
17. "Nike Speech Case Goes to High Court; Justices to Rule on Artistic vs. 'Commercial' Expression," *The Washington Post*, January 11, 2003, p. E1.
18. *Ibid.*
19. www.nikebiz.com
20. "U.S. Supreme Court Agrees to Hear Landmark First Amendment Case," *PR Newswire Association, Inc.* (January 10, 2003), from web.lexis-nexis.com

CHAPTER FIVE

Problems of Justice: The Unfair and the Unfortunate

Acme Title Pawn: High Risk, High Reward

Joe Scruples was reflecting on his current situation with his employer, Acme Title Pawn, while mindlessly mowing his lawn. He had been working at Acme for about a year, but he found himself increasingly worried about his employer. During all of his years of struggling to raise his young family while planning for, attending, and ultimately graduating from college, he never envisioned a career at a firm like Acme Title Pawn. His reservations about the business began to surface by the end of his first day at work, and they have since increased.

Joe is thirty six years old, with a wife and three children. His first full-time job was as an accounts payable clerk at a medical center. After working there for four years, he quit that position to accept another similar position at a printing plant in the town where his soon-to-be wife was employed. He remained employed with that firm, Ace Printing, for a total of nine years until he lost his job as a result of downsizing. By that time he realized that he needed a college education if he hoped to have a meaningful career with job security. He then attended college part-time at night; he supported himself and his family through a succession of jobs, none of which lasted more than a year. He was a clerk in a hospital, an appliance salesman, and an accounts payable clerk for a small manufacturing firm. Approximately one year ago he accepted the position of accounting staff member at Acme Title Pawn.

At the time that he accepted the position, he knew virtually nothing about the title pawn industry, but he saw that this firm would offer him the possibility of increased responsibility, an advantage not offered by his previous positions. Also, the pay for accountants was excellent in this firm. Moreover, they expected sharp eyes and perfect books; there were no accounting scandals here.

Six months into the job with Acme, Joe finally graduated from college with a degree in accounting. It had been a difficult struggle, and he hoped that soon there would be a payoff. Now, he wondered, is this job as good as it gets for someone like me? Joe's concerns were not with the pay or the accounting work. He had become disenchanted with the title pawn industry in general,

---

This case was prepared by Roland B. Cousins and revised by Tom L. Beauchamp. Not to be duplicated without permission of the holder of the copyright, © 2003 by Tom L. Beauchamp. All names and locations in this case are disguised to assure anonymity; however, this case represents an actual situation as experienced by the employee here named "Joe Scruples."

185

and Acme in particular, because of the way the business is run. It seemed apparent to him that the industry preyed on the poor and undereducated—people below where even he had been when he worked in low-level jobs, had young children, and had to pay college tuition.

Joe had learned about so-called "usurious interest rates" in his business law class, but he had imagined that they applied largely to the loan shark on the street corner. The interest rate on his only credit card was 18 percent on the unpaid balance, and he was unaware that legal interest rates could be much greater than that in any industry. He was shocked when he discovered that Acme conducted business by using far higher interest rates—and that it was legal.

If a customer needed a loan, Acme would lend money on the individual's automobile, holding the title as collateral. The maximum amount Acme would lend was 50 *percent* of the car's book value. The creditor was allowed to keep driving the car as long as the specified payments were made.

The standard loan was for one month with an interest rate of 25 percent *per month*. Accordingly, if a customer borrowed $1,000 on the car, then $250 must be paid back at the end of the month, or the car would be seized and sold at auction to satisfy the debt. Occasionally, Acme would extend the credit for several more months as long as the interest was paid every month. A customer borrowing $1,000 for a four-month period would have paid $1,000 in interest and would still owe the $1,000 principal at the end of the fourth month. At that time, or at the end of any month when the principal remained unpaid, the vehicle could be seized. Customers commonly paid over 350 percent annualized interest, though usually the loans were carried only from one to six months.

Because the business of repossession can get very ugly, subcontractors were employed to perform that service in each city in which Acme maintained an office. State laws in most states require that the debtor be paid the difference between the amount owed and the proceeds from the sale of the vehicle, minus any expenses incurred. Acme paid the repossessor an average of $100, a locksmith was typically paid $25, and the cleanup and sale of the vehicle at auction usually cost Acme about $75 to $100. There can also be a transportation charge, depending on the distance from the spot where the vehicle is seized to the location of the auctioneer.

Joe soon learned that the company did not automatically return any excess after the sale to the debtor. Only if the debtor called and inquired was a check sent; but if the debtor did not ask, the check would not be sent unless state law was absolutely explicit on this requirement. Joe knew of a few cases in which the check had been sent without a request, but these seemed to be cases in which there was a likelihood that a complaint by the debtor would be filed with authorities.

Individuals who pawned their car titles generally were people who had no alternative if they were to raise cash. These were people in a financial crisis who were forced to resort to the costliest way to obtain money legally. A typical case is a person who has been out of work, has just moved into the state and found a job, and needs money to live on until the first paycheck comes in two to four weeks.

The title loan industry presents itself in advertisements as a headache-free small business that caters to individuals and that fills a large void in society as a service to those with poor credit ratings or those down on their luck and unable to find financial help. The volume of loans in the states in which Acme maintains offices shows that there is a vast market for such loans. The reason is simple: It is an industry that will make loans to customers to whom no bank will loan—and in small amounts that no bank will make, even if a person has good credit.

Many customers are high-risk. This danger is the official justification for the fact that the 25 percent interest rate is more than twelve times the usury rate for banks in most of the states in which Acme conducts business. Lobbyists have convinced state officials of the high risks of serving customers in this business: Many customers present automobile titles from out-of-state, do not have an in-state driver's license, and have a poor credit history, possibly including bankruptcy. Some customers have stolen the title as well as the automobile, and some run off with the money. In some cases the repossessed vehicle has been wrecked or is in need of repairs that would cost more than the vehicle is worth. The nearest junkyard that pays for vehicles (in contrast to supplying nothing but fee towing) is forty miles away and subtracts towing costs. Joe's immediate supervisor, who has been in the business for six years, has a line that he uses in every training course: "I tell you straight out that we charge extremely high interest rates, but this is the riskiest business I have ever encountered. If you have a tender heart, you will not be in this business a year from now."

Consumer advocates have prevailed in several states in which Acme does not do business. Their argument is that legislation allowing extremely high interest rates sets consumers up to have their cars taken away from them. These states have very different consumer finance legislation.

Although its customers may have bad credit or no credit, Acme does no credit investigation if a clear title is presented. Acme functions as the lender of last resort for most clients, although Joe has suspected that some clients would have other alternatives if they understood the cost of doing business with Acme. Some clients understood, but many others did not understand, the steep character of the interest rates. Often it was unclear what the customer understood.

One day Joe had met a customer in the company parking lot. The customer had come to make the final payment on his loan. He told his story: He was a retired state road worker and had little cash income. One morning his eleven-year old Buick LaSalle encountered significant engine problems, needing an estimated $900 in repairs. He had nowhere to turn except Acme: "You guys really helped me out. We depend completely on that car, and I had no other way to get it fixed. Thanks." As Joe and the retiree talked on, Joe realized that in making this final payment, the customer had now paid, in interest alone, over 175 percent of the money loaned. The percentage of interest on a loan was not meaningful to this man; he understood only how much he had to pay each month and how long it would take to pay off the loan.

Acme tended to locate its offices in African-American neighborhoods in most cities in which it did business. In Florida, Acme's business was quite visible in Hispanic areas. Acme also directed its marketing efforts toward gamblers in areas likely to have down-on-their-luck gamblers, such as Nevada and the Mississippi Gulf Coast. However, there was no discrimination by race, sex, occupation, or anything else in this business; anyone who presented a valid title would get a loan.

The company presently operates in twelve states. If a state in which Acme is operating lowers the legal interest rate that can be charged to less than 22 percent per month, Acme stops doing business in that state. Acme recently suspended operations in North Carolina and Kentucky for this reason.

Because the industry is unregulated, only poor statistics exist on how many title lending institutions there are, how many loans they make per year, what the rate of return on loans is, and the like. One study indicates that there are approximately 400 title loan shops in Florida alone, each with thousands of loan commitments at any one time. In states in which the practice is legal, title loans are treated as pawnshop transactions, but, unlike the case for pawnshops, state statutes do not allow for any form of mediation in consumer disputes with title lenders. There also are no requirements for bonding, and no background checks are conducted of owners or managers. Title loan shop spokespersons like to point out that there is one great difference between their business and conventional pawn shops: The owner deposits only a title, while continuing to drive the car.

Acme had encountered many difficulties in the field, as one would expect considering the nature of the business and its locations. There had been a number of armed robberies at Acme offices even though little cash was kept on the premises. Believing that advertising that stressed "cash for your title" might have misled would-be armed robbers, the company had toyed with the idea of emphasizing a check instead of cash in its ads, especially billboard ads, to discourage robbers.

Very high employee turnover had also been a problem at most branches. Occasionally, an incident of embezzlement was uncovered at a branch. No one at the home office seemed especially surprised when such activity was uncovered. It appeared to Joe that the company did not attract very high-class personnel for most positions, despite the relatively high salaries. Joe thought that the employees at the home office, where he worked, did not seem of a higher caliber than those employed at the branches. Once he had commented to his supervisor on what he perceived to be a lack of professionalism on the part of his coworkers. The accounting manager's response was, "Of course, if there were not something wrong with each one of us, why would we work here?" Joe often thought of that statement.

The founder and CEO of Acme was rumored to have underworld connections. Joe had seen no evidence of this possibility, but it was a widely held perception among the employees. The CEO lived in his "second" home in the Washington, D.C., area, where he worked out of a lavishly appointed private office with only him and two secretaries in Falls Church, Virginia. This office, which was fully funded by Acme, had the finest communications technology, and the boss preferred being in this office to other Acme offices. He was known to be very fond of his $1.55 million home and of the fine restaurants in downtown Washington.

As Joe thought more about his situation, he concluded that he could sum up most of his reservations about working at Acme with a single sentence: It seemed that he was working for a sleazy company in a sleazy business surrounded by rather sleazy individuals. Though perfectly legal, the business was trashy and vulgar—to use words that Joe thought his mother might use.

Joe did still believe that he would acquire responsibilities sooner and move up faster at Acme than at most other firms. The salaries for managers who were even a little higher up were very attractive. Because of the turnover in his department, Joe was already asked to accept additional responsibilities with some frequency. He thought it possible that he could be promoted to the controller's position within five or six years if he continued to work as he had. Management seemed very pleased with his performance; his annual job-performance evaluation had just been filed and was stunningly good.

Joe wondered whether his association with this firm and industry might lessen other job prospects if he stayed another few years, but he was concerned that his job history would present him as a job hopper. He had rarely stayed longer than one year with any employer. He was concerned that leaving Acme at this time would give future prospective employers additional reason to question his stability. Several more years at Acme would strengthen his résumé both in terms of the higher-level responsibilities that he could claim and in the added stability that would be implied by a longer term of employment.

Joe thought that he had to consider the well-being of his family in any decision he made. He would not find it easy to secure another position with much potential in his present geographical area on the Florida-Georgia border. The area had few opportunities of note. Joe and his family were now living about a thousand miles from their relatives. He had accepted a transfer to his present geographical location when he was working for Ace Printing. He had no desire to stay in this location, but just now his wife had a decent position as a clerk in the business office of a local physician's group, and his two older children were active in their schools and extracurricular activities. They had many friends, and Joe believed that there would be a difficult period of adjustment for the children if the family were to move at this time. His wife, too, seemed content with life. She had found satisfaction in her job as well as the community.

Although Joe had not worked in one of the branch offices that deals directly with customers, he had heard plenty of stories around the office about what it was like on the front line. On the basis of what he had heard, he was glad to be working with figures behind the scene, even though the environment in the office was far from ideal. Certain roles in management were clearly not for him.

He could probably arrange to stay in the home office, but even that office seemed fraught with problems, most of which Joe thought were caused by the caliber of Acme's personnel. In the year Joe had been there, he had seen a number of employees go over their supervisor's heads, taking problems to higher levels than necessary and undermining the authority of some supervisors. This practice seemed to be an accepted but stressful way of solving problems and making decisions. There also seemed to be a degree of back-stabbing. Additionally, there had been recurring incidents of executives charging small-change personal items such as phone calls, Fed-Ex delivery charges, and movie rentals on company credit cards. The company continued to pay for such charges in spite of Joe's calling those incidents to the attention of the accounting manager. Sums of money were also borrowed from company accounts with no apparent schedule of repayment.

Joe had an uncle living in Florida who was a professor of business finance. This uncle had a strong interest in alternative sources of consumer financing. A Florida newspaper, the *South Florida Sun-Sentinel,* had published an exposé of charges in the title pawn industry several years earlier, and Joe's uncle had sent him copies of the articles, which Joe had kept in his files. He thought that the articles captured the spirit of the business as he had come to know it. Had he paid more attention to this series when his uncle had sent it to him nine months ago, he might not be faced with his current dilemma. But it did no good to look back. His problem was what he should do now.

H. B. Fuller in Honduras: Street Children and Substance Abuse

PART A

Resistol adhesives are manufactured by H. B. Fuller S.A., a subsidiary of Kativo Chemical Industries, S.A., which in turn is a wholly owned subsidiary of the H. B. Fuller Company of St. Paul, Minnesota.[1] Kativo sells more than a dozen different adhesives under the Resistol brand name in several countries in Latin America for a variety of industrial and commercial applications. In Honduras, the Resistol products once had a strong market position.

Three of the Resistol products are solvent-based adhesives designed with certain properties that are not possible to attain with a water-based formula. These properties include rapid set, strong adhesion, and water resistance. These products are similar to airplane glue and rubber cement. They are primarily used in shoe manufacturing and repair, leatherwork, and carpentry.

Even though the street children of each Central American country may have a different choice of drug for substance abuse, and even though Resistol was not the only glue that Honduran street children used as an inhalant, the term *Resistolero* stuck in that country and indeed has become synonymous with all street children, whether they use inhalants or not.

Social Conditions in Honduras

The social problems that contributed to widespread inhalant abuse among street children can be attributed to the depth of poverty in Honduras. In 1989, 65 percent of all households and 40 percent of urban households in Honduras were living in poverty, making it one of the poorest countries in Latin America.[2]

The average household contains about seven persons living together in a single room. For those in the rooms facing an alley, the narrow passageway between buildings serves both as a sewage and waste disposal area and as a courtyard for as many as 150 persons. Because of migratory labor, high

This case is a blending of two cases, the first prepared by Norman E. Bowie and Stefanie Ann Lenway (see Part A) and the second by Norman E. Bowie and Jeffrey Smith (see Part B)—as adapted and updated for this volume in 2003 by Tom L. Beauchamp (through consultation with Norman Bowie). Published by permission. Not to be duplicated without the permission of the authors.

191

unemployment, and income insecurity, many family relationships are unstable. Often the support of children is left to mothers. Children are frequently forced to leave school and support the family income through shining shoes, selling newspapers, or guarding cars. If a mother becomes sick or dies, her children may well be abandoned to the streets.

Kativo Chemical Industries S.A. and the Street Children

In the early 1980s, Kativo, one of the 500 largest private corporations in Latin America, was primarily a paint company. It decided to enter the adhesive market in Latin America. Its strategy was to combine Kativo's marketing experience with H. B. Fuller's products. Resistol was the brand name for all adhesive products, including water-based school glues.

In 1983, Honduran newspapers carried articles about police arrests of *Resistoleros*—street children who drugged themselves by sniffing glue. Kativo's Honduras advertising agency, Calderon Publicidad, informed the newspapers that Resistol was not the only substance abused by Honduran street children and that the image of the manufacturer was being damaged by using a prestigious trademark as a synonym for drug abusers.[3]

The man on the spot was Kativo Vice President Humberto Larach ("Beto"), a Honduran, who headed Kativo's North Adhesives Division. Offices in nine countries reported to him. He had become manager of the adhesives division after demonstrating his entrepreneurial talents in managing Kativo's paint business in Honduras.

By the summer of 1985, more than a corporate image was at stake. As a solution to the glue-sniffing problem, social activists working with street children suggested that oil of mustard, allyl isothiocyanate, could be added to the product to prevent its abuse. They argued that a person attempting to sniff a glue with oil of mustard added would find it too powerful to tolerate. Sniffing it has been compared to getting an "overdose of horseradish." An attempt to legislate the addition of oil of mustard received a boost when Honduran Peace Corps volunteer Timothy Bicknell convinced a local group called the "Committee for the Prevention of Drugs at the National Level" of the necessity of adding oil of mustard to Resistol. All members of the committee were prominent members of Honduran society.

Beto, in response to the growing publicity about the *Resistoleros*, requested staff members of H. B. Fuller's U.S. headquarters to look into the viability of oil of mustard as a solution, with special attention to side effects. H. B. Fuller's corporate industrial hygiene staff found credible some 1983 toxicology reports that oil of mustard was a serious cancer-causing agent in testing on rats.

In 1986, Beto contacted Hugh Young, president of SAFE (Solvent Abuse Foundation for Education) and gathered information on programs that SAFE had developed in Mexico. Young took the position that the only viable approach to substance abuse was education, not product modification. He argued that reformulating the product would be an exercise in futility because "nothing is available in the solvent area that is not abusable." With these reports in hand,

Beto attempted to persuade Resistol's critics, relief agencies, and government officials that adding oil of mustard to Resistol was not the solution to the glue-sniffing problem. Beto had some luck with Mrs. Norma Castro, governor of the State of Cortes, who, after a conversation with Beto, became convinced that oil of mustard had serious dangers and that glue sniffing was a social problem.

Beto's efforts continued. Early in 1987, Kativo began to establish community affairs councils, as a planned expansion of the worldwide company's philosophy of community involvement. In June 1987, PRIDE (Parents Resource Institute for Drug Education) set up an office in San Pedro Sula. The philosophy of this organization is that through adequate *parental* education on the drug problem, it is possible to deal with the problems of inhalant use. PRIDE introduced Beto to Wilfredo Alvarado, the new head of the Mental Health Division in the Ministry of Health. As an adviser to the Congressional Committee on Health, Dr. Alvarado was in charge of preparing draft legislation and evaluating legislation received by the Honduran Congress. Together with Dr. Alvarado, Kativo staff worked to prepare draft legislation to address the problem of inhalant-addicted children. At the same time, five members of the Congress drafted a proposed law that required the use of oil of mustard in locally produced or imported solvent-based adhesives.

On March 30, 1989, the Honduran Congress voted into law the legislation drafted by the five members of Congress. Beto then spoke to the press about the problems with the proposed legislation. He argued that this type of cement is utilized in industry, crafts, the home, schools, and other places where it has become indispensable. By altering the product, he said, not only will the drug addiction problem not be solved, but also the country's development will be slowed. This law was never implemented, and thus Fuller was never required to add oil of mustard.

H. B. Fuller: The Corporate Response

On June 7, 1989, Vice President for Corporate Relations Dick Johnson wrote a memo to CEO Tony Anderson. He articulated basic values that had to be considered as H. B. Fuller wrestled with the problem:

1. H. B. Fuller's explicitly stated public concern about substance abuse.
2. H. B. Fuller's "Concern for Youth" focus in its community affairs projects.
3. H. B. Fuller's reputation as a socially responsible company.
4. H. B. Fuller's history of ethical conduct.
5. H. B. Fuller's commitment to the intrinsic value of each individual.

Whatever solution was ultimately adopted would have to be consistent with these values. Dick suggested a number of options, including that H. B. Fuller withdraw from the market or perhaps alter the formula to make Resistol a water-based product so that sniffing would no longer be an issue. Fuller preferred the water-based product, but it would likely take years to develop.

Tony suggested that Dick create a task force to find a more immediate solution. Dick decided to accept Beto's invitation to travel to Honduras to view the situation firsthand. Karen Muller, director of community affairs, and Dick Johnson left for a four-day trip to Honduras on September 18, 1989. Upon arriving they were joined by Beto; Oscar Sahuri, general manager for Kativo's adhesives business in Honduras; and Jorge Walter Bolanos, vice president and director of finance, Kativo. Visits to two different small shoe-manufacturing shops and a shoe-supply distributor helped to clarify the issues around pricing, sales, distribution, and the packaging of the product. All agreed that removing Resistol from the market would not resolve the problem, which was extremely complex. The use of inhalants by street children is a symptom of Honduras's underlying economic problems—problems that have social, cultural, and political as well as economic dimensions.

Resistol appeared to be the drug of choice for young street children. However, the street children obtained the drug in a number of different ways. There was not a clear pattern, and hence, the solution could not be found in simply changing some features of the distribution system. Children might obtain the glue from legitimate customers, from small shoe-repair stalls, by theft, from "illegal" dealers, or from third parties who purchased Resistol from legitimate stores but then sold the product to children. For some persons the sale of Resistol to children was profitable. Resistol was available in small packages, which made it more affordable, and the economic circumstances of a country such as Honduras made this packaging economically sensible.

A community relations strategy would therefore be extremely complex and risky. Nonetheless, H. B. Fuller realized that it was committed to a community relations approach to this problem by its mission statement. The company then asked what it would take to achieve a community relations solution in Honduras. It took years to get a grip on the problem.

PART B

On July 17, 1992, the H. B. Fuller Board had the glue-sniffing problem in Honduras on its agenda. Dick Johnson and Karen Muller were to discuss the hiring of street workers to address the social problems created by glue sniffing. The meeting soon took a surprising turn. Fuller Board Chairman Elmer Andersen (a legendary figure in Minnesota, who had served once as governor of the state and who was long prominent in civic affairs) moved that H. B. Fuller leave the market in countries where street children have obtained the product. After some discussion, the Board approved the following resolution:

> WHEREAS, the Board of Directors has carefully considered the business and ethical issues arising out of the abuse of the Company's solvent-based Resistol products by street children in Honduras, Guatemala and certain other Latin American countries; and

WHEREAS, the Company's management and the Board have continually monitored and assessed this situation for a number of years and have considered a variety of alternatives for dealing with these issues,

RESOLVED, that the Company will discontinue the sale of its solvent-based Resistol products where such products have been the subject of significant abuse by children, unless reformulation of such products can minimize or eliminate abuse.

Shortly after the Board passed its resolution, NBC's *Dateline* began to investigate the glue-sniffing problem. On September 8, 1992, *Dateline* ran an uncomplimentary segment on H. B. Fuller. The theme of the story was that H. B. Fuller was profiting from the misery of glue-sniffing street children. CEO Tony Andersen had agreed to be interviewed for the program. Although Andersen was interviewed for nearly an hour, only four minutes were aired. To the viewer, Andersen and H. B. Fuller seemed on the defensive. *Dateline* implied that it was knowledge of the impending *Dateline* story—not concern about street children—that caused H. B. Fuller to leave the market.

The Board resolution was soon implemented as follows: By March 1993, the community action program that had been initiated before the Board decision to withdraw the product had expanded. A full-time coordinator, Maria el Carmen Raudales, had been hired and was sending monthly reports to Beto. Raudales's responsibility was to work with other business, government, and social service agencies and to monitor the specific programs that were paid for locally. By that time the salaries of a physician and four educators who worked directly with street children were being funded. In addition, volunteers built schoolrooms so that some street children might receive an education. Country managers and local UNICEF officials independently began undertaking studies to determine whether Resistol products were being abused in other Central American countries.

Over-the-counter sales of Resistol rubber cement in Honduras and Guatemala were discontinued. Even small shoe-repair "shops" in those countries were no longer able to obtain Resistol. (However, competing brands were still readily available). Although the H. B. Fuller Board believed that the company was aggressively addressing the substance-abuse problem, various critics suggested that Fuller was acting in bad faith. The February 1993 issue of *The Progressive* featured a letter from Annie Baker, a member of a group called the Coalition on Resistoleros, which had served as a focal point for U.S. criticism of Fuller. Baker accused Fuller of violating the Board directive by not ceasing sales to industrial markets and by continuing commercial sales in ten other Central and South American countries plus Mexico. In addition to her remarks in *The Progressive*, Baker faulted Fuller for refusing to add oil of mustard and for putting toluene in its glue. Baker pointed out that toluene is listed in the United States as a hazardous air pollutant, that land disposal of toluene is prohibited, and that OSHA restricts workplace levels (though toluene is a widely used product in U.S. industries).

Not everyone associated with relieving the plight of street children accepted Baker's charges. In a letter to Baker, Marilyn Rocky, Executive Director of Childhope USA Inc.,[4] wrote,

> Believe me I have never seen a street child who couldn't find an immediate substitute when one substance was taken away. They go immediately to the next target of opportunity . . . . petrol, basuco, alcohol, kerosene, and paint thinner . . . . [A]re you going to insist that the companies that manufacture these products must also alter them too? No, that is not the solution. It is not even the problem. The real enemy is the society that considers these children useless and exploitable.

Not all organizations with an interest in the treatment of street children were supportive of Fuller's position. Covenant House, or Casa Alianza, an early supporter, became critical after Fuller decreased the amount of money that it gave to Covenant House for its street-workers program. Bruce Harris, Executive Director for Latin American Programs of Casa Alianza, was a major international critic of Fuller. Harris attributed Fuller's reluctance to add oil of mustard to the fact that it would add costs in the amount of 7 cents per gallon.

At the annual shareholders meeting on April 12, 1993, where demonstrations by the Coalition on Resistoleros took place, CEO Tony Andersen outlined the company's position. He indicated that oil of mustard would not be added to Resistol because such an action would not solve the problem. "Profiles of solvent abusers all over the world universally show them *not* to discriminate between one product or another." Andersen also claimed that Fuller's position was supported by "technical data." At the same shareholder meeting Andersen said, "Within two months (after the Board resolution), our Resistol solvent adhesives were out of the distributorships and off the market in Honduras and Guatemala."

However, Fuller's critics continued to refer to Resistol as the "product of choice." Since Resistol was no longer being produced in the containers that were most conducive to illegitimate use and since its competitors had not curtailed production (indeed had increased production), Fuller maintained that Resistol could not possibly be the product of choice for the majority of Honduran street children. Fuller maintained that news photos of children sniffing glue were almost certainly erroneous in their attribution that the glue being used was Resistol. Yet proving that it was not Resistol was virtually impossible. Fuller maintained that it had done the best that it could do. It managed the supply-side problem by restricting the sale of the product to industrial users, and it managed the social problem through its Community Affairs Councils. Meanwhile, some of its competitors had increased their product supplies.

Nonetheless, criticism of Fuller escalated. A *Dateline* follow-up show was aired on September 28, 1993. A *Dateline* crew had gone to Honduras a few months after the Board meeting and reported that it found children sniffing

Resistol. The report included vivid pictures of street children sniffing glue. Fuller critic Bruce Harris accompanied the *Dateline* crew and pointed, on camera, to a can of Resistol in a small store that sold glue over the counter. During the interview Harris noted that Fuller had reduced its financial support of Casa Alianza's social program in Honduras. Finally, Harris and the retired president of the U.S. firm Testors, a major American manufacturer of model glues, criticized Fuller for not adding oil of mustard. (This criticism had also appeared in the *first Dateline* segment.)

CEO Tony Andersen was angry. In an October 22, 1993, letter to employees, Andersen wrote the following:

> The recent *Dateline* NBC broadcast was the final straw. It's time we stand up and say, "Enough! We're disappointed and dissatisfied with the sensational, trivial, emotional, and grossly inaccurate portrayal the media has given to this serious issue. And we've had enough of the loudly voiced but unfounded claims of our critics who repeatedly espouse simplistic solutions without factual foundation.

In addition, Senior Vice President for Corporate Relations Dick Johnson wrote an angry three-page letter to NBC News President Andrew Lack. He argued that NBC had misrepresented issues and had ignored facts; also, alluding to previous staged events by *Dateline,* he asked pointedly whether an excerpt showing a street vendor pouring solvent adhesive from a jar to a bag for a child was staged. Fuller maintained that NBC provided no reason to believe that it was Resistol that was being sniffed.

Fuller now had a double-barreled problem. First, it was committed to continuing to address the substance abuse problem in Central America, although this massive social problem was not one that it could hope to resolve. Second, it had to deal with hostile reports in the media and other organizations that challenged its policies, programs, and level of commitment. At this point, Fuller basically decided to withdraw from the debate and to ignore its critics. Fuller came to believe that nothing it could do would be sufficient to satisfy critics and that those who opposed it had a vested interest in keeping the controversy alive. Fuller, however, continued to search for new technologies. In April 1994, it stated that it was seeking to find substitutes to solvent-based adhesives that contained toluene. Fuller stated that its ultimate aim was to discover a water-based alternative and that it had entered a partnership to find it. Such a product would have some probability of ending the adhesive-abuse problem. The search for this product is ongoing.

NOTES

1. The subsidiaries of the North Adhesives Division of Kativo Chemical Industries, S.A., go by the name "H. B. Fuller (Country of Operation)," that is, H. B. Fuller S.A. Honduras. To prevent confusion with the parent company, we will refer to H. B. Fuller S.A. Honduras by

the name of its parent, "Kativo." The H. B. Fuller Company was founded in 1887 by Harvey Fuller in St. Paul as a manufacturer of glue, mucilage, inks, blueing, and blacking. The founder was an inventor of a flour-based wet paste that paperhangers found especially effective. Harvey's oldest son Albert joined his father in 1888, and the company grew rapidly, making its first acquisition, the Minnesota Paste Company, in 1892.

2. The following discussion is based in part on James D. Rudolph, ed., *Honduras: A Country Study*, 2nd ed. (Washington, DC: U.S. Department of the Army, 1984).

3. Unless otherwise indicated, all references and quotations regarding H. B. Fuller and its subsidiary Kativo Chemical Industries S.A. are from company documents.

4. Childhope USA Inc. is an international movement on behalf of street children. It is under the auspices of the U.S. Committee for UNICEF.

Stirling Bridge's Unloading of Surplus Tools

Following his graduation from Georgetown University's School of Business, Melvin Gibson accepted a position as a manager with Stirling Bridge Tool and Machinery Company, a multinational corporation that manufactures industrial equipment. Stirling Bridge (SB) was founded in 1887 in Falkirk, North Carolina, by Scottish immigrants who were skilled metalworkers. Begun as a company that manufactured ordinary carpentry tools, both SB's product lines and the geographical areas in which they are marketed has steadily expanded over the decades. SB now manufactures not only its original line of tools but also power tools for use by consumers, light industrial machinery for use by other manufacturing concerns, and heavy industrial machinery for use by the construction industry. SB markets its tools and equipment throughout the United States and Western Europe. In addition, over the past decade, SB has begun selling its products in developing third-world countries and in Eastern Europe.

Melvin has been both happy and successful at SB, rising through the ranks of the power tools division of the company to his present position as vice president.

Melvin reports directly to the President of the Power Tools Division, William Wallace. The power tools division manufactures and markets a wide variety of power tools for use by the typical do-it-yourself consumer. By far its most popular and profitable products are in the Braveheart line of home power tools. This line consists of simple-to-use, long-lasting, and reliable electric hand saws, drills, routers, sanders, and the like. The Braveheart line currently accounts for approximately 80 percent of the power-tool division's profits.

Things had been going well until last year when an unfortunate concurrence of events caused what Wallace regards as a crisis. SB had for three years devoted a great deal of its capital resources to expanding its markets in Eastern Europe. The company feels that it is beginning to understand this market and has established a solid reputation for high-quality equipment. To date, however, this effort has borne little financial success while resulting in a moderately severe cash-flow problem for the company and significant reductions in

This case was prepared by John Hasnas and revised by Tom L. Beauchamp. Not to be duplicated without permission of the holder of the copyright, © 2003 by John Hasnas (George Mason University Law School).

overall profit margins. To make matters worse, Citizen Alert, a consumer interest research group, has launched a vigorous public relations campaign against the Braveheart line of power tools. Edward Longshanks, the president of Citizen Alert, called a press conference to announce that his group considered Braveheart tools to be defective products that pose serious risks of injury to consumers. In support of this claim, Longshanks cited a recent study by Edinburgh University showing a significantly higher than normal rate of hand and facial injuries to people using Braveheart power tools.

This study, its use by Longshanks, and press innuendo infuriated Wallace, who had taken expensive steps to increase the safety of all Braveheart tools as recently as three years ago. Studies he had commissioned had shown that the major cause of injury to power-tool users was the improper installation by the user of moving parts such as drill bits and saw blades. If these parts were inserted at an angle or were not properly tightened, they either could wobble, causing a user's hand to slip when pressure was applied, or could fly off at rapid speeds during use. To solve this problem, SB's engineers devised a locking mechanism for all such interchangeable parts.

This mechanism operated as follows. After inserting the drill bit, saw blade, or other part, the user would turn the tightening key in the normal manner until he or she began to feel resistance. At that point, the user could engage the locking mechanism by turning the key an additional quarter turn, which produced an audible click that indicated the part was safely seated. The user would know that the part was not adequately tightened if he or she had not heard the click. In addition, if the part was improperly angled, the locking mechanism would not allow the extra quarter turn, and the user would not hear the click. Thus, the user could ensure that the tool was safe to operate by making sure that he or she had heard the locking mechanism engage. It was an ingenious innovation, and it had not encountered even a single failure or problem of safety during testing at SB.

The operation of this mechanism was clearly and prominently explained in the instruction booklet that accompanied all Braveheart tools. In addition, a separate warning card was included that, among other things, warned consumers not to operate the tool unless he or she heard the click that indicated that the locking mechanism was engaged. With the addition of the new locking mechanism, Braveheart tools not only met but also exceeded all the safety requirements of the Federal Consumer Products Safety Commission for power tools. In addition, the product line had been examined by Underwriter's Laboratory and had been certified as among the safest power tools on the market when properly used.

Ironically, however, the new locking mechanism seems to have been causally linked to an *increase* in injuries, as revealed by Longshanks' study. Apparently, many purchasers were failing to read both the instruction booklet and the warning card. They were simply using the tools under the assumption that Braveheart tools operated similarly to the other power tools on the market. Thus, they were failing to turn the tightening key the extra quarter turn necessary to engage the locking mechanism. Without the locking mechanism engaged, the removable parts were actually less securely seated than they would be in power tools that did not possess such a mechanism. Hence, they were more likely to wobble or fly off and cause injury.

Following Longshanks' press conference, Wallace made repeated attempts to get the word out about Braveheart's superior safety features. However, the media gave little coverage to his side of the story, and Citizen Alert and other consumer-activist groups denounced all such representations as self-serving apologetics. Within months of the Longshanks' announcement, SB was hit with a rash of lawsuits by injured consumers alleging that the defective design of Braveheart tools was the cause of their injuries. Just last month, the noted personal-injury lawyer, John Balliol, instituted a class-action lawsuit against SB for $300 million, including $150 million in punitive damages.

At that point, SB's CEO, Robert Bruce, directed Wallace to recall all Braveheart tools with the locking mechanism in the United States and return to marketing the earlier model line of tools, which met all current safety codes and had been field-tested for years. Bruce was not impressed by Wallace's argument that the tools with the locking mechanism were of superior quality. As he put it, "It doesn't matter whether the product is safe or not. What matters is whether the consuming public believes the product is safe. Remember what happened with the Audi 5000? At this point in time, SB can afford neither the bad press nor any additional lawsuits. I want all Braveheart tools with the locking mechanism off the shelves as of today."

This was extremely bad news. A large percentage of the tools manufactured last year were still in the stores, and the new-model tools were just coming off the production line. This outcome was a total loss—and a massive one. In addition, the alterations to the production process required to make the tools without the locking mechanism would be costly and would extend the time before a new line of tools could be back in the stores. Under these conditions, Braveheart was facing at least two years of losses and a severe reduction in market share.

Wallace decided that the best way to ameliorate the situation was to speed up the production of the line of tools without the locking mechanism by putting on extra shifts and working around the clock, and to sell the recalled tools with the locking mechanism overseas where there was no risk of lawsuits. He gave Melvin the job of coordinating the overseas sales effort. Last week, John Comyn, SB's chief sales representative operating out of Hawaii, brought Melvin some welcome news. He believes that much of the recalled line of Braveheart tools can be sold in various parts of Polynesia that have particularly favorable market conditions and an almost desperate shortage of sturdy, durable, and reliable tools.

Per capita income has been slowly rising in these formerly nonaffluent areas over the past quarter-century. The economy has been expanding rapidly and producing a virtual explosion of building projects, both by industry and by the citizens themselves. However, because these areas have not yet had the time to develop an indigenous manufacturing base, the targeted regions are chronically short of the tools, machinery, and equipment needed to sustain their ongoing growth. As a result, they are continuously attempting to import modern technologies at an affordable cost.

Comyn had been in the process of negotiating a distribution agreement for Braveheart tools with Clay More, the president of a hardware retailers' trade association in Polynesia, when he learned of the recall of the tools with the locking mechanism. Comyn believes that if the negotiations are handled correctly, SB may be able to dispose of almost the entire line of recalled tools at a reasonable, though very low, profit. Thrilled by this news, Melvin instructed Comyn to set up a conference call with More to negotiate the terms of the deal.

Comyn placed the call, and with Melvin listening in, began the negotiations. Melvin was quite impressed with his bargaining skills. He succeeded in getting More to agree that the members of his association would take more than 90 percent of the recalled tools. In addition, he negotiated a price that, while far lower than SB charged in the United States, was close enough to wipe out most of the expected losses. Toward the end of the bargaining session, the following exchange took place.

> More: Melvin says these tools were recalled from the stores in the United States. Is there anything we should be concerned about?
>
> Comyn: No, not really. The tools are of superior quality and of advanced safety design. They exceed all the requirements of the U. S. Consumer Products Safety Commission and have been approved by Underwriter's Laboratory. They come with easy-to-read instructions about how to use them. What kind of sales support do you need from us?
>
> More: Essentially none. We will end up repackaging the tools anyway. Almost none of our customers can read English, and many cannot read at all. We usually just discard the boxes and foreign inserts anyway. It's not worth the extra cost to translate and print up new materials. We work on pretty thin profit margins as it is. Besides, we're a learn-by-doing sort of culture over here.
>
> Comyn: Anything else we need to discuss?
>
> More: No. You know, you are really doing us a favor. Life has been improving over here, but we simply do not have the tools and equipment to sustain the growth. It may seem strange to you in the West, but people are almost desperate to get their hands on good tools in many parts of our region. The shortage is a big problem for us, and your pricing will allow us to cut down severely on the problem. Moreover, most of the tools that we have been able to import so far are closeouts with rather shoddy safety records; they are neither durable nor reliable. Almost nothing here would meet the standards of your Consumer Products Safety Commission.
>
> Comyn: Glad we could help. There is not much profit in it for us, but at least it will help us penetrate your market. I'll fax you the contracts in the morning.

Comyn has just delivered the sales contracts to Melvin for his approval. In many ways, this deal is a lifesaver. The legal infrastructure is such that there is no risk of civil lawsuits from users of the tools. By making the sale, SB can convert a potentially massive liability into an asset. However, before signing off on the deal, Melvin decides to reflect upon what he is doing in approving this sale. He is a little bothered by the fact that the consumers are not likely to learn to activate the advanced safety features of these tools—which, he is convinced, are wonderful safety features. But how in the world, he asks, could these workers ever be given the proper instructions?

AIDS, Patents, and Access to Pharmaceuticals

During the past twenty-five years, instances of HIV/AIDS have grown dramatically. Approximately 42 million people worldwide currently live with HIV infection. It is projected that by the year 2010, the figure will increase to 60 million—possibly as high as 110 million (United Nations and World Bank estimates).

Realization of the threat that AIDS presents has prompted many responses in the last quarter-century from both government and business. The pharmaceutical industry began to see prospects for drug therapies circa September 1984, when the U.S. National Cancer Institute (NCI) conducted a screening program to discover a drug that would kill, or at least deactivate, the human immunodeficiency virus (HIV) that causes AIDS. Five months later, the Burroughs Wellcome Company in North Carolina, later GlaxoSmithKline (GSK), sent samples of zidovudine (formerly azidothymidine, or AZT) to the NCI for virological, immunological, and pharmacological testing.

THE HISTORICAL DOMINANCE OF AZT

On March 19, 1987, the FDA approved the drug for sale, and a year later (on February 9, 1988) Burroughs Wellcome obtained an exclusive license to market AZT under the brand name Retrovir. As with all patents, Burroughs Wellcome received exclusive proprietary rights over AZT for seventeen years, until February 9, 2005.

Before approval, however, federal regulations require that new drugs be tested extensively. Because of the grim prognosis of those infected with the disease, questions of fair access to drugs arose immediately. One standard test is to select two similar groups of patients and give one the new drug and the other a harmless placebo. Burroughs Wellcome, in compliance with federal regulations, created a placebo-controlled trial of AZT to determine its efficacy and its toxicity for HIV-infected patients. Critics maintained that a placebo-controlled trial under such extreme circumstances was unethical, because the

This case was prepared by Tom L. Beauchamp, with assistance by Jeffrey P. Kahn, John Cuddihy, David L. Parver, Kier Olsen, and Ahmed Humayun. Not to be duplicated without permission of the holder of the copyright, © 1992, 1996, 2003 by Tom L. Beauchamp.

trial itself denied 10,000 patients the only promising drug for treating AIDS. These critics argued that the demands of scientific testing could not be resolved with justice and compassion for HIV patients. However, defenders of the trial insisted that it was necessary to determine both what AZT's efficacy was and whether its negative side effects would outweigh its benefits. Dr. Samuel Broder of NCI denied that "compassion and science are in conflict," on grounds that "we have to be concerned with people who have AIDS both now and in the future." He noted that "serious errors—irredeemable errors . . . can be introduced if we don't undertake appropriately controlled studies. It would be a catastrophe if we dismissed a 'good drug' or if we allowed a 'bad drug' to become the standard of therapy."[1]

When AZT entered the market, Burroughs Wellcome was its sole producer. As such, Burroughs Wellcome was free to set the price of its drug. Pharmaceutical companies typically recover research and development costs by charging whatever the market will bear before competition and new drugs enter the market, even if the cost exceeds some consumers' budgets. This practice has long been controversial. Burroughs Wellcome originally listed a $10,000 retail price (at the time, the company wholesaled the drug for $8,300) for a year's supply, with a projected use by some 30,000 patients. By October 1989, the AZT full-dosage price had been lowered approximately $650 per month, to $7,800 per year retail; and by late 1991, the retail price had dropped (partially through the lowering of dosage) to approximately $3,000 per year.

Industry analysts believe that Burroughs Wellcome's original cost for bringing AZT onto the market ranged from $80 million to $180 million. Sales quickly exceeded $220 million annually after it entered the market. In 1990, sales earned the Wellcome Foundation, the British-based parent company, approximately $287 million.[2] Early in 1990, it was thought that sales could soon reach $1 billion annually. Retrovir's volume sales increased 53 percent in 1990 from 1989 levels.

Critics charged that the company's AZT price was unreasonably high and created a potential hardship for patients who lack any real alternative. Burroughs Wellcome defended the AZT price as fair and necessary because of the costs it incurred, citing the lengthy and expensive process of manufacturing AZT, as well as intensive and financially burdensome labor and technology. However, the company has refused to provide precise figures on costs to the U.S. Congress, claiming that these figures are proprietary confidential. Burroughs Wellcome has stated that it committed $80 million to the drug's research and development, including $10 million in free AZT administered to 4,500 clinical trial patients.[3]

Often individuals with AIDS—many of whom are young, indigent, and uninsured—have been unable to pay AZT's market price. Therefore, public programs such as Medicaid have borne much of the treatment cost in the United States. Burroughs Wellcome also had to fight off legal challenges to its patents from Barr Laboratories. Barr, a pharmaceuticals firm based in Pomona, New York, filed an abbreviated new drug application with the FDA on March 19, 1991, asking permission to produce a generic equivalent to

Retrovir. In response, Burroughs Wellcome sued Barr for patent infringement in federal court. Barr contended that a generic version of AZT would sell for 40 percent less than the current prices. Edwin A. Cohen, at that time Barr Laboratories's president and CEO, said, "We would like to see zidovudine become available at the lowest possible price." On July 17, 1991, NIH Director Bernadine Healy announced that the NIH had granted Barr a "nonexclusive patent license to market AZT."[4] According to one pharmaceutical consultant, "Burroughs Wellcome [could] lose at least half their business in the first year a copy drug reaches the market."[5]

The lawsuit continued, but in a November 1994 ruling, Burroughs Wellcome prevailed in this legal contest. The U.S. Court of Appeals upheld a July 1993 federal ruling that established Burroughs Wellcome's continued role as *exclusive* patent holder.[6] Criticism mounted that this decision would negatively affect patients who, as a result of Burroughs Wellcome's control of the AZT market, must either die or continue to pay what critics consider exorbitant prices for the drug. In response, in February 1995, the Food and Drug Administration granted approval to Barr to create and market the generic form of AZT upon expiration of Burroughs Wellcome's patent rights in 2005.[7]

In 2002, GSK also faced a lawsuit. This case, filed against it by the AIDS Healthcare Foundation, represented another effort to break the control that GSK possessed over the market. The Foundation alleged that the AZT patent was illegally obtained.[8] As the lawsuit wore on, many people looked away from these issues (still unresolved) and toward another problem: the legal right to produce a cheaper version of these drugs.

THE ARRIVAL OF NEW DRUGS ON THE MARKET

Throughout the 1990s, several companies continued their efforts to study the efficacy of AZT and to develop other products to combat AIDS.[9] One study, conducted by the National Institute of Allergy and Infectious Diseases and reported in September 1995, suggested that AZT used alone was less effective than DDI (dideoxyinosine) alone, a combination of DDI and AZT, or a combination of zalcitabine (DDC) and AZT. As compared with the use of AZT alone, the other three treatments were more effective in preventing death and progression of HIV infection to full-blown AIDS.[10] This and other evidence indicated that AZT alone could no longer be considered the mainstay in the search for effective AIDS treatments.

Researchers were working feverishly to explore still other approaches to AIDS therapy.[11] One advance was thought to hold particular promise for AIDS treatment, namely, a class of drugs called protease or proteinase inhibitors, which work by disabling an enzyme crucial to the flourishing of the HIV virus.[12] Several pharmaceutical companies were working on the manufacture of the drug. Some companies hoped to be able to offer the treatment to desperate patients even during fairly early stages of testing. By initiating a lottery system in June 1995, Hoffmann–La Roche became the first manufacturer to offer free of charge (to 2,280 AIDS patients) their version of the inhibitor, known as Invirase or sequinivir. The lottery was expanded to include 2,000 additional patients in November. Merck & Co. followed suit by making the drug Crixivan available free of charge to 1,400 people. Abbott Laboratories also offered such a gateway program, to provide its experimental drug to 1,400 people.

Recent developments in AIDS research have yielded other drugs that are effective in delaying the onset of AIDS in HIV-positive patients and in treating AIDS patients. Although research is still progressing and no panacea for AIDS has emerged, some new drugs can change AIDS from a fatal illness to a chronic disease for many patients. (Notable are *nucleosides* and *nonnucleosides.*) These drugs are usually taken in combination as so-called drug "cocktails."

Despite the far more competitive marketplace that has now been established, the high cost of AIDS treatment renders full and easy access to adequate treatment an ongoing struggle. First-class treatment in the United States is back up to around $10,000 a year per patient. This price makes first-class treatment affordable to only a relatively small class of people. The United States government has taken some steps to ameliorate this problem of access to AIDS treatment. Those who do not have drug insurance or are not eligible for Medicaid are provided for, at some level, through a federal act that disperses funds to states to spend on AIDS drugs.[13] The government also reimburses $750 million a year under the AIDS Drug Assistance Program. Thus, domestically—though not in all international markets—the problem of access to AIDS treatment is mitigated partially by this scheme of federal support.

However, the complexities and costs of AIDS treatment still make it an impractical option for many patients, most prominently for two high-risk groups: (1) the poor, homeless, and drug-addicted in the United States and, even more so, (2) the poor in the developing countries of Africa and Asia. In the latter regions, anything short of the most meticulous use of drug cocktails can lead to the development of drug-resistant strains of AIDS.[14] Dr. Deborah Cotton, a clinician and researcher at Massachusetts General Hospital, says that taking AIDS drugs "requires a degree of complexity I've never seen before . . . . It is hard for even the most organized person to comply . . . . The worst thing to do is partially treat. It is safer for me to not treat some people."[15] Both financial barriers and the rigorous drug schedule cause problems of access and increase the possibility of the spread and worsening of the virus.

CHANGES IN THE INTERNATIONAL MARKET

Internationally, the high cost of AIDS treatment has had devastating consequences. In Africa, 25 million HIV-infected patients and 5 million patients with AIDS need some form of treatment.[16] The lack of an adequate social and governmental infrastructure and the absence and/or misuse of financial resources have left third-world countries without resources to respond effectively to the dangers that AIDS poses. The situation continues to be complicated by the existing price structures in developing countries and price structures in countries that produce the drugs. International AIDS groups, including the Nobel-peace-prize-winning Doctors-Without-Borders, are working to reduce the cost of AIDS treatment in Africa and are appealing to pharmaceutical companies for help. They have provided financial analyses intended to show that a combination of three AIDS drugs that jointly sell for approximately $15,000 per year in the United States could be sold profitably to poor countries for approximately $780 a year.[17]

In response to domestic critics and international pressures, pharmaceutical companies have attempted to adjust their price structures to offer AIDS drugs at lower prices. In May 2000, at the urging of the World Health Organization, five multinational drug companies offered to sell their AIDS drugs to poor nations at considerably reduced prices. However, negotiations had to be conducted nation by nation, and these negotiations have moved slowly: Uganda, Rwanda, and Senegal were the lone nations to reach agreements quickly. By 2002, only about 10,000 of several million needy persons in Africa were receiving AIDS drugs. New offers by pharmaceutical companies were expected to reach, under the completed agreements, only approximately 100,000 persons, a small percentage of those in need of the drugs.[18]

AIDS activists continue to maintain that drugs can be priced more cheaply than the pharmaceutical companies acknowledge. In response, in May 2001, Bristol-Myers Squibb announced that it would sell the two AIDS medicines that it manufactures "below cost" to sub-Saharan African countries. However, various empirical disputes over costs and pricing have not been resolved. Activists claim that it is unclear "whether the company calculated its cost as the actual manufacturing expense, or a sum that includes other costs such as research and publicity. While Videx [a Bristol-Myers Squibb drug] has been selling for $3 a dose in South Africa, the same drug can be obtained in Thailand for 36 cents."[19] These price differences have also made headlines in smuggling cases. Smugglers—and even some nations and organizations—have sold AZT supplies that they purchase cheaply to European countries and others who will pay a higher price.[20]

Third-world governments have taken modest steps to provide the needed drugs. Since 1997, almost all AIDS patients in Brazil have received free treatment, using the same three-drug cocktail that is available to patients in developed countries like the United States. A 1996 patent law in Brazil specifies that any medicine commercialized in the world before May 14, 1997, is unpatented.[21] This includes all first-generation antiretroviral drugs. This patent-busting solution has been proclaimed a success in Brazil, where the government estimates that approximately 146,000 hospitalizations were avoided in the period 1997 through 1999, saving the Ministry of Health $422 million.[22]

India provides another example of the rejection of the supremacy of patents in the face of AIDS. Since India's Patent Act of 1970, only the production processes of drugs, and not the pharmaceutical products themselves, can be patented for seven years. Moreover, the law allows the government to intervene if the patent holder does not allocate production licenses under "fair conditions."[23] The Indian pharmaceutical firm CIPLA gained attention in the global market in February 2001 when it offered to sell a generic, three-drug AIDS therapy for an annual cost of U.S. $350 per patient.[24] Later in 2001, the company announced that it would export its three-drug therapy to a "dozen" countries, including Nigeria, Algeria, Cameroon, Ivory Coast, and Cambodia; and it was in talks to expand its sales to other African and Southeast Asian nations. CIPLA also announced that it was cutting its prices on AIDS drugs for the fourth time in nine months. The last of the four reductions cut prices by 39 percent.

Pharmaceutical companies have opposed all forms of patent-busting. Although they understand the tragic effects of the AIDS epidemic on developing nations, they do not consider violating patents to be a proper solution to the problem. An arrangement for CIPLA to sell cheap retrovirals to Uganda and Ghana failed to develop when GSK warned CIPLA that it was violating patent rights. Phil Thomson, spokesman for GSK, stated that "Patent protection is fundamental to continued research and development in these areas. . . . We have to aim to protect our patents across the developing world."[25]

Pharmaceutical manufacturers as well as the World Trade Organization insist that without patent protection and the profits that accrue from it, there would be no incentive to spend money on research that develops new therapies. Their preferred response to the AIDS epidemic is to offer drugs at discounted prices to developing nations, negotiated on an individual and a competitive basis. They are opposed to the establishment of a formal pricing system, since it "would not reflect differences in cost structures, would undermine the principles of price competition and legitimate commercial confidentiality, and would violate antitrust laws."[26]

In 2001, CIPLA offered to pay Bristol-Myers Squibb Co. and Pfizer Ltd. 5 percent royalties for permission to sell knockoff versions of patented AIDS drugs, and it made a similar offer to other major drug companies.[27] The willingness of pharmaceutical companies to entertain such an offer, however reluctantly, is indicative of recent shifts in the understanding of intellectual property rights. This point was emphasized on March 20, 2001, when the World Trade Organization adopted the principle that developing countries may legitimately use generic drugs in times of health crises without the permission of patent-holding major pharmaceutical companies.[28]

Recognizing that international opinion was shifting, pharmaceutical companies began more competitively to negotiate prices with individual governments. Prices of antiretroviral drugs to treat HIV/AIDS dropped 54 percent in 2001 in Latin America and the Caribbean countries as a result of agreements between ministries of health and drug manufacturers.[29] In Haiti, for instance, the cost of a retroviral drug dropped from $21,489 to $1,606. More recently, in his State of the Union address, President Bush announced an unprecedented plan to allocate $15 billion to assist twelve countries in Africa and two in the Caribbean in the fight against HIV/AIDS. This 200 percent increase in funding over five years represents the growing trend of more developed nations joining the fight in lesser developed countries. The money has been designated for education, health care infrastructure in these countries, UN programs, and expanding access to drugs. Most surprising is that the administration has listed CIPLA's three-drug therapy as among the generic treatments recommended for purchase. Despite this significant increase in funding, the Bush plan reaches only a relatively small portion of those affected.[30]

Many expect that this trend of lower prices and improved access to new drugs will continue. However, the majority of AIDS sufferers still face barriers to treatment. Many governments continue to avoid direct confrontation with the issues surrounding AIDS treatment costs, and millions of AIDS patients remain both ineligible for public assistance and financially unable to purchase the drug.

NOTES

1. The following sources were used to develop the early history of the problems presented in this case study: "AIDS Drug Is Raising Host of Thorny Issues," *The New York Times*, September 28, 1986, Section 1, p. 38; M. A. Fischl, D. D. Richman, M. H. Grieco et al., "The Efficacy of Azidothymidine (AZT) in the Treatment of Patients with AIDS and AIDS-Related Complex: A Double-Blind, Placebo-Controlled Trial," *New England Journal of Medicine* 317 (1987), pp. 185–91; D. D. Richman et al., "The Toxicity of Azidothymidine (AZT) in the Treatment of Patients with AIDS and AIDS-Related Complex: A Double-Blind, Placebo-Controlled Trial," *New England Journal of Medicine* 317 (1987), pp. 192–97; Robin Levin Penslar and Richard D. Lamm, "Who Pays for AZT?" *Hastings Center Report* (September/October 1989), pp. 30–32; Philip J. Hilts, "AZT to Be Widely Given Out to Children with AIDS Virus," *The New York Times*, October 26, 1989, pp. A1, A22; Philip J. Hilts, "F.D.A., in Big Shift, Will Permit Use of Experimental AIDS Drug," *The New York Times*, September 29, 1989, pp. A1, A16; Martin Delaney, "The Case for Patient Access to Experimental Therapy," *Journal of Infectious Diseases* 159 (1989), pp. 412–15.
2. The Wellcome Group, *Annual Report 1990*, p. 17.
3. T. E. Haigler, Jr., president and CEO, Burroughs Wellcome, in testimony before the Subcommittee on Health and the Environment of the House Committee on Energy and Commerce, March 10, 1987, p. 12.
4. Public statement of Bernadine Healy, director, National Institutes of Health, July 17, 1991; see also *Scrip*, No. 1637 (July 26, 1991), p. 9.
5. Lourdes Lee Valeriano, "Barr Laboratories Applies to the FDA for Approval to Make an AIDS Drug," *The Wall Street Journal*, April 19, 1991, p. 4.
6. Wade Lambert, "Legal Beat: AZT Patent Ruling," *The Wall Street Journal*, November 23, 1994, p. B4. See also *Burroughs Wellcome v. Barr Laboratories, Inc.*, 93–1503, U.S. Court of Appeals for the Federal Circuit, Washington, DC.
7. "Barr Laboratories Wins F.D.A. Approval for Generic AZT," *The New York Times*, February 28, 1995, p. D4.
8. *AIDS Healthcare Foundation v. GlaxoSmithKline.* "AIDS Advocacy Group Seeks to Invalidate AZT Patents," *Health Care Fraud Litigation Reporter*, 8:5 (December), 2002, p. 6.
9. Concorde Coordinating Committee, "Concorde: MRC/ANRS Randomised Double-Blind Controlled Trial of Immediate and Deferred Zidovudine in Symptom-Free HIV Infection," *The Lancet* 343 (April 9, 1994), pp. 871–81; William R. Lenderking, Richard D. Gelber, Deborah J. Cotton et al., "Evaluation of the Quality of Life Associated with Zidovudine Treatment in Asymptomatic Human Immunodeficiency Virus Infection," *The New England Journal of Medicine* 330 (March 17, 1994), p. 742.

10. Lawrence K. Altman, "Experts to Review AZT Role as the Chief Drug for H.I.V.," *The New York Times*, September 17, 1995, pp. 1, 38.

11. Anne Rochell, "'AZT Isn't Whole Ballgame Anymore,'" *The Atlanta Journal and Constitution*, July 23, 1994, Science Section E, p. 1.

12. See the following articles for background on this section: "AIDS Drug to Be Given Away," *The New York Times*, June 22, 1995, p. A17; Justin Gillis, "Merck to Provide New AIDS Drug," *The Washington Post*, July 17, 1995, p. A7; Justin Gillis, "Two Firms Will Offer Wider Access to Experimental AIDS Drugs," *The Washington Post*, September 21, 1995, p. A3; "Lottery for AIDS Drug," *The New York Times*, July 18, 1995, p. C3; "Lottery for New AIDS Drug Expands," *The New York Times*, September 19, 1995, p. C12; "New AIDS Drug to Be Offered Via Lottery," *The Los Angeles Times*, June 22, 1995, p. D2; "Roche Holding Ltd," *The Wall Street Journal*, September 18, 1995, p. B9; Michael Waldholz, "Unit of Roche Sets Up Lottery for AIDS Drug," *The Wall Street Journal*, June 21, 1995, p. A5; Michael Waldholz, "Merck Joins Roche in Offering Test Drug Free to Some AIDS Patients," *The Wall Street Journal*, July 17, 1995, p. B3.

13. Sheryl G. Stolberg, "Africa's AIDS War," *The New York Times*, March 10, 2001, p. A1.

14. Editorial, "Campaign for an AIDS vaccine," *The Boston Globe*, January 29, 1997, p. A12.

15. Michael Lasalandra, "Some Say Miracle AIDS Drugs Not for Everyone," *The Boston Herald*, July 22, 1997, p. O11.

16. Sheryl G. Stolberg, "Africa's AIDS War," *The New York Times*, March 10, 2001, p. A1.

17. Sabin Russell, "Price Cut Urged For AIDS Drugs In Poor Nations," *The San Francisco Chronicle*, November 29, 2000, p. A16.

18. *The New York Times*, March 10, 2001.

19. Karen De Young and Bill Brubaker, "Another Firm Cuts HIV Drug Prices," *The Washington Post*, March 15, 2001, p. A1.

20. Rajeev Syal, "Scandal of Africa's Aids Drugs Re-Sold to Britain," *Sunday Telegraph* (London), December 29, 2003, p. 1.

21. Tina Rosenberg, "Look at Brazil," *The New York Times Magazine*, January 28, 2001, Section 6, p. 26.

22. http://www.aids.gov.br/assistencia/aids_drugs_policy.htm

23. http://www.dse.de/zeitschr/de600-3.htm

24. http://www.irinnews.org/AIDSreport.asp?ReportID=1041&selectRegion=Africa

25. A Christian Science Monitor Roundup, "Patents, profits, and AIDS care," *The Christian Science Monitor*, February 28, 2001, World Section, p. 1.

26. http://www.phrma.org/press/print.phtml?article=207

27. Daniel Pearl, "Companies Weigh Offer of Royalties," *The Wall Street Journal*, February 16, 2001, p. B1.

28. http://www.medguide.org.zm/aids/aidsafr13.htm

29. According to a survey by the Pan American Health Organization (PAHO), "Healthcare Access: AIDS drug prices drop 54% in Latin America, Caribbean," *AIDS Weekly*, August 12, 2002, Section: Expanded Reporting, p. 16.

30. Danna Harman, "How Best to Spend New AIDS Money," *The Christian Science Monitor*, January 31, 2003, p. 1.

AT&T's Policies
on Affirmative Action

AT&T has had a long and tumultuous relationship with issues of affirmative action. Its policies have swung from nonvoluntary compliance in the 1970s to voluntary programs and enthusiastic endorsement of affirmative action in recent years.

HISTORICAL ORIGINS

In 1970, the U.S. Equal Employment Opportunity Commission (EEOC) pursued AT&T on grounds that it engaged in discriminatory practices. The EEOC claimed that the firm engaged in "pervasive, system-wide, and blatantly unlawful discrimination in employment against women, blacks, Spanish-surnamed Americans, and other minorities."[1] The EEOC argued that the employment practices of AT&T violated several laws, including the Civil Rights Acts of 1866 and 1964, the Equal Pay Act of 1963, and the Fair Employment Practices Acts of numerous states and cities. AT&T denied all charges brought against it, claiming that its record demonstrated equality of treatment for both minorities and women.

In the spring of 1972, the U. S. Department of Labor intervened in this dispute and assumed jurisdiction in the matter. After a period of negotiation, a final agreement was reached on December 29, 1972. The Department of Labor proposed an out-of-court settlement, and AT&T entered a Consent Decree, which was accepted by a Philadelphia court on January 18, 1973. This agreement resulted in AT&T's paying $15 million in back wages to 13,000 women and 2,000 minority-group men and giving $23 million in raises to 36,000 employees who had presumably suffered because of previous policies. Out of this settlement came an extensive, companywide affirmative action recruitment and promotion program. AT&T set rigorous goals and intermediate targets (later often referred to as "quotas") in fifteen job categories to meet first-year objectives. The goals were determined by statistics regarding representative numbers of workers in the relevant labor market. The agreement also stated

This case was prepared by Tom L. Beauchamp and revised by Joanne L. Jurmu and Ahmed Humayun. Not to be duplicated without permission of the holder of the copyright, © 1992, 1996, 2003 by Tom L. Beauchamp.

that if, during this campaign, its progress was to fall short of deadlines, AT&T would then have to depart from normal selection and promotion standards by more vigorously pursuing affirmative action goals.[2]

At the time of this agreement, AT&T had a union contract that established ability and merit as the primary qualifications for positions but that also required that seniority be given full consideration. This contract conflicted with features in the Consent Decree, which called for an affirmative action override that would bypass union-contract promotion criteria if necessary to achieve the affirmative action goals. The decree required specifically that under conditions of a target failure, a *less* qualified (but *qualified*) person could take precedence over a more qualified person with greater seniority. This condition applied to promotions, not to layoffs and rehiring, where seniority continued to prevail.

It was in this context in 1974 that there arose a case in affirmative action and reverse discrimination known as *McAleer* v. *AT&T*.[3]

MCALEER AND THE COURTS

Daniel McAleer was a $10,500-per-year service representative who handled orders for telephone service in AT&T's Washington, D.C., Long Lines Division. In 1974, he asked for a promotion that he did not receive. Instead, a staff assistant named Sharon Hulvey received the promotion. Although less qualified than McAleer, Hulvey received the promotion because of the affirmative action program at AT&T. McAleer claimed that he had been discriminated against on the basis of sex. He then brought a lawsuit against AT&T to ask for the promotion, differential back pay, and $100,000 in damages (on grounds of lost opportunity for further promotion). Joined by his union (Communications Workers of America), he also claimed that AT&T had undermined the ability of the union to secure employment rights to jobs and fair promotions under the relevant collective bargaining agreement.

The McAleer case came before Judge Gerhard A. Gesell, who held on June 9, 1976, that McAleer was a faultless employee who became an innocent victim through an *unfortunate but justifiable* use of the affirmative action process. More specifically, Gesell ruled that McAleer was entitled to monetary compensation (as damages) but was not entitled to the promotion because the discrimination that the Consent Decree had been designed to eliminate might be perpetuated if Hulvey were not given the promotion. The central thrust of Gesell's ruling is as follows:

> After the filing of the Philadelphia complaint and AT&T's contemporaneous answer, and following an immediate hearing, the Court received from the parties and approved a Consent Decree and accompanying Memorandum of Agreement which had been entered into by the governmental plaintiffs and AT&T after protracted negotiation. This settlement was characterized by Judge Higginbotham as "the largest and most impressive civil rights settlement in the history of this nation."

... "Affirmative action override" requires AT&T to disregard this standard [seniority] and choose from among basically qualified female or minority applicants if necessary to meet the goals and timetables of the Consent Decree and if other affirmative efforts fail to provide sufficient female or minority candidates for promotion who are the best qualified or most senior . . . .

This entire process occurred without the participation of Communication Workers of America (CWA), the certified collective bargaining representative of approximately 600,000 nonmanagement employees at AT&T and the parent union with which plaintiff Local #2350 is affiliated. Although it was consistently given notice in the Philadelphia case of the efforts to reach a settlement, and although it was "begged . . . to negotiate and litigate" in that proceeding, 365 F. Supp. at 1110, CWA persistently and repeatedly refused to become involved . . . .

Judge Higginbotham presently has before him and has taken under advisement the question of modification of the Consent Decree because it conflicts with the collective bargaining agreement . . . .

It is disputed that plaintiff McAleer would have been promoted but for his gender. This is a classic case of sex discrimination within the meaning of the Act, 42 U.S.C. 2000e-2(a)(2). That much is clear. What is more difficult is the issue of defenses or justifications available to AT&T and the question of appropriate relief under the circumstances revealed by this record. McAleer seeks both promotion and damages. The Court holds that he is entitled only to the latter.

General principles of law also support plaintiff McAleer's right to damages. It is true that AT&T was following the terms of the Consent Decree, and ordinarily one who acts pursuant to a judicial order or other lawful process is protected from liability arising from the act . . . . But such protection does not exist where the judicial order was necessitated by the wrongful conduct of the party sought to be held liable . . . .

Here, the Consent Decree on which the defendant relies *was necessary only because of AT&T's prior sex discrimination.* Under these circumstances the Decree provides *no defense against the claims of a faultless employee such as McAleer.* . . . [Italics added]

Since McAleer had no responsibility for AT&T's past sex discrimination, it is AT&T rather than McAleer who should bear the principal burden of rectifying the company's previous failure to comply with the Civil Rights Act of 1964. An affirmative award of some damages on a "rough justice" basis is therefore required and will constitute an added cost which the stockholders of AT&T must bear.

In the year that Judge Gesell's decision was reached, the same Judge (A. Leon) Higginbotham that Gesell mentions handled a union petition to eliminate the affirmative action override from the Consent Decree. Higginbotham went out of his way to disagree with Gesell, saying that he had wrongly decided the case. He found AT&T to have *immunity* as an employer because of its history with and commitments to a valid affirmative action plan. McAleer therefore had no right to damages. However, because he was hearing only a *union* case, Higginbotham's ruling did not directly overturn or otherwise affect Gesell's ruling. AT&T's lawyers—Mr. Robert Jeffrey, in particular—felt strongly that Judge Gesell's arguments were misguided and that Judge Higginbotham did the best that he could at the time to set matters right, though, paradoxically, Higginbotham's opinion did nothing to alter or overturn Gesell's.

Soon thereafter AT&T and McAleer settled out of court for $14,000, with $6,500 of it going to legal fees for McAleer's attorney. Both McAleer and Hulvey continued their employment at AT&T. Jeffrey, AT&T's lawyer, maintained that this case was an aberration. From the moral point of view, Jeffrey believed that both Judge Gesell's ruling and the law being promulgated at the time in the White House deserved severe ethical scrutiny and criticism.[4] Nonetheless, policies of affirmative action became entrenched, and AT&T shifted ground from reluctance about affirmative action to strong support for it.

AFFIRMATIVE ACTION IN THE 1980s AND 1990s

AT&T, together with many large firms in the U.S., adopted voluntary (that is, self-imposed rather than mandated) affirmative action plans to foster the promotion and hiring of women and minorities throughout the 1980s and 1990s. When such plans are adopted, questions often arise about the practice of substituting one type of discrimination for another. In March 1987, the U.S. Supreme Court decided a case involving alleged reverse discrimination that many believe set a strong precedent for future affirmative action plans. In this case, *Johnson* v. *Transportation Agency*,[5] the majority held that the affirmative action plan being assessed was proper because it

1. Was intended to *attain*, not *maintain*, a balanced workforce;
2. Did not unnecessarily trammel the rights of male employees or create an absolute bar to their advancement; and
3. Expressly directed that numerous factors be taken into account, including qualifications of female applicants for particular jobs.

Justice Brennan stated in the Court's opinion that "our decision was grounded in the recognition that voluntary employer action can play a crucial role in furthering Title VII's purpose of eliminating the effects of discrimination in the workplace and that Title VII should not be read to thwart such efforts."[6] Many firms viewed this and related Supreme Court decisions[7] as encouraging the continuation of affirmative action plans already in place and the adoption of new plans where they have not previously existed. However, corporate America and American courts continued in the 1980s and 1990s to be divided over both the morality and the legality of affirmative action plans such as the one that generated the McAleer case. Many firms continued to adopt plans almost identical to the one that led to the promotion of Hulvey rather than McAleer, whereas other firms insisted that these policies involve immoral forms of discrimination.

In March 1988, AT&T's shareholders were in sharp disagreement over the company's employment history and affirmative action program. One set of shareholders fought for a stronger affirmative action program, whereas another set recommended phasing it out. AT&T addressed such questions through various changes of policy, and by 1996, it was using an affirmative action plan that was aimed primarily at identifying *underutilized groups at particular AT&T locations*. Hiring and promotional targets continued to be stated as percentage goals (e.g., 40 percent women in management positions); but the particular groups targeted and the numbers to be hired or promoted were considered only relative to the geographic location of particular AT&T facilities. What was an underutilized group at one facility might not be underutilized at another. The "normal hiring pool" was itself location-relative. Because targets had become exclusively location-specific, the old companywide targets were eliminated.[8]

AFFIRMATIVE ACTION AT AT&T
IN THE TWENTY-FIRST CENTURY

As of March 2002, AT&T had a publicly announced "equal opportunity/affirmative action" policy that anyone could access through the internet. Among its several provisions is the following:

> AT&T's policy charges managers with the responsibility to implement affirmative action initiatives that are consistent with AT&T's obligation as a government contractor on behalf of women, minorities, persons with disabilities, special disabled veterans, veterans of the Vietnam era, and other veterans.[9]

In its policy, AT&T acknowledges a positive obligation to the public and to its actual and potential employees to enforce affirmative action plans on behalf of disadvantaged and underutilized sections of the workforce. AT&T stands for a proactive promotion of affirmative action, but it places responsibility for this task in the hands of regional managers who are charged with implementing the company's general equal opportunity/affirmative action initiatives, as they find it necessary to do so. To facilitate this task of the regional managers, AT&T publishes annual summaries of percentages of female, minority, and disabled sections of its workforce, arranged according to the different tasks they perform.[10] In this manner, affirmative action has become an integral part of AT&T's hiring policy and company culture. However, the policy is implemented by region, rather than nationally or internationally, and the company no longer sets explicit target goals of the sort that dominated its early affirmative action efforts.

NOTES

1. U.S. Equal Employment Opportunity Commission, "Petition to Intervene," Federal Communications Commission Hearings on A.T.&T. Revised Tariff Schedule, December 10, 1970, p. 1.
2. The stipulations of the agreement were met by the company before an established 1979 deadline.
3. Sources consulted for background include *McAleer* v. *American Telephone and Telegraph Company*, 416F.Supp. 435 (1976); Earl A. Molander, *Responsive Capitalism: Case Studies in Corporate Social Conduct* (New York: McGraw-Hill, 1980), pp. 56–70; "A.T.&T. Denies Job Discrimination Charges, Claims Firm Is Equal Employment Leader," *The Wall Street Journal*, December 14, 1970, p. 6; "A.T.&T. Makes Reparation," *Economist* 246 (January 27, 1973), p. 42; Byron Calame, "Liberating Ma Bell: Female Telephone Workers Hit Labor Pact, Says Men Still Get the Best Jobs, More Pay," *The Wall Street Journal*, July 26, 1971, p. 22; "FCC Orders Hearing on Charge That A.T.&T. Discriminates in Hiring," *The Wall Street Journal*, January 22, 1971, p. 10; "Federal Agency Says A.T.&T. Job Bias Keeps Rates from Declining," *The Wall Street Journal*, December 2, 1971, p. 21; Richard M. Hodgetts, "A.T.& T. versus the Equal Employment Opportunity Commission," in *The Business Enterprise: Social Challenge, Social Response* (Philadelphia: W. B. Saunders Company, 1977), pp. 176–82.
4. According to Mr. Jeffrey of the legal staff in AT&T's Washington, DC, office, in a phone conversation on March 10, 1982.
5. *Johnson* v. *Transportation Agency, Santa Clara County, California*, 480 U.S. 616 (1987).
6. *Ibid.*
7. *Fullilove* v. *Klutznick*, 448 U.S. 448 (1980); *United Steelworkers* v. *Weber*, 443 U.S. 193 (1979); *United States* v. *Paradise*, 480 U.S. 149 (1987).
8. Information based on phone conversations with Mr. Frank Bloomfield, Equal Opportunity Affirmative Action Manager for the Network Service Division, December 10, 1991, and Ms. Joanne Marleowicz, Corporate Equal Opportunity Affirmative Action Manager, December 10, 1991, and May 7, 1996.
9. http://www.att.com/hr/life/eoaa/index.html
10. http://www.att.com/hr/life/eoaa/eeodata_2000.html

Rumpole's Revenge, or Women in Catering

After graduating from the Birmingham Baptist School of Business, it had been the dream of Leo McKern to travel in Europe, starting with a job in the region. Accordingly, Leo was happy to accept the offer of a managerial position with R&M Catering, Inc., one of the most successful and fastest-growing catering service companies in the United Kingdom.

A relatively new company, R&M has quite an interesting history. The company was founded in 1993 by Hilda Rumpole, a woman then in her mid-fifties. Up until that time, Hilda had been married to Horace Rumpole, a rather dissolute barrister, and had spent her life caring for her home and her son Nicholas, who now lives in Miami, where he is a popular professor at the University of Miami. Horace had spent his career representing indigent criminal defendants and, as a result, had accumulated almost no savings. He had enjoyed spending a significant fraction of his small income at the local pub.

When Horace died in 1992, Hilda was left with no resources other than the proceeds of a small life insurance policy. After discussing her situation with Dodo MacIntosh, an old school friend who had some experience in the catering business, Hilda decided to go into business with Dodo and therefore used the life insurance proceeds to open the R&M Catering Company. For small jobs she began by using her own kitchen, but for large jobs she hired a staff and rented the basement kitchen in the old stone church next door. After she had worked this way for three years, she then bought her own facility less than a mile from her home. At this point, having become the clear leader and organizing force, she bought out Dodo.

Hilda was a woman with a forceful personality and a commanding presence. She had bought her first facility and renovated it at a remarkably low cost, doing work such as the painting and the installation of shelves herself. She also had a proven ability to gain considerable cost advantages for R&M by driving hard bargains with suppliers and service providers. In addition, she seemed to be able to gain customers simply through the force of her personality. It was often said that potential customers seemed almost afraid to say no to her. She hired some very good consultants on business expansion, and as a re-

This case was prepared by John Hasnas and revised by Tom L. Beauchamp. Not to be duplicated without permission of the holder of the copyright, © 2003 by John Hasnas (George Mason University Law School).

sult, by 1999, R&M had grown into the largest catering company operating in London.

Hilda, however, was not one to rest on her laurels. Hard upon the heels of her success in London, she opened branches of R&M in Manchester, Leeds, and Liverpool. Hilda retained her consultants, but personally oversaw the founding of each new branch, choosing the branch managers, negotiating the initial contracts, and supervising operations until things were running to her satisfaction. When these branch operations proved successful, Hilda further expanded the business to Glasgow and Edinburgh in Scotland, and Belfast in Northern Ireland.

As the size of the company grew, so did the demands upon Hilda as CEO. When she took the company public in 1996, she retained 51 percent of the stock, guaranteeing that she could remain in control of the company for as long as she liked. By working tirelessly, she has managed to stay on top of all aspects of the company's operations, and each branch bears the stamp of her leadership. However, by last year, it became apparent that additional managers were needed throughout the company, and Leo was hired as a manager in the home branch in London.

Essentially, his job is to begin to bring far more order to the chaotic disorganization caused by the company's rapid expansion. Clear, consistant, and comprehensive corporate *policy* has never been developed in this company, starting as it did in a home kitchen. For example, as far as Leo can tell, R&M has nothing that can pass for a personnel policy. In the early years of the company, Hilda did all the hiring. For the top positions, she rarely advertised; instead, she hired as many of her old school friends as she could trust. Many of them had been interested in getting into the business because of either a failed marriage or the death of a husband. Hilda had been an active member of two clubs filled with such women, and she had gotten to know them well.

Thus, R&M had evolved to the point that it had a corporate management composed chiefly of middle-aged women who were somewhat bored with their lives and typically not very happy with their husbands or their financial circumstances. Hilda filled most of the lower-level delivery positions and waitperson positions with men, in part because she was particularly effective in negotiating favorable wage rates with men and in part because she enjoyed being in a position in which a woman made all the major decisions.

As the company expanded, hiring patterns continued to follow Hilda's preferences and personality. Although she began hiring many younger people for management positions, an inordinate number of them continued to be divorced, separated, or widowed women who had experienced disappointing marriages. In addition, women did a little bit better than men for wages, even when men and women were in comparable positions. Over the years, not much has changed. When Hilda left London to oversee the development of the new branches, Phillida Erskine-Brown, herself married to a philandering husband, took over as general manager of the London branch. Whether consciously or unconsciously, Phillida seems to have continued Hilda's hiring preference for women who have suffered some significant negative experience with men. Although many men and happily married women are employed by R&M at the managerial level, a disproportionate number of those hired for or promoted to such positions are divorced women. In addition, although the lower-level service positions continue to be filled predominantly by men, the service employees who are promoted to supervisory positions are usually women.

A typical illustration of the latter situation was the promotion of Liz Probert to project manager. She oversees all aspects of a specific catering contract. Liz came to R&M two years ago after being emotionally devastated when an affair she had been having with a married barrister ended badly. Fearing a scandal, the barrister had ended their romance when he came up for appointment as Queen's Counsel. Originally hired as a waitress, Liz later became a food preparer and eventually began taking catering orders over the telephone. She also became friendly with Marigold Featherstone, a project manager with whom she found she had much in common. Last month when a project manager's position opened up, Featherstone supported Liz for the position, and Liz received the promotion.

One of Liz's coworkers is Tony Timson, who has been employed at R&M for five years. Beginning as a waiter, he has also been a delivery driver, a food preparer, and a telephone order-taker. Tony believed that he knew the business well, and when the project manager's job opened up, he expected to get it. Although Liz was certainly qualified for the job, Tony had a more extensive knowledge of R&M's services and had three years more experience. He was bitterly disappointed when he was—unfairly, in his view—passed over for the promotion.

Leo has also noticed that women who hold the white collar positions in the company form a very close-knit group. Perhaps because they have so much in common and are members of the same clubs, they are very friendly with each other. They regularly take tea together and often get together after hours at small neighborhood restaurants. They seem to derive a great deal of pleasure from discussing the shortcomings of their husbands, ex-husbands, or ex-boyfriends, and in fact, this seems to be one basis on which their bond is formed.

Leo has detected that this bonding basis spills over into the way the women relate to the male employees of R&M. For example, Sam Ballard is the company's chief accountant. Ballard is a conservative, staid, middle-aged, married man who is overweight, has a very pale complexion, and is extremely religious. His wife Marguerite does not work outside of the home. Ballard apparently reminds some of the female senior managers of their current or former husbands. Because of his complexion, they refer to him among themselves as "Soapy" and will sometimes use this nickname within his hearing. In addition, they will often tease him about his churchgoing ways with comments such as "Heard any good hymns lately?" or "What's the latest word from God, and how's she doing these days?" Some make facetious comments about his home life such as "You're not neglecting the Mrs., are you?"

Another example is George Frobisher, a project manager who is one of the few men to have been promoted to his position from the lower-level service jobs. Frobisher comes from a working-class family, and although married, he likes to spend much of his leisure time at a local pub called Pommeroy's Wine Bar. Many of the female senior managers, perhaps on the basis of their personal histories, view this habit as evidence of a bad moral character and suspect that he neglects his wife. Their manner toward Frobisher is cool and aloof, and often downright hostile. Most of the women tend to be curt with him, and occasionally there is heard a derogatory comment about his drinking habits. Leo has also noticed that Frobisher seems to have more of the less desirable catering contracts assigned to him than do the women project managers.

On the whole, Leo strongly suspects that attitudes prevalent among R&M's female senior management negatively affect their male subordinates' chances for advancement. However, he has watched carefully, and none of this treatment seems to have a negative impact on R&M's financial success. Male employees in the lower-level service jobs frequently become frustrated by their lack of advancement and leave the company. However, because these are low-skill positions that require no training, they are easily replaced. Further, because the entrance salary for a newly hired employee is lower than that earned by one who has been on the job for a while, the turnover in lower-level personnel actually produces cost savings for the company. In addition, the bonding among the female senior employees that results from their common life experiences also seems to be economically beneficial. The high degree of camaraderie and trust among the women allows them to cooperate effectively and informally with little dissention. Most have no problem about coming to work early and staying late. The company has as yet experienced virtually no governance costs associated with satisfactorily resolving employee disputes. Further, because the women seem to regard R&M as their second (and better) family, there is an extremely low absentee rate among them. The absentee rate for men is slightly higher, but corporate expectations have produced a low rate for the men as well.

Last week, when Hilda was in town, Leo had a meeting with her and Phillida to discuss his preliminary suggestions with regard to reforming and rationalizing parts of R&M's corporate policy. When the discussion turned to personnel policy, Leo mentioned his observation that divorced and separated women seem to receive some preference in hiring. Before Leo could go any further, Hilda said, "Yes, yes. That's just one of my little charities. Now that I run a business, I'm in a position to help those who, usually through no fault of their own, find themselves in difficult straits. I like to think that I'm doing my small part to liberate women from the stereotypical gender roles society assigns to them. Women should no longer be forced to choose between a demeaning marriage or the impoverishment of divorce and single motherhood as I was. Besides, R&M never hires or promotes anyone who is not qualified and fully capable of doing the job." While Hilda was speaking, Leo noticed Phillida nodding in agreement.

Leo was about to say something in response when Hilda said, "Let's move on to the accounting procedures," in a tone of voice that clearly would brook no alternatives. Discussion never returned to R&M's personnel policies before Hilda ended the meeting to catch a flight to Edinburgh. Leo was left with the distinct impression that Hilda had no interest in formulating a policy regarding hiring and promotion. She knows what she is doing; her mind is made up; and she does not mind speaking her mind to Leo.

The NYSEG Corporate Responsibility Program

We are responsible to the communities in which we live and work and to the world community as well. We must be good citizens and support good works and charities. . . . We must encourage civic improvements and better health and education.[1]

Many large corporations operate consumer responsibility or community responsibility programs, which aim to return something to the consumer or to the community in which the company does business. The motivation is at least twofold: These programs create a positive image of the company, and they make life much better for various unlucky members of the community. However, these programs are not good for corporate profits. They operate at a net loss and are, in effect, a form of corporate philanthropy.

New York State Electric and Gas Corporation (NYSEG) has created a program to fulfill what its officers consider to be the company's social responsibility to its public, in particular its consumers. When this program started two decades ago, NYSEG was a New York Stock Exchange–traded public utility with approximately 60,000 shareholders. Recently NYSEG became a subsidiary of the Energy East Corp., a superregional energy services and delivery company with over 5,800 employees. Energy East Corp. serves 1.4 million electricity customers and 600,000 natural gas customers in the northeastern United States. It is traded on the New York Stock Exchange.

In general, eastern public utilities have not enjoyed strong returns to shareholders in recent years because of relatively mild winters, increased plant costs, and a lower electric market price. However, Energy East has been able to increase earnings per share and dividends per share every year. Operating revenues have also gone up significantly. Energy East has been aggressively attempting to increase profitability by selling power plants and focusing on energy delivery. It has expanded its services rapidly and intends to continue the expansion. NYSEG itself continues to deliver electricity to over 800,000 customers and natural gas to around 250,000 customers across more than 40 percent of upstate New York.

This case was prepared by Tom L. Beauchamp and Kelley MacDougall, and revised by John Cuddihy and Jeff Greene. Not to be duplicated without permission of the holder of the copyright, © 1991, 1996, 2003 by Tom L. Beauchamp. This case is indebted to Cathy Hughto-Delzer, NYSEG Manager, Consumer Affairs.

NYSEG's corporate responsibility program has not, as yet, been altered by the change to Energy East Corporation or by the relatively weak financial returns for utilities in recent years. NYSEG designed the program—and continues it today—to aid customers who are unable to pay their utility bills. The program does more than simply help customers pay their bills. It locates and attempts to remedy the root causes of bill nonpayment, which almost invariably involve financial distress. However, NYSEG attempts to reach beyond financial exigency. It seeks to rescue people in the community who are in unfortunate circumstances because of industrial injury, the ill health of a spouse or child, drug dependency, and the like. The company offers its assistance whether or not it is reasonable to suppose that the assistance provided will restore a paying customer.

To implement this plan, NYSEG has created a system of consumer advocates—primarily social workers trained to deal with customers and their problems. Since the program's 1978 inception, NYSEG has maintained a staff of several consumer representatives. Each of them handles approximately one hundred cases a month, over half of which result in some form of financial assistance. The remaining cases are referred to other organizations for assistance.

The process works as follows: When the company's credit department believes that a special investigation should be made into a customer's situation, the employee refers the case to the consumer advocate. Referrals also sometimes come from human service agencies and from customers directly. Examples of appropriate referrals include unemployed household heads; paying customers who suffer serious injury, lengthy illness, or death of a wage-earner; and low-income senior citizens or those on fixed incomes who cannot deal with rising costs of living. To qualify for assistance, NYSEG requires only that the customers suffer from hardships that they are willing to work to resolve.

Consumer advocates are concerned to prevent the shutoff of service to these customers and to restore them to a condition of financial health. They employ an assortment of resources to put them back on their feet, including programs offered by the New York State Department of Social Services and the federal Home Energy Assistance Program (HEAP), which awards annual grants of varying amounts to qualified families. In addition, the consumer advocates provide financial counseling and help customers with their medical bills and educational planning. They arrange for assistance from churches and social services, provide food stamps, and help coordinate Veterans Administration benefits.

NYSEG also created a direct financial-grants program called Project Share, which is funded by a foundation created by NYSEG and by direct contributions from NYSEG employees, retirees, and customers. The latter can make charitable donations through their bills. They are asked voluntarily to add one, two, or five extra dollars to their bill each month. This special Fuel Fund is intended to help customers pay for energy emergencies, repairs to heating equipment, home weatherization, and water heater replacements. Grants of up to $200 are available to households in which someone is over sixty years old, has a disability, or has a serious medical condition—and with insufficient means of paying basic bills. The special fund of money created is overseen by the American Red Cross, which receives applications, determines eligibility, and distributes the collected funds. By 2002, over $4 million has been distributed to over 20,000 customers since Project Share began in 1982.[2]

The rationale or justification of this corporate responsibility program is rooted in the history of public utilities and rising energy costs in North America. Public utilities originally provided a relatively inexpensive product. NYSEG and the entire industry considered its public responsibility limited to the functions of providing energy at the lowest possible cost and returning dividends to investors. NYSEG did not concern itself with its customers' financial troubles. The customer or the social welfare system handled all problems of unpaid bills, which was considered strictly a matter of business.

However, the skyrocketing energy costs in the 1970s changed customer resources and NYSEG's perspective. The energy crisis caused many long-term customers to encounter difficulty in paying their bills, and the likelihood of power shutoffs increased as a result. NYSEG accepted the responsibility to assist its valued customers by creating the Consumer Advocate system. NYSEG believes that its contribution is especially important now because recent reductions in federal assistance programs have shifted the burden of addressing these problems to the private sector.

The costs of NYSEG's involvement in the program are paid for from company revenues, which in principle (and in fact) entails that returns to shareholders are lowered. However, these costs are regarded by company officers as low. The program has few costs beyond office space and the consumer advocates' salaries and benefits, which total a half-million dollars. All expenses are treated as operating expenses. To augment Project Share's financial support, NYSEG shareholders have voted the program an annual, need-based grant. In the past, these shareholder gifts have ranged from $40,000 to $100,000 annually. NYSEG shareholders also fund related personnel and printing costs. The company itself has also supported Project Share through direct contributions to the Red Cross.

The company views some of the money expended for the corporate responsibility program as recovered funds because of the customers retained and the bills paid through the program. NYSEG officials assume that these charges would, under normal circumstances, have remained unpaid and would eventually have been written off as losses. NYSEG's bad-debt level is 20 percent lower than that of the average U.S. utility company. The company believes that its corporate responsibility policy is *both* altruistic *and* good business, despite the program's maintenance costs. Though these costs well exceed recovered revenue, the service builds excellent customer relations. In other words, staffing and otherwise paying for these programs is a net financial loss for the company and its shareholders—what many businesses would call a "losing proposition"—but managers and shareholders do not (in public) complain about these unnecessary expenses, and most seem to feel good about the extra services the company provides to its customers.

It is unknown what view Energy East Corp. will ultimately take of this program, which it acquired from prior management at NYSEG. The program could be disbanded, cut back, or enlarged to serve all of Energy East's several utility services.

NOTES

1. "The Johnson and Johnson Way" (from the Johnson and Johnson Company credo).
2. www.nyseg.com/nysegweb/main.nsf/doc/share and www.nyseg.com/nysegweb/faqs.nsf/pwrprtnr (as posted January, 2003)